Betraying Dignity

The Fairleigh Dickinson University Press Series in Law, Culture, and the Humanities

Series Editor: Caroline Joan "Kay" S. Picart, M.Phil. (Cantab), PhD, J. D., Esquire
Attorney at Law; Adjunct Professor, FAMU College of Law;
former English & HUM professor, FSU

The Fairleigh Dickinson University Press Series in Law, Culture, and the Humanities publishes scholarly works in which the field of Law intersects with, among others, Film, Criminology, Sociology, Communication, Critical/Cultural Studies, Literature, History, Philosophy, and the Humanities.

On the Web at http://www.fdu.edu/fdupress

Publications

Orit Kamir, *Betraying Dignity: The Toxic Seduction of Social Media, Shaming, and Radicalization* (2019)

Marouf A. Hasian, Jr., *Lawfare and the Ovaherero and Nama Pursuit of Restorative Justice, 1918–2018* (2019)

George Pate, *Enter the Undead Author: Intellectual Property, the Ideology of Authorship, and Performance Practices since the 1960s* (2019)

Victor Li, *Nixon in New York. How Wall Street Helped Richard Nixon Win the White House* (2017)

Marouf A. Hasian, Jr., *Kafkaesque Laws, Nisour Square, and the Trials of the Former Blackwater Guards* (2017)

Michaela Stockey-Bridge, *The Lure of Hope: On the Transnational Surrogacy Trail from Australia to India* (2017)

Ted Laros, *Literature and the Law in South Africa, 1910–2010: The Long Walk to Artistic Freedom* (2017)

Peter Robson and Johnny Rodger, *The Spaces of Justice: The Architecture of the Scottish Court* (2017)

Doran Larson, *Witness in the Era of Mass Incarceration: Discovering the Ethical Prison* (2017)

Raymond J. McKoski, *Judges in Street Clothes: Acting Ethically Off-the-Bench* (2017)

H. Lowell Brown, *The American Constitutional Tradition: Colonial Charters, Covenants, and Revolutionary State Constitutions 1578–1786* (2017)

Arua Oko Omaka, *The Biafran Humanitarian Crisis, 1967–1970: International Human Rights and Joint Church Aid* (2016)

Marouf A. Hasian, Jr., *Representing Ebola: Culture, Law, and Public Discourse about the 2013–2015 West Africa Ebola Outbreak* (2016)

Jacqueline O'Connor, *Law and Sexuality in Tennessee Williams's America* (2016)

Caroline Joan "Kay" S. Picart, Michael Hviid Jacobsen, and Cecil E. Greek, *Framing Law and Crime: An Interdisciplinary Anthology* (2016)

Caroline Joan "Kay" S. Picart, *Law In and As Culture: Intellectual Property, Minority Rights, and the Rights of Indigenous Peoples* (2016)

Betraying Dignity

The Toxic Seduction of Social Media, Shaming, and Radicalization

Orit Kamir

FAIRLEIGH DICKINSON UNIVERSITY PRESS
Vancouver • Madison • Teaneck • Wroxton

Published by Fairleigh Dickinson University Press
Copublished by The Rowman & Littlefield Publishing Group, Inc.
4501 Forbes Boulevard, Suite 200, Lanham, Maryland 20706
www.rowman.com

6 Tinworth Street, London SE11 5AL

Fairleigh Dickinson University Press gratefully acknowledges the support received for
scholarly publishing from the Friends of FDU Press.

British Library Cataloguing in Publication Information Available

ISBN 9781683932031 (clcth)
ISBN 9781683932055 (pbx)

Library of Congress Control Number: 2019949747

In loving memory of my parents, Shulamit and Amior Kamir, who supported me unconditionally, always, and inspired my steadfast commitment.

In fond memory also of Daniel Kaplan of Ann Arbor, who offered me a home away from home.

Contents

Acknowledgments

This book would not have been written if not for the generous support and encouragement of Anna Triandafyllidou, head of the Cultural Pluralism research in the Global Governance Programme of the Robert Schuman Centre for Advanced Studies at the European University Institute (EUI) in Florence. Anna gave me the incredible opportunity to spend two semesters (the winters of 2014 and 2015) in Florence, researching and writing this book, and enjoying the intense, vibrant academic life at the EUI. The institute's library, workshops, and fantastic members and visitors enriched me and this project tremendously.

Sven Steinmo, of the EUI, generously contributed through rigorous conversation and warm hospitality, together with Rita Kungel, for which I am deeply grateful.

Warm-felt thanks go to the colleagues at the EUI who read previous drafts of various chapters and kindly engaged in helpful dialogue: Carlos Closa, Gaby Gumbach, Sabrina Marchetti, Audrey Macklin, Dick Moon, and Eitana Guia. Friends outside the institute were equally generous and helpful in patiently reading and charitably commenting on the countless drafts of chapter 1: Orna Ben Naftali, Steve Kaplan, Rick Lempert, Carl Lewis, Sophie Moonen, and Robert Rotberg.

Having written the book in the winter of 2015, I hesitated for three years whether to publish it. If not for Caroline Picart, the editor of the Law and Culture series in Fairleigh Dickinson University Press, that this book is a part of, I might never have braved its publication. Her gentle yet insistent probing encouraged me to publish.

Sam Brawand, my excellent copyeditor, received a somewhat messy manuscript and turned the pumpkin into a fairy-tale carriage. I am grateful for her professionalism, patience, and kindness.

Kind, heartfelt thanks to James Boyd White, who generously read the entire manuscript and gave me good, supportive advice. It is rare to have a truly upright person for a mentor, and I am grateful for it.

This is an opportunity to thank Bill Miller, who taught me to understand honor and unwittingly changed my life. And to Joseph Weiler who introduced me to James Boyd White, to Bill Miller, and to the EUI.

I thank Rivka Elisha, director of the Israeli Center for Human Dignity and my good friend, for developing the notions of dignity and respect together with me since 2004. I also thank Yakir Englander, a colleague and a dear friend, for brainstorming many issues of glory with me.

Thanks to Rebecca Johnson, who invited me to the University of Victoria Law School in the fall of 2017, to present chapter 1 of this book, and to the wonderful students who engaged in deep conversation.

Elijah (Lije) Millgram kindly offered valuable and timely conversation, observations, advice, and editing for which I am deeply grateful.

My wonderful family, friends, and cats have always been there for me, loving, supportive, and forgiving even when I was preoccupied and impatient. I cannot thank them enough. Special thanks to Dina Wardi and to my sister Anat Yacobi and her family, Ruchama-Tehila, Israel, David, and Avraham-Ram, for their relentless backing and compassion.

Last but not least: this book is dedicated to my beloved parents, to whom I am forever grateful. My beloved grandparents had died long before I ventured on this expedition, but their love and support, as well as their integrity and strength, never ceased to inspire me. All four endured World War I, and two, together with my mother, survived World War II as well. The insightful lessons they learned and shared live on in my heart, in my scholarship, and in my activism. It is undoubtedly the source of my commitment to human dignity and respect. I am grateful to all four: Lola (Leah) Kanner-Frim and Arthur Frim, my mother's parents, and Haya Glicklich-Kachko and Nachum Kachko, my father's. I lament their beloved families and entire communities that perished in the Holocaust.

Introduction

Why Worry about Dignity, Honor, and Values

The specific argument I make in this book is that in the second decade of the twenty-first century, many people around the world are fleeing the social and political culture established less than a century ago, after two world wars, which I call a dignity-based culture.[1] As we abandon this new culture, we return to an older cultural structure that has been around for millennia, which, following anthropologists, I call an honor-based culture. Most of us find ourselves adopting new versions of that old cultural structure masquerading as novel and exciting. We are mostly unaware of the ancient logic and mentality of honor that underlie these contemporary social and political organizations.

In making this argument, I present both the culture that we are fleeing and the cultural structure that many of us are unwittingly returning to. I further present two additional, closely related types of cultures that are central to Western civilization. They are based on the fundamental values that I call *glory* and *respect*, and present in the following sections. I, therefore, begin this book by describing four cultural types, based on four fundamental values—*honor, glory, dignity*, and *respect*—and hope to properly distinguish them from each other. This enterprise is nothing less than an attempt to sketch out a way to think and to talk about the deepest nature of social and political cultures, and of each and every one of us, who are creatures of these social and political cultures. It is this endeavor that I invite you to join.

This ambitious venture requires that we be absolutely clear on the precise meanings of human dignity and honor, glory, and respect. This is no simple task. For decades now, much attention has been given and an abundance of meanings have been attributed to human dignity, at the expense of its adjacent and antithetical notion, honor, which has been drained, neglected, and ignored. The result is that we do not know (or at least cannot agree on) what dignity means, because the term has been overwhelmed with too many meanings, and we do not know what honor is, because we no longer give it enough thought to form a clear sense. Worse still—we confuse the two, sometimes speaking of dignity as if it included the defining components of honor. Under such circumstances, it is hard to consider an argument that builds on the bipolarity constituted by these two underlying values and the social norms built on them.

This is further complicated by the fact that in the decades of accelerated growth, the term "dignity" has absorbed the two additional notions, which I refer to as glory and respect. I attempt to untangle the conglomerate, over-reaching notion of dignity by framing a narrow, coherent definition of this concept that would distinguish it from narrow, coherent definitions of the contiguous honor, glory, and respect.

If all this were not enough, the subject matter of this book is a concept that has fallen out of grace: *value*. Readers forced to encounter this term cringe with disdain. It has been so tainted and discredited that any reference to it is almost unacceptable. Colleagues and friends who kindly read previous drafts of this book's chapters all strongly recommended substituting "value" with something more appealing. But there are two reasons that prevent me from accepting their good advice.

First, the term "value" merges two meanings: one is "standard," and the other "worth." It is precisely this combined meaning that I examine throughout the book. Human dignity is a particular standard by which we measure conduct; it is also a specific type of worth that we attribute to individuals. Honor is a different standard by which we measure conduct, and a different specific type of worth that we attribute to individuals. The same holds true for glory and respect. It is as *a standard to measure conduct and a type of worth we attribute to people* that I present each of these four concepts, comparing them to each other and distinguishing between them. It is, therefore, as values that I analyze them and values that I must call them. No other term can do the work.

Second, our disdain for "value" is one of many reasons that we escape from dignity and plunge into honor. Distancing ourselves from anything that has to do with values, we stopped thinking about them, and forgot their importance and consequence in all levels of our lives. Values guide our conduct, our visions, our choices, and our interpretations of everything in our lives. When we ignore them, we are completely unaware that we forsake one value-based system and replace it with another. Avoiding the notion of value would be stepping into the trap that I try to caution from.

Since I must speak of values, I ask my readers to suspend their disdain for the duration of this book's reading. My hope is that reencountering values, the systems of meaning that they generate, and the enormous importance they have in our lives, readers might reconsider their negative predisposition toward this sphere. In the meantime, if the word "value" sounds too disconcerting to you and disrupts the process of reading, please think of it as "moral value," or "ethical value," or anything else that works for you.

In the famous first chapter "A Disquieting Suggestion," of his 1984 book *After Virtue: A Study in Moral Theory*, Alasdair MacIntyre asked his readers to imagine the complete destruction of the natural sciences.[2] Following the catastrophe, enlightened people seek to revive science, although everyone has forgotten what it had been. So they try to use the fragmentary notions of science that they still recall, but do so out of context. They discuss relativity theory, evolutionary theory, and phlogiston theory, but it is completely meaningless. "For everything that they do and say conforms to certain canons of consistency and coherence and those contexts which would be needed to make sense of what they are doing have been lost, perhaps irretrievably."[3] They re-create a world in which the language of natural science continues to be used, but completely out of context. MacIntyre's point is

> that in the actual world which we inhabit the language of morality is in the same state of grave disorder as the language of natural science in the imaginary world which I described. What we possess, if this view is true, are the fragments of a conceptual scheme, parts which now lack those contexts from which their significance derived. We possess indeed simulacra of morality, we continue to use many of the key expressions. But we have—very largely, if not entirely—lost our comprehension, both theoretical and practical, of morality.[4]

MacIntyre first published this bleak view in 1981. His criticism was directed toward the worldview that emerged and became hegemonic in the West since the Enlightenment. As an adherent of this very enlightenment culture, I suggest that forty years after MacIntyre's lament, this culture too has been abandoned together with any reference to any type of morality. We have distanced ourselves from the ethical sphere to such a degree that we no longer use even its key expressions, such as "value," which has become mostly meaningless and even embarrassing. This paves the way, among many other things, to the unwitting abandonment of dignity and the embracement of honor. Ultimately, since this is the very topic of this discussion, I must use the term "value" and hope that readers agree to revive its fundamental meaning.

Honor, glory, dignity, and respect, four complex value terms that generate four systems of meaning, deserve full elaboration, which I attempt to provide in chapters 2 to 5. The final chapter builds on these cultural presentations to make the argument with regard to the contemporary flight from dignity culture to honor-based ones. Chapter 1 offers an overview discussion of all four values and cultures, as well as the book's layout and argument.

The rest of this introduction contains two sections. One describes the journey that brought me to the distinction among honor, glory, dignity, and respect and the four types of cultures that they give rise to. The second section offers a concise definition of the four terms as I use them in this book.

FOUND IN TRANSLATION: THE SOURCE OF THE QUADRANGLE PERSPECTIVE

My interest in dignity goes back to 1995. Thanks to the indefatigable efforts of Aharon Barak, who later became Israel's Supreme Court chief justice, the state of Israel enacted, in 1992, its Basic Law: Human Dignity and Liberty. This was a deliberate attempt to follow the lead of the Universal Declaration of Human Rights (UDHR) and the Basic Law for the Federal Republic of Germany (Grundgesetz für die Bundesrepublik Deutschland), and to make their notion of dignity the centerpiece of Israeli law. Israel's legal system almost immediately pronounced the new Basic Law to be the country's Bill of Rights.[5]

At that time I was pursuing my doctoral studies in law and culture, under the supervision of James Boyd White, at the University of Michigan's law school. Upon my return to Israel in 1995, on my first year of academic teaching of law, I was instructed to prepare and teach a first-year course on the Israeli legal system. It was then I realized that the legal system had changed dramatically in my absence, and was now speaking the new language of human dignity. Never having studied dignity systematically, I failed to fully grasp its essence. Finding little legal material on this new discourse, I turned to philosophical literature, only to discover that, in the words of Michael Rosen, "there does not exist a large, systematic body of contemporary philosophical literature on dignity."[6]

Having exhausted conventional academic sources, I turned to the foundational text of Hebrew Judaic culture, the Hebrew Bible, in search of every appearance of the Hebrew word that indicates "dignity" in Israel's Basic Law: the word *kavod* (כבוד). I was hoping that this research would shed light on the primal, authentic usage—and hence meaning—of the elusive term. But this fascinating endeavor merely added to my confusion, as it led me in seemingly many different and unconnected directions.[7]

Seeking new grounds, I turned to interpretation via translation and looked up how the Hebrew Bible's *kavod* was translated into English in different versions. It was at this point that I discovered that the Hebrew *kavod* was sometimes translated into *honor*, sometimes into *glory*, sometimes into *respect*, and sometimes (in contemporary translations) into *dignity*. Apparently, the ancient Hebrew concept *kavod* combined four notions that in English were somehow related—yet distinct. The only thing that was irrefutable was that every usage of *kavod* implied, in one way or another, weight, as the Hebrew root *k.v.d* connotes weight. The closely related Hebrew word *kaved* means both "heavy" and "liver," which was believed by the ancients to be both the body's heaviest and most significant organ. Therefore, *kavod* meant "weighty," heavyweight, in the sense of important: central, crucial, substantial.

Following the conceptual-linguistic intuition of the Hebrew Bible's translators to English, I examined separately the meaning of the *kavod* references that were respectively translated as honor, glory, respect, and dignity. This led me to the revelation that the Hebrew *kavod* served as a catchphrase for "heavyweight value" of four types: one that refers to a person's hierarchical social standing; another that refers to innate human essence; a third that refers to our divine virtue; and a fourth that attributes merit to our specific human traits. *Kavod* encompassed all these different types of value. The translations taught me that the English language does not seem to have a corresponding catchphrase, but assigns specific labels to each such type of heavyweight value. It calls the hierarchical social value *honor*, our divine virtue *glory*, the value of humanity *human dignity*, and the merit of specific human attributes *respect*.

Because they are analogous to siblings, sharing family resemblance, these values have often been confused in many ways, some innocent and some manipulative. But in a family portrait, each of them has its own distinct face, stature, and manner. If we imagine *kavod* to be the surname of this family of values, then their first names are honor, glory, dignity, and respect.

Were this so simple, this family portrait would have been unanimously acknowledged. In fact, several obstacles have occluded this interpretive option, preventing the systematic comparative investigation of the four basic values. First, only the prism of the Hebrew *kavod* invites a common examination of all four. Without *kavod*, it would be highly unlikely to address them together. Second, none of these four English terms has exclusively denoted a single meaning; over the course of history, each of them has been used to convey several of the four meanings. This historical reality has blurred the boundaries between the four distinct meanings, while simultaneously obscuring each of them.

Third, each of these notions has been carefully studied and developed by a different academic discipline. Honor has been examined very thoroughly in anthropology; glory in theology; dignity has been scrutinized in philosophy, legal philosophy, and law; and respect (not necessarily under this name) in philosophy, especially ethics, and psychology. Political science is the discipline that compares informal social institutions (codes of behavioral norms) and their histories and evolution. Circumscribed by disciplinary boundaries, the four basic values had little opportunity to convene.

As luck would have it, my studies in Michigan included several courses on honor and on honor cultures and societies with an enthusiastic expert in this field, Professor William (Bill) Ian Miller. As a student of philosophy and a lawyer (both in Jerusalem, Israel), I was exposed to Kantian ethics, the moral philosophy of Immanuel Kant,[8] as well as legal discourse on dignity. Sporadic studies of Jewish culture enabled me to learn some of the history of glory, and a lifelong keen interest in philosophy, psychology, and feminism drew me to thinkers such as Erich Fromm and Charles Taylor, as well as feminist scholars, who gave much thought to what I call respect. Most significantly, as a native speaker of Hebrew, the Hebrew *kavod* was my starting point. I was, therefore, situated at a crossroads that enabled me to consider the four concepts of dignity, honor, respect, and glory together, in light of *kavod*, distinguishing them from each other and defining each separately.

My first opportunity to present the four-faced framework took place in an international conference on the constitutional meaning of human dignity in Jerusalem, in 1999. Five years later, I published my first book on the topic, in Hebrew, *Israeli Honor and Dignity: Social Norms, Gender Politics and the Law*, laying out the framework and applying it to the analysis of Zionist history and Israeli society.[9] That same year, Rivka Elisha and I founded the Israeli Center for Human Dignity, an NGO that has been active in bringing its insights to many Israeli students, soldiers, inmates, social activists, employers, employees, and interested individuals and groups of every kind. Teaching and ceaselessly participating in discussions about honor, dignity, respect, and glory has spoken volumes. Another source of enrichment has been my Talmudic study with Yakir Englander, which has shed much light on the meanings of glory, but also of the other values.

For almost twenty years, my research and writing on this topic have been mostly in Hebrew. The last few years have seen a sudden explosion of English-written scholarly work on dignity.[10] I hope that this interest in the topic might create the opportunity to share my Hebrew-based perspective with the English-speaking world.

The many English-written treatises on human dignity have made a significant contribution to this field, each emphasizing a distinct point of view and developing a unique argument. Many of them share a presupposed commitment to the cultural linguistic history of the English term "dignity" and to its prevalent contemporary usages. I respect and appreciate this commitment but do not share it. I believe that the current preoccupation with the multitude of meanings attributed to dignity perpetuates the overburdening of the concept rather than clarifying it. My motivations and goals are different: I focus on defining, analyzing, and distinguishing the narrow, universalistic notion of dignity that, I believe, was pronounced by the United Nations' UDHR as the foundation of the global post–World War II era.

The concept that the UDHR chose to call *dignity* is, of course, linked to some of the meanings previously associated with this English word. But I believe that the dignity of the UDHR is distinct from a host of meanings that may have been associated with the English term. I believe that a focus on the precise meaning of the UDHR's notion requires some distancing from the linguistic history and common usage of the English term per se. I suggest that the UDHR's term, the dignity that has come to be the central value of constitutional and international human rights discourses, is a concept that, although attached to the English word "dignity," does not necessarily carry the word's entire cultural and linguistic baggage. This universal concept is commonly associated with the English word mostly because English is the lingua franca (common language) of the contemporary era and of the international human rights discourse. I dare to propose that we use the term "dignity" not as an English term, but as a term of Esperanto (international language) of values and norms (the same holds true for the notions of honor, glory, and respect in the context of this discussion).

ANALYTICAL DEFINITIONS OF HUMAN DIGNITY AND RESPECT, HONOR, AND GLORY

This section offers a concise version of the narrow definitions of human dignity, glory, respect, and honor that this book assumes and explores. Careful comparative review of the four concepts invites the weighing of their similar and different pros and cons. It further invites contextualized consideration of the respective value systems (i.e., foundational attitudes, ideologies) that have been built on them, and the potential tensions and possible alliances between them.

For me, each of the following values is a social construction. That is, I view the discourses of dignity, honor, respect, and glory as strictly epistemological.

Human Dignity

Human dignity is the inherent value the enlightenment-based worldview ascribes to anyone who belongs to the human family. It is equally innate to the human makeup of every human being. We can think of it as the moral hallmark of human quality that is similarly imprinted in each of us. In this context, the terms value, worth, virtue, and merit mean the opposite of measurable price: they mean priceless, innate ethical assets.

Dignity is an ethical *ought* and not an empirical *is*; it is normative and not descriptive, quality and not quantity. Human dignity does not depict people's empirical value; it constitutes them as normatively worthy by virtue of their humanity.

In line with Kantian philosophy, since human dignity is the moral value of human subjects as such—it must always be acknowledged, preserved, and upheld fully and unconditionally. It is absolutely prohibited to forgo human dignity and treat any member of the human category disregarding their intrinsic human value—that is, to treat any human as an object, as a mere means to an end.[11]

On December 10, 1948, the United Nations General Assembly adopted the Universal Declaration of Human Rights (UDHR), which determines in its first article that "all human beings are born *free and equal in dignity and rights.*" In its opening statement, the declaration proclaims that "recognition of the *inherent dignity* and of the *equal and inalienable rights* of all members of the *human family* is the foundation of *freedom, justice and peace* in the world."[12]

Liberty and equality were embraced as the foundation of the modern age as early as the late eighteenth-century American and French Revolutions. A century and a half later, the UDHR's first article clarifies that *it is in human dignity and rights that we are all equal.* It goes on, in Articles 2 and 3, to establish that the recognition of this inherent equal dignity and rights is *the basis of freedom*, liberty.

This clarification came in the aftermath of World War II and the unprecedented brutality that members of the human family forced on each other. Horrified by humankind's unleashed potential for cruel self-destruction, the world realized and declared that future human survival and prosperity ("freedom, justice and peace in the world")[13] depended upon a universal acceptance of the tenet of human dignity. A year later, this same tenet was made the centerpiece of (then Western) Germany's new constitution (Basic Law). With time, additional constitutions (such as South Africa's) and international treaties (mostly European) adopted human dignity as their underlying principle, or their foundational attitude. Half a century later, human dignity is widely accepted—now also in the English-speaking world—as the foundation of contemporary human rights–oriented culture.

Glory

Following centuries-long theological discourse, I use the word "glory" to convey the value that Judeo-Christian theologies attribute to humans as manifesting God's exceptional virtue. In the biblical narrative, God created Adam in his own divine image and likeness. In so doing, God endowed Adam with sacred, metaphysical glory, that is, with God's exclusively transcendental, infinite value. Glory was thus Adam's innate, eternal, inestimable value as God's earthly image.

Jewish and Christian theologies differ on whether sin, the Fall, and subsequent exile from Eden deprived Adam of divine human glory. Christian theologies define Jesus Christ as the second, perfect Adam and true image of God, his Father. According to this line of thought, since the Fall, divine human glory is not necessarily inherited by all humans from their ancestral first couple; however, it may be acquired through the acceptance of Christ and his gospel. Either way, in the Judeo-Christian tradition, humans who manifest the divine image of God partake in his glory.[14]

Over millennia, Jewish and Christian treaties have offered innumerable interpretations and variations on this theme. They all share the precept that human beings' innate, most precious value does not derive from tentative membership in social orders, but from the absolute divine hallmark imprinted in humans by their creator. This notion is pervasive, almost self-evident, in Christian-based European and latter American culture.[15]

Although this type of human value was traditionally called "glory," since 1948, many refer to it as "dignity." I believe that the notion of glory was the Judeo-Christian transcendental precursor of the UDHR's humanistic, secular, enlightenment-based notion of human dignity. I suggest that clear terminological and conceptual distinction between them is now inseparable from our civilization's separation of state from church/religion; of secular ethical values from theological ones; and of civic codes of norms from religious ones.

Respect

If cherishing human dignity is valuing the way in which we are all identical, revering *respect* is valuing ways in which we are different from each other. To draw on the metaphors mentioned above—we are all members of the human family, and human dignity is the family (normative) attribute that we all share. Yet none of us is merely that. On the foundation of our common humanity we each build a specific, complex, multifaceted human configuration that we think of as our personal identity. Its building blocks are myriad realizations of our characteristics, abilities, feelings, desires, choices, and attempts. Personal identity is built over time; it is fluid and ever changing. It is somewhat self-determined: a manifestation of our human autonomy. Every personal identity is a unique human achievement. In contemporary culture we encourage, cherish, and value it.

We endorse individual manifestations of our human potential because we revere individuality and pluralism. But what is the value that we ascribe to such individual, distinctive personal identities per se? The term "human dignity" assigns worth strictly to the generic stamp of fundamental humanity in each of us; to our human common denominator. I suggest that we employ the noun "respect" to denote the value we assign the richness of our different identities. Although the verb "to respect" is used for a wider range of meanings, the noun seems best suited to express the type of value that I wish to distinguish from dignity.

Respect belongs to the same universalistic, humanistic, liberal, and secular enlightenment-based foundational attitude as human dignity. But whereas human dignity conveys the veneration of an abstract idea of a singular, generic human structure—respect implies accepting recognition of multiple, concrete, unique individual identities. Human dignity endows absolute, unconditional merit and protection to the kernel of the universal human. Quite distinctly, respect can only attribute relative, tentative, and conditional value to countless actual manifestations of human plurality. Due to their endless variability, they necessarily interfere and clash with each other. If they are all to be cherished, such relish, that is, respect, must be provisional.

Respect-based rights must be more tenuous than those guaranteeing human dignity. At the same time, they correspond with a far greater variety of human needs, preferences, choices, and aspirations.

The widespread confusion of human dignity and respect blurs the crucial distinction between the necessarily absolute human dignity–based fundamental human rights and the manifold provisional respect–based rights. This confusion breeds pervasive misunderstandings, instigating a variety of accusations aimed at human dignity–based culture.

Honor

Human dignity and respect are inseparable from contemporary enlightenment-based civilization, as is the universalistic, humanistic, secular foundational attitude that they underlie. Other cultures did not and do not necessarily cherish and uphold these values and their derivatives. Instead, they have relied on alternative value systems to ascribe value, worth, to their members. The most popular and successful of those types of systems has been that of *honor and shame*. Most traditional societies in most parts of the world adhered—and often still do—to honor-and-shame foundational attitudes, their logic, psychology, and economy.

In honor-and-shame societies, honor is the relative value attributed to and felt by a member of society vis-à-vis his peers. This type of value is neither universal nor innate to all members of a group per se; quite the contrary, it implies comparative social status, prestige, rank, and standing in the hierarchical structure of a specific group. It is admired and sought after, because its accumulation promises superiority over others, hence better living and improved prospects of survival and prosperity. In honor-based societies, shame is dishonor: the absence of honor due to inherent lack or circumstantial loss.

In most honor-and-shame societies, honor is partially bequeathed and mostly gained through a careful and disciplined adherence to the norms defined by the relevant honor code. A meticulous observance of the appropriate honor norms entitles a person to honor; failure bestows shame and often harsh consequences. Honor is ceaselessly achieved, enhanced, accrued, and inevitably lost, while shame is dreaded and avoided at all costs.

Different honor societies adhere to different honor codes, that is, to different sets of social norms. In many traditional honor societies, proud self-assertion, bravery, and loyalty to group and leader were prevailing honor norms. Yet other honor societies cherished and credited scholarship, modesty, self-restraint, or entrepreneurship. In all of them, adherence to the group's specific honor code impacted every individual's standing, hence honor. There is a tendency to assume that all honor societies and their codes revered militant boldness, and that if a society does not encourage assertiveness— then it is not an honor-based one. This misinterpretation probably results from popular acquaintance with militant honor cultures (think of the Wild West, the Japanese *bushidō* [the way of warriors] culture, or Europe's dueling aristocrats). It misleads people to consider honor societies that revere self-restraint, education, financial success, or other nonmilitant values as dignity—or other value-based cultures. But what distinguishes a dignity culture from an honor one is that one ascribes to every human being absolute, universal, immeasurable worth, whereas the other ascribes to each of its members worth and standing according to their relative adherence to the group's honor norms.

In an honor-revering society, peers are in perpetual competition for honor, always measuring themselves against all others. The logic of the honor competition is, as Bill Miller aptly put it, that of a zero-sum game.[16] Since social hierarchy is a pyramid and honor corresponds to a position in the pyramid, one member's promotion must entail another's demotion. Each player's every move, therefore, affects all others' honor and relative standing.

Although anthropological literature usually refers to *traditional* honor-and-shame societies, honor mentality is very much alive in contemporary social groups all over the world. It is explicitly evident in formally hierarchical institutions, such as the military, a police force, or a penitentiary system (where ranks are symbolic badges of one's honor). It is more subtle, but no less ubiquitous in academic institutions, public settings, private organizations, and the international arena.

The logic of an honor-and-shame foundational attitude differs dramatically from that of a universalistic, humanistic, dignity-based one. Nonetheless, many people around the world are intimately familiar with both, combining them or fluctuating between them in innumerable ways. This is also true of groups, from classrooms and sports teams to countries and nations. The prevailing confusion of the terms "honor" and "dignity" intertwined with unwarranted dismissal of honor have made it almost impossible to discern honor-based interactions, emotions, responses, and attitudes from human dignity–based ones, and to analyze them accordingly.

Commitment to a value system is commitment to a moral standard that generates norms, requires certain types of conduct, and prescribes how we estimate people's worth. It entails an adherence to the norms that derive from that value system. A person who abides by a specific honor-based value system is likely to adhere to the specific norms it implies. A Japanese samurai who embraced the *bushidō* value system also lived by the *bushidō* honor code: he was likely to carry himself as the norms suggested, speak to his leader in accordance with the relevant norms, treat his wife in compliance with the right norms, deal with peers and foes as specified by the norms, and fight in light of the norms and die accordingly. The same is true of a person committed to a value system based on human dignity, glory, or respect, whether or not he or she is fully aware of it.

I believe that in one way or another, despite our disdain toward moral terminology, we are each committed to one or several of these fundamental values: honor, glory, dignity, and respect; that we adhere, at least to some extent, to their corresponding informal institutions. I believe that these values, whether or not we are fully aware of them, and however we may call them in English or in other languages, both frame and impact our respective visions of the world and of ourselves, our understanding and evaluation of situations and events, and our needs, longings, and aspirations. They inform the norms that we adhere to, reject, or create, and finally—our actions and omissions. On a larger scale, they motivate and account for aspects and elements of historical forces and developments. I suggest that by increasing our awareness and understanding of them, we can practice autonomy and free choice in evaluating and criticizing them, and in preferring one over the other.

NOTES

1. The phenomenon of fleeing freedom and dignity is not unique to the twenty-first century; it has been taking place for many decades, as chap. 6 presents in detail. This book focuses on the contemporary, twenty-first-century flight from freedom and dignity, examining its specific features.

2. Alasdair MacIntyre, "A Disquieting Suggestion," in *After Virtue: A Study in Moral Theory*, 2nd ed. (Notre Dame, IN: University of Notre Dame Press, 1984; first published 1981), 1–6.

3. MacIntyre, "Disquieting Suggestion," 1.

4. MacIntyre, "Disquieting Suggestion," 2.

5. Israel, Basic Law: Human Dignity and Liberty, 12th Knesset, March 17, 1992 (hereafter noted as Israel Basic Law); United Nations General Assembly, Third Session, Universal Declaration of Human Rights (UDHR), Resolution 217A, Paris, December 10, 1948,http://www.un.org/en/universal-declaration-human-rights/(hereafter noted as UDHR); and Germany, Basic Law for the Federal Republic of Germany, Bonn, May 8, 1949 (hereafter noted as German Basic Law).

6. Michael Rosen, *Dignity: Its History and Meaning* (Cambridge, MA: Harvard University Press, 2012), xiv.

7. For online searching and reference, please see the Hebrew Bible (HB), 2019,https://biblehub.com/.

8. Kantian philosophy will be discussed later in chap. 4. For a more detailed explanation, see Immanuel Kant, *Groundwork of the Metaphysics of Morals* (1784), trans. Thomas Kingsmill Abbott (Peterborough, ON: Broadview, 2005).

9. Orit Kamir, *Sheela Shel Kavod: Yisraeliyut U Kvod Haadam* [Israeli honor and dignity: Social norms, gender politics and the law] (Jerusalem, Israel: Carmel, 2004).

10. Among the many important new books are: Donna Hicks, *Dignity: Its Essential Role in Resolving Conflict*, foreword Archbishop Emeritus Desmond Tutu (New Haven, CT: Yale University Press, 2011); George Kateb, *Human Dignity* (Cambridge, MA: Harvard University Press, 2011); Michael Rosen, *Dignity: Its History and Meaning* (Cambridge, MA: Harvard University Press, 2012); Jeremy Waldron, *Dignity, Rank, and Rights*, ed. Meir Dan-Cohen (Oxford: Oxford University Press, 2012); David G. Kirchhoffer, *Human Dignity in Contemporary Ethics* (Amherst, NY: Teneo, 2013); Matthias Lutz-Bachman, *Human Rights, Human Dignity, and Cosmopolitan Ideas* (Burlington, VT: Ashgate, 2014); and Marcus Düwell, Jens Braarvig, Roger Brownsword, and Dietmar Mieth, eds., *The Cambridge Handbook of Human Dignity: Interdisciplinary Perspectives* (Cambridge: Cambridge University Press, 2014). Interestingly, 2014 also saw the publication of Aharon Barak's two-volume monograph on dignity in Hebrew, titled *Human Dignity: The Constitutional Right and Its Daughter-Rights* (Jerusalem, Israel: Nevo).

11. Kant, *Metaphysics of Morals*, Ak. 6:462.

12. UN General Assembly, UDHR, Article 1; Preamble; emphasis mine.

13. UDHR, Preamble.

14. Since in Judaism and Christianity, God is usually referred to in masculine terms, I do so as well. This by no means indicates a stand on the matter.

15. Not having studied Islam or other religions in this context, I cannot responsibly refer to their perceptions of the human being's value. My reference to glory in the context of Islam is sporadic and tentative; I sincerely hope that it is not inaccurate. I respectfully leave the task of applying the distinction between honor, glory, dignity, and respect in Islam and Muslim societies to experts.

16. William Ian Miller, *Humiliation and Other Essays on Honor, Social Discomfort, and Violence* (Ithaca, NY: Cornell University Press, 1993), 116.

Chapter One

Escape from Dignity to Honor

An Overview

More than seventy years after the end of World War II, there is a sense that the period of relative peace and well-being that followed two world wars, the modern-day *Pax Romana*, may be fading away.

OUR EXISTENTIAL CONTEMPORARY CONDITION

In the twenty-first century, rapid technological developments have caused professions and jobs to become redundant and superfluous; the global economy grows increasingly ruthless; and climate change and poverty have boosted massive immigration from third-world countries into developed countries. Apparently in response, liberal democracies seem to become more populist, totalitarian, chauvinistic, or militant; radical right-wing and even neo-Nazi parties and groups gain momentum; international alliances such as the European Union lose ground; and in considerable parts of the world, religious fundamentalism escalates into monstrous jihadist crusades.

At the same time, individuals in prosperous communities worldwide lose themselves in the mazes of social media and networks, sometimes enduring and perpetrating destructive shaming and bullying. Additionally, young people in elite universities cultivate what has been called victimhood culture: a zealous version of identity politics that, pursuing equality and diversity, intensifies both conformity, the fear of deviation from political correctness, and polarization between divergent groups.

I suggest that many of these sociocultural phenomena—the surge of totalitarianism and fundamentalism as well as the advent of victimhood culture and our digital obsession—are symptoms that reflect an essential feature of our time; a contemporary condition, that I call *escape from dignity*.

This book unpacks the existential condition that gives rise to populism and neo-fascism on the one hand, and victimhood culture on the other; to jihadist[1] ecstasy as well as to Facebook[2] obsession. I define this condition as fear of life under human dignity–based culture, and the consequential flight from it. Flight from dignity leads many to step into traps of new, pathological versions of honor-based culture. Such traps are set by universally powerful, interest-driven systems that thrive on the growth of these new and well-disguised versions of an honor-based culture.

I suggest that, in the name of comprehensibility, we use the word "dignity" narrowly, to exclusively denote the innate worth of any human being as such. By the expression, dignity-based culture, I mean the post–World War II version of liberal, individualistic, human rights–centered ethos. This worldview set out to safeguard humanity from the recurrence of brutal oppression and genocide. It is articulated in international documents, sanctifies human worth, and speaks the language of human rights. Conversely, these interest-driven systems that lay traps to seduce us into new forms of honor mentality are predominantly totalitarian, fundamentalist, or populist ideologies and regimes that have been on the rise in the twenty-first century. Yet they can also take the shape of power-hungry commercial conglomerates or university administrations (that sometimes facilitate and exacerbate the acceleration of excessive victimhood culture).

The malady of our time is, therefore, an escape from humanism, that is, dignity-based culture, and the unwitting embrace of pathological new versions of hierarchical and competitive collectivism—versions of honor-based culture. Escape from dignity-based humanism weakens individual autonomy, liberal democracies, and regional and international alliances; the embrace of multiple new versions of honor-based culture strengthens populist regimes, powerful commercial conglomerates (such as Facebook), and the spread of victimhood culture.

ESCAPE FROM FREEDOM

This book's argument, encapsulated in its title and presented at length in chapter 6, resonates with Erich Fromm's 1941 visionary manifesto *Escape from Freedom*.[3] As the world was in the grip of World War II, Fromm analyzed what he viewed as the universal fear of freedom and the consequential flight from it toward the arms of new versions of totalitarianism and conformism. Almost eighty years later, my argument with regard to the turn from dignity to honor via politics and social media echoes and builds on that landmark insight.

In a nutshell, Fromm claimed that after centuries of struggle, in modern times some parts of humanity achieved relative individual freedom. The overwhelming powers of religion, feudalism, patriarchal family, and oppressive state were curbed, mostly within European culture, and the individual person was somewhat free to define and to determine him- or herself. Yet, alone with this newly gained freedom, facing a senseless world and unknown future, the individual was now filled with paralyzing fear: the fear of freedom. This existential fear was experienced as isolation, loneliness, and alienation. Startled, men and women yearned for the security they now imagined that they had once felt in the arms of all-embracing tribe, nation, culture, or religion. They tried to reestablish these traditional, organic collectives—only to find that this was no longer possible; there was no way back to the (imagined) lost paradise. In their desperation, people created new versions of collectivism and belonging that became modern totalitarian social orders. In some parts of the world, people chose various forms of Fascism, including Nazism; in other parts, people allowed themselves to be brainwashed by commercials, and lost themselves in boundless, competitive consumerism.

According to Fromm, both of these paths (Fascism on one side and obsessive consumerism on the other) are damaging and self-destructive. The only healthy, sustainable way of life is for every person to pursue their unique version of individual freedom and self-determination. To accomplish this, he argues, we must not merely liberate ourselves from oppression (establish our "negative freedom"), but also learn how to engage in the creative process of self-construction and expression (manifest "positive freedom"). We should not merely rejoice in our flight from slavery (under feudalism, patriarchy, nationalism), but also learn to fulfill our individual freedom through love and creation. Only freedom that manifests itself in the authentic singular blossom of each and every individual can be strong and enduring enough to prevent a massive escape to totalitarianism and other forms of new slavery. This is why, in Fromm's view, liberal society must actively encourage and facilitate full self-development of all its members.

Escape from Freedom was written as World War II was destroying freedom and life worldwide. When the war finally ended, the nations that defeated Fascism pledged allegiance to the concept of human dignity that they erected: the equal, inherent, absolute worth of every human being. They proclaimed that human dignity was the source and goal of fundamental human rights, and that both human dignity and rights would be universally celebrated and cherished. In so doing, they established a new form of social order that was to be universal: one that aims to protect the absolute, inherent value of every human being by guaranteeing everyone's human rights. That moment of hope was meant to launch a new humanistic era worldwide and to establish a new universal culture. And indeed, the following decades have, in many ways, improved the lives of many people around the globe.

Yet, many of Fromm's insights regarding the fear of freedom and the escape back to oppression seem, once again, as relevant today as they were when he first presented them. This is why this book returns to them.

Writing during World War II, Fromm articulated his argument using the terminology of freedom (positive and negative). In the postwar era of human dignity and rights, this book offers an analogous argument, using the terminology of human dignity. Much like Fromm contrasts freedom with oppression and the free world with oppressive social systems, I contrast dignity with honor, and dignity-based culture with variations of honor-based culture. Honor is the value ascribed to a person within a hierarchical social structure that evaluates people based on their status and relative social standing. It is also the name of the fundamental principle that organizes such social systems. An honor-based social organization is different from a dignity-based social organization, much like a free society differs from an oppressive one.

Using terminology of *dignity* and *honor*, this book presents the following argument. Overwhelming change and uncertainty that plague the turn of the twenty-first century have shaken the proclaimed universal allegiance to human dignity and rights. In times of upheaval and uncertainty, dignity apparently seems too thin, abstract, and impersonal to many people around the globe. They feel lonely and unprotected in the face of devastating changes. This leads many to seek comfort and safety in traditional social systems based on honor. Yet they find that there is no going back to severed primordial ties and no rekindling of traditional, organic honor-based clans, tribes, and extended families. The fear of existence in a world based on individualistic dignity, enhanced by the longing for the imagined comforts and warmth of a collectivistic world based on honor, has been directing people to follow two new paths. One of these paths recommends authoritarian, semitotalitarian social orders, established and run by populist, neo-fascist, or fundamentalist parties and leaders. The rise of Daesh (the so-called Islamic State of Iraq and the Levant), neo-fascism, Trumpism, and Vladimir Putinism indicates the fascination with this type of escape. The other path leads to the arms of all-consuming virtual social media, to virtual versions of Islam, or to the identity politics of victimhood culture.

It is easier to accept that people who join jihad or a radical right-wing party seek the warmth of an honor-bound society. It is far harder to acknowledge that the comforts of honor may be sought in the normative, widely accepted, and now readily available arena of virtual social networks. Yet in Facebook and its ever-more *cool* satellites, people who may have initially sought dignity and respect are enticed through sophisticated underlying structures to seek constant affirmation of their standing and importance and to then build their sense of worth and meaning on perpetual, immediate virtual participation and feedback. They relinquish their privacy together with the experience of individual separateness, instead submitting to the networks' demands of permanent availability and constant response. Some engage in ruthless, age-old honor games of shaming peers and competitors, now practiced in virtual manners. In return, they feel that they receive acknowledgment and affirmation of their worth, belonging, and status as limbs of something bigger than themselves. Ultimately, they trade in the pain of lonely seclusion (associated with existence in the dignity-based culture) for ceaseless confirmation of themselves as members of tightly knit (virtual) networks, confirmation typical of honor-based groups.

Simultaneously, they serve the profit-seeking program, which thrives on their commoditization into sellable *data*—on their transformation from subjects to objects, and thereby, on their deprivation of human dignity. The well-hidden commercial platform, which profits from its members' submissive participation in the virtual honor game, rewards them for their dehumanized maintenance of the system with virtual honor points, in the shape of their numbers of followers, the times their posts are shared, or retweets.

Victimhood culture was labeled by Bradley Campbell and Jason Manning as a new moral culture, distinct from both its predecessors: dignity-and-honor-based moral cultures.[4] I suggest that this classification relies on a misinformed definition of honor and honor culture. In fact, based on their own detailed presentation of contemporary campus life in elite US universities, victimhood culture is yet another new version of honor culture. Students in elite universities develop extraordinary sensitivity to what they perceive as slights to collectives that they define themselves as members of (Hispanic, African American, LGBTQ, and others). They wage war on offenders, and enlist social media and university administrations to redeem their collectives' honor and to shame their rivals. In so doing, they merely use new tools (such as social media and university administrations) while subscribing to the logic of honor and engaging in feuding: a prevalent and harmful honor game.

In terms of post–World War II human dignity and rights, I suggest that both routes described in the previous paragraphs replace the humanitarian—dignitarian—vision with boundless hunger for and pursuit of (personal or collective) honor. Like Fromm, I believe that we must fight for our enlightenment-inspired world, and we must do so by strengthening and expanding the hold of our human dignity–based culture. Fromm claims that to fight totalitarianism we must actively and unapologetically reinforce not merely our negative freedom (the liberty from slavery), but also our positive freedom (self-manifestation). I assert that the humanist mission is not merely intended to safeguard human dignity, but to further encourage the development of every person's particular and singular self-realization. Only fully self-actualized individuals can be strong enough to cope with change and uncertainty without fleeing to honor-based totalitarian social orders or to an obsessive preoccupation with social media. I designate the noun "respect" to denote the virtue of self-manifestation. This book, therefore, urges to fortify the culture of dignity by expanding it into "dignity-and-respect culture."

A VIGNETTE DEMONSTRATING THE BROAD UTILITY OF THE QUADRILATERAL DISTINCTION BETWEEN HONOR, DIGNITY, GLORY, AND RESPECT

The previous section discussed honor, dignity, glory, and respect, mostly in the context of social structures that large groups of people adopt and adhere to. This section focuses on their application to the individual level and to interactions within small groups such as family and friends. Commitment to any of these notions begins on this personal level. Escape from dignity and pursuit of honor is relevant on a personal level as much as on a national one.

In the course of writing the first draft of this chapter, my friend Alex told me of an incident that had taken place during a visit at an academic institution some years back. Walking into the dining hall one day, Alex noticed an acquaintance, Bill, dining with two other colleagues. The convention in the institution was that colleagues, including visitors, joined each other for lunch, unless expressly requested not to. Making eye contact and smiling, Alex asked whether it was all right to join, to which Bill replied with an unqualified "yes." Alex joined, yet Bill did not interrupt the conversation to make introductions, and Alex thus merely nodded to the others at the table.

At an appropriate moment Alex ventured a comment, yet the three colleagues ignored the input and continued with their conversation. A few moments later Alex once again attempted to join the discussion, and was once again ignored. Feeling increasingly awkward, Alex wondered whether the colleagues considered this a private tête-à-tête, or a work lunch. Growing self-conscious, Alex withdrew and pretended to be absorbed in thought. The environment felt alienating and potentially hostile. Finally, since the colleagues continued as if they were alone at the table, Alex gobbled the meal as quickly as possible and had coffee privately in his office, reluctant to spend more time in the dining hall. The experience left its mark and caused caution and many secluded lunches away from potentially hurtful interactions.

The casual incident at the cafeteria (which I have since learned strikes a chord with many), is, of course, hardly significant enough to warrant concern. Yet in essence, this mundane social interaction can be deeply significant, and differs only in detail and scale from countless others. The result, a perceived offense to a person's worth that may invoke strong emotions and actions, constituting anything from tension, sadness, timidity, to conflict, hostility, confrontation, and even full-blown violence. Interactions among groups and nations are no different. In fact, I would argue that most discords, personal and collective, past and present, contain some offense to human worth. Examining a subtle but ostracizing social interaction as that in Alex's story is unlikely to incite strong moral or political responses that cloud our vision; it may, however, best demonstrate the quadrilateral-perspective framework that I propose and its usefulness.

Encountering my four-part distinction, Alex wondered how he could apply it to the incident he had experienced; how the distinction between honor, dignity, respect, and glory could help him deal with his hurt and frustration.

I suggest we use *human dignity* strictly to mean every person's intrinsic, immeasurable, inviolable value as a human being and a member of the human family. To figure out whether the offense he suffered was to human dignity, Alex would need to ask himself whether the colleagues' dismissal of him was dehumanizing, and whether it rendered him (or attempted to render him) less human than others. Did the colleagues' rude conduct indicate that he, or any person, may have lesser inherent value than others? Did their cold shoulder deny the universality of intrinsic human worth?

In the Judeo-Christian world, many assign humankind innate value because, created in God's image, man manifests his glory. To distinguish this theological perspective from a universalistic, enlightenment-based one, I refer to this type of human worth as *glory*, and distinguish it from the narrow definition of human dignity. To address this aspect of Alex's worth, he would need to assess whether the colleagues' conduct toward him tarnished the divine spark, that metaphysical, transcendental glory imprinted in each of us by the creator. Simply put: scarring a person's body is often considered an offense to the divine human glory. Did the colleagues' behavior scar Alex's soul enough to be considered such an offense?

Perhaps the hurt felt by Alex was the emotional response to lack of recognition, acceptance, and appreciation of his *specific*, concrete personal identity and quality. I use the noun "respect" to denote the merit of a person's unique individuality as such. To investigate this perspective, Alex would have to consider whether his pain was caused by the blunt refusal to acknowledge his value as the thoughtful, intelligent, original, articulate, and witty individual he has worked to be.

From yet another perspective, perhaps Alex's deep sense of discomfort was shame and humiliation: one's inevitable response to loss of *honor*. Following the long-standing anthropological convention, I designate the term "honor," as well as the words "shame" and "humiliation," to refer exclusively to a person's relative value in social terms of hierarchical standing, status, rank, and prestige within a specific, tightly knit group. We may ask, was the colleagues' blunt exclusion a public signal, simultaneously constituting and exposing Alex as unworthy of their notice? Were they nonverbally declaring and revealing that Alex's standing in the social hierarchy of the profession or the department was dramatically lower than theirs? Perhaps publicly placing themselves out of his reach elevated the colleagues' professional and societal honor at the expense of their visitor's, triggering Alex's sense of shame and humiliation.

Why bother to define whether the offense was to dignity, glory, respect, or honor? Because it may assist both Alex and the rest of us, the surrounding society, in understanding the type of harm done and in deciding what means are best suited to redress it. If we frame the injury as offending Alex's honor, we may define the incident as a case of *shaming*, describe the injury as loss of face, and suggest that Alex avenge himself on the others, or that the academic department in which the incident occurred consider whether its honor culture breeds a hostile work environment. If we determine that the incident constituted a violation to human dignity, we may urge Alex to file a complaint to a human rights tribunal. If we conclude that divine human glory was disgraced, we may wish to rebuke the colleagues for contemptuous treatment of the image of God. Finally, if we agree that respect is at stake, we may advise Alex to leave the hostile, disrespectful environment and seek a more emotionally nourishing one.

Of course, we may decide that the conduct offended several of these values and requires multiple responses. Or, expressing a more specific moral view, we may decide to focus exclusively on the protection of human dignity, discarding offenses to honor, or to glory, or to respect (likewise, we may, of course, choose to protect exclusively each of the other values).

It is possible and likely that we will differ on the analysis of any incident: some of us will see it foremost through the lens of honor, and others through the lens of respect, or dignity, or glory. The common terminology cannot overcome such differences. It may, however, provide for a common language to understand and discuss them. It enables constructive, respectful conversation.

As Alex considered the possibilities, he concluded that there was no offense to human dignity, as the colleagues' behavior did not challenge the value of humanity per se—at least not to a significant extent. He said that glory was not a part of his worldview, and his pain was not related to his divine merit. There was no doubt in his mind that his exclusion undermined his social standing, that is, his honor, yet he said that this aspect was not a major concern for him. He concluded that the incident deprived him, above all else, of the recognition, acknowledgment, and acceptance that we tend to think one requires in order to flourish. Having been allowed to participate in the discussion, Alex may have actively pursued and practiced self-determination and growth. Denial of this opportunity may be the gravest damage caused by the described interaction. It is, therefore, the value system, set of emotions, code of conduct, and moral logic that correspond with *respect* to which he now turned in seeking to rectify the damage he incurred.

The analysis gets more complicated when class, race, gender, and sexual orientation come into play. I have so far led you to assume that Alex, like Bill and the colleagues, were all white men. But what if Bill and his colleagues were indeed white men, while Alex was a woman of color, a transgendered person, or physically challenged? In such cases, she—as well as many of us—may evaluate the offense differently. We may focus on the offense to universal human dignity, feeling that the colleagues' conduct challenged Alex's equal human value. We may also consider the exclusion as a more significant offense to the honor of the group of which Alex is a member.

Unless we all use the same terminology to discuss and to argue this point, we may all speak of dignity, while we each respond (in emotions and conduct) to a different grievance. Such blindness breeds mutual misunderstanding and further offense. It may lead to an individual or group's withdrawal or aggression. Common terminology may help us not merely to understand each other's differing views on the situation but also to accept them. It is easier to accept that someone evaluates the situation differently if one knows that their point of view is respect based, whereas another's is honor based. Such tolerance may also lead one to search for solutions that would satisfy adherents of both honor and respect. It may even enable one to accept more calmly a decision based on a different value than the one they would have ascribed the situation.

In the second decade of the twenty-first century, young people in US universities refer to offenses such as the one experienced by Alex as "microaggression."[5] Such labeling is not conducive to identify which value system was harmed, and whether it is one that we wish to uphold. Some microaggressions may offend human dignity, while others give slight to the honor of a person and a group to which they belong. Some microaggressions may ignore the respect that a person requires to flourish, and others may offend the image of God embedded in humankind. If we are adherents of dignity, we may not want to consider slights to honor as seriously as offenses to dignity. The label, microaggression, blurs these important distinctions, preventing us from identifying the value system, the foundational attitude that we want to promote and sustain as a common denominator.

Furthermore, the consequence is that any slight to honor is likely to be considered a serious transgression and grievance; hence, the honor-based system is unwittingly strengthened and entrenched—perhaps at the expense of other value systems. I believe this is one way in which many flee dignity, embracing honor on both the individual and the social levels.

The quadrilateral-perspective framework invites us to examine, in every situation, what the damage is in terms of each value system, that is, foundational attitude, and which perspective or perspectives we wish to uphold and act on. This framework is applicable to more emotionally and politically charged social situations than the cafeteria incident. So, for example, airport security checks have repeatedly aroused forceful protestations, claiming that bodily searches compromise human dignity. Defining dignity narrowly, distinguishing it from glory, honor, and respect, we may want to consider whether it is human dignity that the security checks defy, or whether they curtail personal self-determination (hence effecting respect) or publicly demean people of high standing (hence staining honor). Perhaps certain practices of security checks may offend some people's honor, while others offend both honor and human dignity. The operative normative question would be: Do we want to consider honor in this context, or do we focus solely on the protection of dignity?

Force-feeding of hunger striking prisoners similarly gives rise to heated debates regarding human dignity. Clearly, force-feeding undermines prisoners' respect and honor: food is forced unto them against their personal will (offending respect), exposing their helplessness and vulnerability (insulting honor). Preservation of divine human glory may support forced feeding, to prevent human death at all costs. But does human dignity likewise require the forced feeding, or does it mandate protection of the integrity of prisoners' bodies and will even at the expense of their lives? In order to determine this difficult issue, we would need to choose whether life itself or liberty is predominant in the makeup of human dignity. If we choose to exclusively apply glory or honor considerations—we may ignore these nuances of dignity philosophy, and either approve of forced feeding (to uphold glory) or prohibit it (to uphold honor).

Multicultural interactions are particularly likely to be fraught with misunderstandings regarding offenses to personal and collective human worth. Precise distinction of dignity from honor may enable members of Western communities to better understand the humiliation and outrage felt by members of honor-cherishing communities, even when narrowly defined human dignity does not seem to be compromised. To give a familiar example: publishing a humorous caricature of the prophet Muhammad may seem, from a dignity-and-respect-based point of view, as an act of personal autonomy and self-manifestation, deriving from human dignity and respect and protected by human rights. From an honor-based perspective this same act may seem as outrageously shaming, calling for vengeance and cleansing of the prophet's—and his followers'—offended honor. It might trigger an honor-based attack on the culture of human dignity and rights. From a glory-based perspective, a caricature of God's prophet may be seen as abomination.[6] Do we want to uphold dignity and respect at all costs, or to balance them against considerations arising from honor and glory?

Likewise, a request to unveil a woman's face may be understood, from a dignity-based perspective, as upholding basic human dignity. From a glory-based perspective, the demand to expose body parts may be perceived as offensive to divine human glory, and from an honor-based point of view imposition of such a demand may be humiliating to the unveiled woman, to her father, husband, family, or culture. Additionally, some women protest against the unveiling from a respect-based perspective, claiming that their personal free choice to veil their faces should be respected. Some such women claim that preservation of the abstract human dignity might come at the expense of offense to concrete respect. Which of the two should prevail in such a clash?

In order to address a sensitive situation, it is initially necessary to agree on common terminology that makes it possible to distinguish between these different perspectives. This paves the way to communication, negotiation, and hopefully mutual tolerance and reflexive decision-making. In such an atmosphere, attempts may be made to find a solution that accommodates several of the competing values. Even if eventually the defense of human dignity is chosen at the expense of honor, glory, or respect, or vice versa, it can be formulated and explained in the most comprehensible and respectful manner, and perhaps be more acceptable to those whose stands were overruled.

EVOLUTIONARY NARRATIVE
UNDERLYING THE BOOK LAYOUT

I am an avid believer in stories. This book, therefore, makes the argument regarding escape from dignity by narrating the story of the evolution of honor, glory, human dignity, and respect, and the normative codes that they inspired. In slightly other words, political scientist Sven Steinmo's, this book tells the story of informal institutional evolution.[7] The narrative culminates in the current escape from dignity back to honor-bound informal institutions. It is a long and winding road that I take, in belief and hope that the travel provides as much pleasure as the arrival at the destination.

This is roughly how the story goes: Once upon a time there were many young societies all over the world that played and developed the ambitious, competitive game of honor and shame. Over time, they established and nurtured many honor-based societal and intersocietal informal institutions. Members of these societies derived their sense of self, self-worth, and meaning from the honor codes they were born into and spent lifetimes learning, mastering, developing, and cherishing.

On the fringes of some such cultures, some religious ideologies suggested the subversive normative idea that at least in one sense all humans were of equal value: the valuable image of the world's divine creator was imprinted in each and every one of them, disregarding the clan they belonged to, the territory they lived on, or their position within their group's honor game. Let us call the notion of divine human value *glory*.

One way of telling the history of Christian Europe is as the struggle to integrate these two value systems (honor and glory based) and their respective informal institutions. The medieval Crusades were one such particularly dramatic attempt. Much later, as late as the nineteenth century, Europeans in the United States of America were divided over the question whether people of African origin could and should be considered as members in communities defined by honor- or glory-based rules. It took the bloody Civil War to apply (at least formally) both honor-and-glory-based informal institutions to all US citizens. As late as the first half of the twentieth century, in the heart of Europe, Nazi ideology dismissed glory altogether, trying to revive an exclusively honor-based world in which Aryans are at the top of the honor hierarchy, and some Others (including Roma, Jews, LGBTQ, and people with disabilities) are excluded from it altogether (and hence from the right to live).

The modern era started when human individuality gradually became an increasingly revered and celebrated value. As philosopher Charles Taylor notes in his *Sources of the Self: The Making of the Modern Identity*, the Renaissance creative artist became a role model: humans were encouraged to pursue, find, choose, liberate, and express their unique true selves.[8] Such selves were assigned growing respect.

Yet simultaneously, as societies grew into nations and nation-states, and the foundational attitude of honor and shame merged with the modern ideology of nationalism, the competition for national honor became increasingly powerful, dangerous, and costly. National honor overshadowed the developing reverence of the unique individual human self. It took two world wars and roughly a hundred million lives lost for the nations of the world to realize that survival of the species and the universe required relinquishment—or at least the curtailing of the honor-and-shame-based informal institutions and the war games that they entailed.

As the basis for an alternative, foundational attitude that would organize the new world order and its institutions, the modern nations agreed to secularize the idea of glory (the religious concept of divine imprint in human beings) and label it "human dignity," meaning equal fundamental human value, per se, imprinted unconditionally in every member of the human family. They stated this agreement in a United Nations Universal Declaration of Human Rights (UDHR), and on this basis toiled to build new informal institutions: norms that would define and defend basic universal human rights.[9] Review of the UDHR reveals that it embraces both dignity and respect; yet it was the minimalistic dignity, and not the more ambitious respect, that received the most attention.

The revolutionary process announced by the UDHR has been developing in significant parts of the world. Yet, often lacking meaningful, systematic fortification of respect, many people experience and view contemporary, dignity-based informal institutions as disappointingly thin and formalistic. Disillusioned and alienated, even as they seek dignity and respect, many find refuge in honor-based informal institutions, which now abound in the virtual spheres of social media and the internet. A few are sucked into honor traps in the service of fundamentalist or nationalist ideologies; some join the honor wars of *victimhood culture* on elite US campuses.

This story, as told in this book, suggests that the dignity-oriented global culture's next logical step is sketching and constructing systematic norms that would affirm and secure richer and more diverse human rights that reflect, uphold, and enhance respect. This would strengthen and empower individuals, enabling them to thrive as such, rather than escape dignity and replace it for honor-based systems.

Further, the secularized human dignity shed most of the sublime, spiritual residue that divine human glory had traditionally enjoyed. The absence of the spiritual dimension reduces the secular concept's attraction for many people, making the libidinous honor seem more alluring in comparison. Dignity culture, therefore, might search for its own versions of spirituality and passion.

In the presentation of honor-and-shame societies, the notion of glory, and the concept of human dignity, this book's contribution is mostly in the descriptive mapping out of what has been amply researched and analyzed in several disciplines, naturally preferring certain interpretations to others. The less trodden path is the book's evolutionary narrative in its entirety, the suggested quadrangle perspective, and the conceptual-normative distinction between dignity and respect.

Chapter 2 introduces honor as a foundational attitude in honor-and-shame societies, demonstrating how adherence to the honor principle motivates members of such groups. It presents their experience of relentless competition for social precedence and recognition and the feeling that they must excel and conquer at all costs. The chapter narrates the acceleration of honor conflicts as European honor groups grew from clans and city-states into nations. Chapter 3 follows the development of the alternative, subversive value system nourished by the Judaic and Christian cultures. This value system centers on glory—God's divine merit that is embedded in humankind and adorns us with inherent worth. This notion (in its pure form) fosters mutual reverence among fellow humans, as well as the adherence to divine commandments regarding the treatment of the human body and soul. The chapter follows the fusion of glory and honor in European culture. Chapter 4 narrates how, after two world wars, the world, led by the United Nations, realized that honor has become vastly deadly and dangerous. After World War II, the conquering Allies decided to repress the thirst for honor and to mitigate it with a modern, universal, atheistic variation on glory: human dignity. This new formulation drew on Kantian philosophy[10] and was shaped in binary opposition to honor.

Chapter 5 presents respect, defined as the value bestowed on diverse manifestations of personal characteristics. Individuality has been venerated for several centuries, and its recognition has been defined by philosophers such as Charles Taylor and psychologists such as Erich Fromm. This chapter suggests that respect, the value of concrete, specific individuality, is the unpronounced basis of the next phase of human rights; it is the offspring hidden in the folds of the UDHR's sanctification of dignity. The merit accorded human specificity, respect, is the value that is yet to be fully spelled out, acknowledged, elaborated, celebrated, and made the foundation of the next generation of human rights.

Lastly, chapter 6 presents the flight from dignity by referring to fundamentalism and populist nationalism (including Trumpism), on the one hand, and social media (including victimhood culture) on the other hand, as overwhelmingly powerful and enticing honor-based platforms. *Donald Trumpism* is presented as an American dignity-escape and honor-seeking response to the growing international Muslim fundamentalism. Victimhood culture is discussed as yet another US honor-bound, social media–inspired subculture that is currently locked in a feud with Donald Trumpism. The chapter alludes to Fromm's analysis in his book *Escape from Freedom*. It suggests that fundamentalism and populist ideologies (including Trumpism) and social media (including the related victimhood culture) constitute the early twenty-first century's most alluring honor traps, much as, according to Fromm, Fascism and the culture of advertisement lured the masses away from freedom in the first half of the twentieth century.

While I paid homage to Fromm's book *Escape From Freedom*, it is, of course, not the only source of inspiration for this one. Over the long course of developing the dignity-honor-respect-glory argument, I have read dozens of books and articles that all contributed, in one way or another, to fine-tuning my thoughts. Zygmunt Bauman's *Liquid Modernity*, Yuval Noah Harari's *From Animals into Gods: A Brief History of Humankind*, and Harari's *Homo Deus: The History of Tomorrow* are but three shining examples.[11] In a conscious attempt not to overburden the reader of this book with an incessant flow of names, titles, references, and nuances, I deliberately trimmed down quotes and references. In fact, to minimize the reader's feeling of cacophony and confusion, I attempted to construct each of the book's sections as a dialogue with a single other (usually academic) voice. This, sadly, forced me to leave out many important contributions to the many topics this book touches on. It brought me to leave out minority and dissenting voices and focus on founding text. I am acutely conscious of this, and hope to make up for it in the future. I am, of course, grateful and indebted to all the many thinkers and writers on whose shoulders I gratefully stand.

The book of Genesis (11:4–9)[12] tells the ancient-world story of the tower of Babel that our ancestors attempted to build together. Their aspirations were thwarted by God's confounding their language, causing them to break into groups speaking diverse dialects. This divine intervention produced such disruptive misunderstanding that the ancients had to abandon their plan of building a universal city and tower. Separated by words, they gave up on the collective dream to reach the stars.

In 1948 we tried again, this time aspiring to build a universal value system and social institutions that would ensure our human rights and survival together. In the UDHR, we stated that *"a common understanding of these rights and freedoms is of the greatest importance for the full realization of this pledge."*[13] Yet, once again, many things came between us, among them our conflicting interests and ideologies, mutual suspicions, fragility, impatience, alienation—and languages.

We aim for human dignity, but each of us hears something different; we want to build together a dignity-based world for our common well-being—but fail to hand each other the proper tools. In our frustration we turn away from our common project and escape to various illusions of safety and comfort in numbers and honor. This book cannot bridge over conflicting interests, ideologies, and mutual suspicions; it cannot overcome or remedy fragility, impatience, and alienation. But it aspires to remind us of the possibility of a common language with which we intended to build our universal future, based on human dignity, respect, and rights. It voices the plea that we do not give up, abandoning it for self-destructive alternatives, but rather that we fortify our universal, humanistic project by expanding our commitment to human dignity into commitment to the combined vision of dignity and respect.

NOTES

1. *Jihad* is, of course, the term denoting Muslim religious wars, and indeed the bloodcurdling images of Daesh (the so-called Islamic State of Iraq and the Levant) soldiers beheading prisoners are the epitome of our collective nightmare. Yet fanatic, fundamentalist Christianity (in the United States for example); fanatic, fundamentalist Judaism (in Israel and the West Bank); and fanatic, fundamentalist Hinduism (in India) can also be said to be waging religious wars—jihad—on contemporary, liberal, dignity-based, rights-oriented culture.

2. I refer to Facebook since, at the time of writing this book, it is the largest and most influential platform of its kind.

3. Erich Fromm, *Escape from Freedom* (1941; repr., New York: Avon Books, 1965).

4. Bradley Campbell and Jason Manning, *The Rise of Victimhood Culture: Microaggressions, Safe Spaces, and the New Culture Wars* (Cham, Switzerland: Palgrave Macmillan, 2018), 12.

5. Campbell and Manning, *Rise of Victimhood Culture*, 3–20. See discussion in chapter 6.

6. I am referring here to the attack on the journal *Charlie Hebdo* in Paris, France, on January 7, 2015. See Adam Withnall and John Lichfield, "Charlie Hebdo Shooting: At Least 12 Killed as Shots Fired at Satirical Magazine's Paris Office," *Independent*, January 7, 2015,https://www.independent.co.uk/news/world/europe/charlie-hebdo-shooting-10-killed-as-shots-fired-at-satirical-magazine-headquarters-according-to-9962337.html.

7. Political scientist Sven Steinmo has written extensively on the evolution of informal institutions. See, for example, Steinmo, "Evolutionary Narratives," in *The Evolution of Modern States: Sweden, Japan, and the United States* (Cambridge: Cambridge University Press. 2010), 1–29; Orion A. Lewis and Sven Steinmo, "How Institutions Evolve: Evolutionary Theory and Institutional Change," *Polity* 44, no. 3 (July 2012): 314–39.

8. Charles Taylor, *Sources of the Self: The Making of the Modern Identity* (Cambridge: Cambridge University Press, 1989), 22.

9. United Nations General Assembly, Third Session, Universal Declaration of Human Rights (UDHR), Resolution 217A, Paris, December 10, 1948, Preamble, http://www.un.org/en/universal-declaration-human-rights/ (hereafter noted as UDHR).

10. See Immanuel Kant, *Groundwork of the Metaphysics of Morals* (1784), trans. Thomas Kingsmill Abbott (Peterborough, ON: Broadview, 2005).

11. Zygmunt Bauman, *Liquid Modernity* (Cambridge, UK: Polity, 2000); Yuval Noah Harari, *From Animals into Gods: A Brief History of Humankind* (Charleston, SC: CreateSpace, 2012), and *Homo Deus: The History of Tomorrow* ([Toronto, ON]: Signal, 2015).

12. For references to Hebrew or Christian biblical verses, see: Hebrew Bible (HB), 2019, https://biblehub.com/; and King James Bible (KJV), 2019, https://biblehub.com/.

13. UDHR, Preamble; emphasis mine.

Chapter Two

The Honor Game

The peacock's disproportionately large tail is a potential death trap: the bigger and heavier the tail, the slower and more vulnerable its owner. Fanned, the tail renders its owner completely helpless. Nevertheless, peacocks seem decidedly self-satisfied fanning their inefficient tails, and onlookers exclaim in awe at what we consider a magnificent sight. What is the logic of that?

THE HANDICAP PRINCIPLE

Biologists Amotz and Avishag Zahavi suggest in their 1997 book *The Handicap Principle* that the bigger and heavier the tail, the more powerful the statement conveyed through its fanning: *"anyone who dares fan this heavy tail, and is still alive—must be really self-assured, hence—surely a superior peacock."* The Zahavis consider this an example of what they call *the handicap principle*. According to this principle, when a member of a group burdens itself in a seemingly inefficient way, it might be signaling to its group that it can afford to do so, that is, it is strong, confident, and superior enough to dare act extravagantly. As a reward, the self-handicapping member gains social status within the group; and as a result, the group rewards it with recognition and appropriate eminence.[1]

The peacock's tail fanning is a flamboyant example of what the Zahavis describe as a prevalent phenomenon. Their flagship example is the social conduct of the Arabian babbler, a bird that the Zahavis have studied closely since the 1970s. Babblers live long lives (several decades) in stable, enduring, tightly knit, and very strictly hierarchical groups. They follow precise and intricate rules, which dictate performance of various social roles, such as feeding other members, protecting the group's territory, and standing on

17

guard for hunters. Adherence to the rules and execution of the social roles they prescribe bestow status and rank.

The hierarchy is structured so that the higher the status, the greater the responsibilities and tasks it carries with it. At the same time, high status also involves desirable perks: rich food, fertile playmates, and choice of tasks. Upward mobility is, therefore, attractive to most members, who are willing— and often eager—to work hard and compete to improve their social standing. When two or more group members compete for status, they try to outperform each other, each taking on more social tasks, and the harder—the better.

To maintain status, a member performs the tasks that accord with its relative standing in the hierarchy. To gain higher status, a member performs ever more arduous, demanding, and sometimes dangerous social roles. Desiring upward mobility, most group members are constantly engaged in purchasing, substantiating, securing, and seeking more status in the group, through ceaseless adherence to rules and to strenuous performance of social tasks. Everyone's social work is performed as they all perpetually observe and monitor each other, keeping track and score. It is the watchful community, applying its unwritten rules, that determines, in unity, who gains status and how much. All are implicated and affected by each such move, so all have a vested interest in monitoring everyone and in exact application of the rules.

The babblers are not alone: the Zahavis describe numerous behaviors of a great variety of species that subscribe to the logic of the handicap principle and manifest it. According to this logic, the greater (and often more dangerous) the task performed, the higher social rank it secures for its performer. And the higher a member's social rank, the greater the tasks it has to perform to maintain and improve its status. This logic, inducing members to perform ever-increasing social tasks, serves the group's interests, forever encouraging individuals to compete for growing social responsibilities—even at their own peril. In return for their accelerating efforts, the group awards its obedient members status, standing, and rank, that is, worth within its social hierarchy.

Self-endangering group-promoting conduct among animals is often celebrated as altruistic. According to the Zahavis, such conduct must be understood in the context of strong communitarianism (that is, strict flock, pack, or herd structure), firm hierarchical social order, and group acknowledgment of elaborate social rules related to the social hierarchy. From this perspective, self-endangering animals are not merely self-sacrificing: they follow social rules as a way of competing for social status at all costs.

Like many animals, a babbler's rank within the group is more important to it than anything else; gaining and maintaining status and social recognition is motivation that trumps even the will to live. Apparently, the typical babbler does not consider life outside its group. It is first and foremost a team player; as such, it does whatever possible to fortify and to improve its place within the team. In return, the group awards it the appropriate status reflecting its social conduct. This gratifies the individual—while preserving the system. The process is dynamic, self-perpetuating, and *stagnation proof*, because when another group member outshines our babbler by performing even more arduous social labor, it will rise in the hierarchy, pushing our poor babbler back and down. Our babbler will have to work even harder to regain its rank, let alone ascend in the hierarchy. Such competition among members may be exhausting for the individuals, but it serves the group and the system well.

The context is, therefore, that of competition for status within group hierarchy, and the heavier the burden a group member endures performing social tasks in line with the group's rules, the more social status that individual gains. If so, you may ask, why does the peacock fan its tail? This flamboyant self-handicapping practice serves no practical social task (such as feeding or guarding), so why perform and reward it? I daresay that the colorful practice seems to be a pure symbol of the abstract, general handicap principle itself—much like the maintenance of a luxurious, costly mansion, designed, above all else, *for show*—to signal the endurance of high costs, connoting high status. A grand mansion sets a high standard, discouraging potential competitors.

If the babblers—or the peafowls—were human, if they were building mansions instead of fanning tails, anthropologists would refer to the handicap principle that they subscribe to as *honor*. The specifics of each group's social interactions, deriving from the handicap/honor principal, manifesting and upholding it, would be considered *an honor code*.[2] I suggest that the honor structure performs parallel functions in human societies as does the handicap principle in the animal kingdom. If you reread this section substituting people for babblers, peafowls, and members of other flocks, packs, and herds—you may get a good sense of honor and the logic of the social world it structures.

EXTRAPOLATING THE HONOR PRINCIPLE

In the mid-twentieth century, cultural anthropologists observed, documented, and interpreted systemic honor-based social conduct in small, secluded, traditional Mediterranean communities, typically those of remote Greek, Italian, Spanish, and North African villages. The founders and most prominent leaders of this trend were John George Péristiany and Julian Pitt-Rivers, others following in their footsteps.[3] The research of honor-based culture was mostly associated with the Mediterranean region and its long-standing sociocultural practices.[4] Gradually, additional parts of the world were scrutinized using this perspective. Increasingly, cultural anthropologists realized that not only the Middle East, the Arab and Muslim worlds,[5] Indian cultures,[6] and Japan[7]—but also Latin America,[8] southern US states,[9] and even northern and western European cultures[10] (such as Iceland,[11] France,[12] Germany[13]) could be studied, described, and analyzed as honor cultures. Typically, each anthropological study researched and documented, in great detail, the specific mechanisms of a singular honor society—just as the Zahavis' meticulous study documented the specific systemic manifestations of the handicap principle within a particular group of babblers.[14]

From their detailed studies of particular flocks and herds, the Zahavis extrapolated the general handicap principle. Similarly, comparing varieties of specific honor societies, some scholars of human societies have been extrapolating a general, abstract concept of the honor principle. Just as the handicap principle is an organizing structure that underlies the operation of herds and flocks, and their members—so, too, honor is an underlying, organizing logic that motivates and informs the function of human social groups and their members. A feature of human societies, honor may be defined not merely as a principle, but also as the core of a value system, that is, as a fundamental value, that underlies an honor society's informal institution: its honor code.[15]

The theoretical elaboration of honor as a sociocultural organizing principle can be traced back to Pitt-Rivers and Péristiany and their fellow contributors to the anthropological research of Mediterranean communities. But in the following decades, academic interest in honor waned and faded, and the subject was mostly abandoned. Study of honor societies must have seemed too structural for poststructural anthropologists. Concomitantly, upstanding philosophers and sociologists such as Charles Taylor, Pierre Bourdieu, and Peter Berger contrasted honor with dignity, declaring that honor-based dynamics were replaced, together with the premodern regimes that they served, by the modern logic and ethics of human dignity.[16] Viewing these declarations both interesting and important, let me quote them in some length.

A researcher of North African honor, Bourdieu stated in no uncertain terms that

> the ethos of honor is fundamentally opposed to a universal and formal morality which affirms the equality in dignity of all men and consequently the equality of their rights and duties. Not only do the [honor] rules imposed upon men differ from those imposed upon women, and the duties towards men differ from those towards women, but also the dictates of honor, directly applied to the individual case and varying according to the situation, are in no way capable of being made universal. This is so much the case that a single system of values of honor establishes two opposing sets of rules of conduct—on the one hand that which governs relationships between kinsmen and in general all personal relations that conform to the same pattern as those between kinsmen; and on the other hand that which is valid in one's relationships with strangers. This duality of attitudes proceeds logically from the fundamental principle . . .

according to which the modes of conduct of honor apply only to those who are worthy of them.[17]

Sociologist Berger has similarly contrasted dignity with honor:

> Both honor and dignity are concepts that bridge self and society. . . . The concept of honor implies that identity is essentially, or at least importantly, linked to institutional roles. The modern concept of dignity, by contrast, implies that identity is essentially independent of institutional roles. . . . In a world of honor, the individual discovers his true identity in his roles, and to turn away from the roles is to turn away from himself—in "false consciousness," one is tempted to add. In a world of dignity, the individual can only discover his true identity by emancipating himself from his socially imposed roles—the latter are only masks, entangling him in illusion, "alienation" and "bad faith." . . . In a world of honor, identity is firmly linked to the past through the reiterated performance of prototypical acts. In a world of dignity, history is the succession of mystification from which the individual must free himself to attain "authenticity."[18]

Philosopher Taylor has also similarly commented that

> it is obvious that this concept of dignity is the only one compatible with a democratic society, and that it was inevitable that the old concept of honor was superseded. . . . With the move from honor to dignity has come a politics of universalism, emphasizing the equal dignity of all citizens and the content of this politics has been the equalization of rights and entitlements.[19]

Honor was thus declared antithetical to the contemporary, universal, equal human dignity, hence irrelevant to the present. (As presented in chapter 1, while I completely agree that honor is antithetical to dignity, I am far less confident that it is indeed a structure of the past, or of North African societies.)

No less important seems to be the prevailing sentiment that honor is simply not an organizing principle to take pride in; it is grossly politically incorrect. Indeed, the few scholars who research honor plead with their readers that as unattractive as it may be, honor must be acknowledged and understood. In the words of Kwame Anthony Appiah, author of the 2010 *The Honor Code*, "It is surely better to understand our nature and manage it than to announce that we would rather we were different . . . or, worse, pretend that we don't have a nature at all. We may think that we have finished with honor, but honor is not finished with us."[20]

Robert L. Oprisko, author of the 2012 *Honor: A Phenomenology*, put it more bluntly: "Honor's evolution as a concept has instilled it with qualities that are politically incorrect, display some of the less flattering qualities of humanity, and perpetuate inequality. . . . Honor is a social fact, even if some would choose to ignore it."[21]

I was first introduced to the study of honor in 1993, through Professor William (Bill) Ian Miller's course on saga Iceland at the University of Michigan in Ann Arbor. A keen scholar of Old Icelandic literature, Miller went on to fashion a vivid perception of honor as a sociocultural organizing structure.[22] Over the last twenty years I have applied Miller's notion of honor to countless sociocultural texts and situations, testing, exploring, and developing it in the process. My Miller-based conceptualization of honor is not significantly different from that presented by other honor scholars, such as Oprisko. Nevertheless, our percepts differ in emphasis and nuance,[23] and—most notably—in terminology. So, for example, Oprisko's usage of the terms "glory" and "dignity" differs significantly from mine.[24]

It is, of course, colorful and captivating to introduce and discuss particular manifestations of honor—as is the mention of the peacock's fanned tail. No scholarly analysis will arouse my reader's appetite for honor more than bloody anecdotes of honorable duels between medieval knights or romantic gentlemen; grim tales of Old Icelandic or timeless Bedouin blood feuds; or epic stories of *bushidō*-bound samurai (or their dutiful wives) stoically committing honor suicide. Yet my objective here is to present you with a concise overview of honor per se; the organizing principle/fundamental value extrapolated from the study of numerous specific honor societies and their concrete cultural practices. The goal is to acquaint you with the logic of honor that underlay most societies of antiquity, a logic that is still very much present, potent, and alluring even today, politically incorrect, academically shunned, and commonly suppressed and denied as it may be. To perk up the familiarization process, I implore you to summon the images of an honor culture of your choice, and cast your favorite John Wayne, Zorro, or Zorba the Greek character as the leading man of honor of the enfolding tale, as you embark on the voyage into the ideal-type honor society.

SHAME: THE ABSENCE OF HONOR

Honor, in honor societies, is a precious *good*, often regarded as a man's most valuable possession.[25] Acquiring, accumulating, and defending one's honor and avenging attacks on it may be more important than life itself. Honor corresponds with and manifests esteem, prestige, high status, and rank. Accumulation of honor means excellence, distinction, precedence, superiority, and the admiration—and envy—that follow. Absence of honor means shame: when you lack honor you possess shame, and/or exhibit it, and/or are forced to own and admit to it. Loss of honor means exposure of shame (that always lurks beneath honor or behind its back), or perhaps the accumulation of shame. Shame (or having it revealed) means inferiority; it is degrading, deserving of contempt.

In comparison with honor, shame seems passive: if it is the absence of honor, *dishonor*, then logically it must simply be *lack*. Nevertheless, it is not merely used as an abstract concept. In an honor society, shame is something you feel, have, are, or are deeply afraid of becoming. Like honor, shame is typically animated or essentialized and deeply personalized, hence viewed and experienced as a vivid characteristic, a condition, or a symbolic commodity. It is often referred to as a *stain* on one's reputation, or the exposure of an element that should have not been exposed.

A stain of shame or an exposure of shame *shames* you: just as you take on the (positive) identity of your (manifest) honor, you take on the (negative) identity of your (exposed) shame. If you have (or manifest) honor, you are honorable; if you have shame (or your shame has been exposed), you are shameful. Having or being shame is very real: you burn with the pain of your shameful existence. You seek to run, hide, or rid yourself of it. If honor is something to covet and to pursue, shame is something to avoid at all costs and to hide or shed if you have (or if your shame has been exposed).

HIERARCHY, CLASS, AND THE HONOR CURRENCY

Historical and contemporary honor-based societies around the world differ in many respects, including their specific social rules and the particular behaviors that they consider honorable or shameful. Nevertheless, they all subscribe to the fundamental dichotomy between honor and shame as an essential criterion for assessing and fixing human value, and they all determine their members' comparative social rank based on such attribution of honor-and-shame-based value. What makes each of them an honor society, then, is the axiomatic attribution of worth and distribution of hierarchical status among group members in accordance with their respective honor or shame. In fact, the attribution of value, that is, honor or shame, and distribution of rank are perceived as inseparable or indistinguishable.

Typically, since antiquity, an honor-and-shame society was a relatively small, secluded, self-sufficient, strictly hierarchical social organization. Hierarchy was crucial: it provided order and a sense of certitude and security. It prevented anarchy and diminished instability and anxiety. Hierarchy determined each member's place, standing, duties, rights, and prospects within the group. Further still, it determined worth and identity. Fixing people's comparative standing, hierarchy dictated their mutual responsibilities, expectations, and valuation. It was a master's responsibility to feed the servant and wife, and they had corresponding responsibilities to serve him in the socially accepted ways determined by custom and rules. Those who complied and fulfilled their roles were good master, servant, or wife, and were accordingly entitled to high slots in their respective echelons of social hierarchy (the wife in comparison with other wives of similar stature, the servant in comparison with other servants of his status, and the master in comparison with other masters such as himself). If they did not follow procedure, they were not-so-good master, servant, or wife, deserving lower standing in their respective echelons of hierarchy.

Within the hierarchies of their groups, people knew who they were, what to do, and how to do it. The hierarchy provided them a sense of identity, certainty, and comfort. Your low status as a peasant may have precluded your marrying a noble lady or gentleman, but it reassured you and your entire community that you did have a secure place, a clear role, a recognized meaning, and distinct value within your group. As long as you played by the rules, you could sleep soundly at night—and dream of the noble lady or gentleman that you could not approach in real life. The ability to know one's place granted a lot of people peace of mind, securing the peace in their communities.

Most traditional honor societies prescribed to pyramid structured hierarchies: the higher the rank, the fewer the slots.[26] Typically, underneath the very top, layers of the pyramid formed classes of rank and honor.[27] Within these layers, people could be challenged and judged by their peers, gaining honor and status and losing them to their equals. If the top 20 percent of the pyramid was considered aristocratic, then it was recognized as a distinct honor class. Its members would compete for rank and honor among themselves. If the next 40 percent of the pyramid was considered the middle class, then its members competed for honor among themselves. While honor societies differed in the strictness of their class distinction, most adhered to the structural distinction itself.

In this context, honor was the currency determining, manifesting, and symbolizing your standing in the hierarchy, hence your worth, identity, role, and responsibilities. Each position in the hierarchy corresponded with a certain portion of the group's honor. If you held an allotted slot in the hierarchy, you were also entitled to a certain measure of honor: the portion of the group's honor that corresponded with the slot you held. To move up in the hierarchy, you had to gain more honor: having more honor entitled you to hold a higher position that corresponded with the greater amount of honor you now had. If you lost honor, you moved down in the hierarchy, to the position that corresponded with your diminished amount of honor.

Honor served as the chips of the game: if you had four red chips, you were entitled to the slot that had (in the collective social consciousness) four red circles marked on it; if you had ten gold chips, you could move up to the slot that had ten gold circles marked on it; if you possessed merely two green chips, you would be pushed down to the slot acknowledged as befitting those chips. (Aristocratic blood might have granted you two blue chips as birth-right, which you could only lose if you encountered immense shame. Gold chips might have only been available to an aristocrat performing social tasks reserved for people of that social class.)

HONOR NORMS

In a game in which chips buy, manifest, and secure your right to a slot, and the slot, entailing your status, rank, and standing, corresponds with your social roles, responsibilities, worth and identity—there must be rules deter-mining how to gain chips and how they are lost. These are the honor norms, constituting a group's honor code. To serve their purpose, such rules must be meticulous, clear, commonly acknowledged, and uniformly adhered to by group members.

Honor codes often specify with considerable precision the honor or shamefulness assigned to almost every important social behavior. Compli-ance with the standards and norms prescribed by an honor code guarantees the acquisition of honor, and thus the achievement of status. Failure to com-ply with these demands instills shame and humiliation, leads to mockery or punishment by others, and diminishes status in the social hierarchy. Comply-ing with different honor norms to different degrees bestows different amounts of honor or shame, earning different degrees of status.

For example, in many traditional honor societies, the more sons a man raises and the greater their achievements—the more honor he accumulates and the higher his status. The honor norm is that many successful sons are a vehicle to gain esteem and prestige. Even a clear and simple rule as this one invites endless negotiation over interpretation: Is the neighbor whose three sons shepherd together fifty sheep more or less honorable than the neighbor whose five sons are a priest, a criminal, and three poor peasants? Negotia-tions over interpretation of such a rule breed tension, hostility, and some-times violence. Yet they also allow a community to engage in and constantly reconsider its values and ways of life. Such negotiations allow an honor society the flexibility to change and move, for example, from appreciation of shepherding to esteem of commerce, or from regard for education to rever-ence of wealth. Such changes can be accommodated by an existing honor system; they do not necessarily affect or undermine it.

Raising many sons is useful for a traditional society—as well as for any of its members. Even if society did not reward the raising of many sons with honor and status, many members would surely desire and attempt to have them, in order to ensure their clan's survival and prosperity. Yet, often, honor norms ascribe honor to behaviors that are deemed useful to the group—but not necessarily to the individual member. Manifestation of heroism in battle is an obvious example. No self-preserving, self-interested man would consider it useful to participate in a bloody battle against the enemies of his group, if he could rely on others to do so in his place. Yet most societies have typically considered it in their best interest to recruit as many soldiers as possible, encouraging their members to partake in military exploits. Most societies, therefore, have defined it honorable to enlist, fight, and manifest courage and bravery in the battlefield. The more courageous a warrior's conduct in the face of the enemy, the more honor he secures for himself. Concomitantly, societies have condemned the refusal to fight as shameful cowardice, losing a man his social standing.

If you are weary of my repetitive use of the male pronoun "he," and of examples relating exclusively to men, let me reassure you it is no oversight. Please hold your breath until you reach the section referring to honor's gendered politics.

Patriotic bravery has been rewarded with symbolic and material honors (including land, slaves, medals, and desirable social positions), whereas the shame of cowardice has rendered shunning, if not ex-communication. Volunteering to fight, risking one's life for one's community is not, under such circumstances, a self-sacrificing act motivated by pure altruism. It is a calculated risk taken in the course of honor and status seeking. Like the babbler and many other creatures, members of honor societies have preferred honor and status (for themselves or their relatives) to life itself. They choose standing within the group over anything else (that is, over a life of shame within the group or a life outside it).

The requirement to extend generous hospitality to strangers is another familiar example of an honor norm. In antiquity, when wild beasts and humans roamed by night, inns were scarce and roads were risky, traveling was a highly dangerous adventure. A society interested in encouraging trade had to reassure its members that leaving their relatively secure dwellings and the comfort zones of their clans, they would find refuge in the hospitality of foreigners. Imagine, for example, a Bedouin tribe scattered in a desert, and a member of a certain clan riding on his camel to trade with another clan. Come night, or sandstorm, or bandits, the adventurous merchant seeks refuge with a stranger. The stranger's immediate interest is to send the foreigner away: he is not family, and feeding him would be unnecessarily costly. Hence, the Bedouin honor code requires that strangers at one's doorstep be taken in and cared for with great precision. Following this honor norm bestows honor and esteem on the host; ignoring it means shame and loss of status. Stories of lavish hospitality at great cost to the hosts can be found in the Bible, in Icelandic sagas, and in Western and Bedouin folklore. They are not stories of altruism, but of social adherence to honor codes.

Generous gift giving, at weddings, for example, is yet another universally recognizable example of an honor norm. It is in no wedding guest's best interest to spoil the young couple with a generous gift. But a society interested in encouraging young people to start families (thus maintaining order and stability) might want to redistribute wealth among members so that more established households contribute to each emerging new family. Many traditional societies have, therefore, mandated that wedding guests bestow generous gifts upon the young couple. Such generosity is rewarded with reputation and prestige, whereas too small a gift is considered shameful stinginess. To reinforce these social determinations, some traditional societies (e.g., in the Caucasus) have developed wedding shaming rituals. At the end of a wedding ceremony all gifts are opened and publicly displayed, and the most generous guest is acknowledged as most honorable and seated in a special, honorary seat. Other guests, who could have contributed more than they did, are implicitly shamed through comparison.

SHAMING: THE TAKING AWAY OF HONOR

In many honor societies from antiquity to this day, adherence to honor norms that dictate, for example, the display of courage in battle, generous hospitality to strangers, and openhandedness in wedding gift giving, constitutes the high road to acquiring, preserving, manifesting, and reinforcing honor and social standing. Yet not everyone has the opportunity, means, or patience to display bravery in combat or generosity in gift giving or hospitality. For the impatient, honor societies offer a shortcut: they can gain honor by seizing it from others who have it.

When member A takes honor from member B, it is as if he replaces B's honor with shame, bestowing on B shame in the amount of honor he has taken away from him. It is as if A takes away from B x number of gold chips (representing honor), exchanging them with x number of white chips (representing shame). It is as if A uncovers the (x amount of) shame that was concealed by B's—now removed—(x amount of) honor. In so doing, A shames B.

To prevent mayhem and bloodshed, such honor taking must, of course, also be governed by precise rules. The rules dictating whether, when, how, and how much honor can be seized from another group member comprise a distinct category of honor norms: the norms of shaming.

The foremost, overarching rule of shaming is that exposure of *honor fraud* bestows upon the *honor whistle-blower* the honor he redeemed from the fraudulent member who held on to it undeservedly. The underlying logic manifested in this interaction is as follows: An honor society considers itself as having a certain amount of honor (a bank of honor chips, if you wish). Each individual is entitled to his share of honor according to his birthright and conduct and befitting his status in the hierarchy. Member A, for example, is entitled to two blue chips because he was born to an honorable family, five green chips because he worked hard, and ten gold chips because he volunteered to fight the enemy and lost a limb. When an individual pretends to deserve more honor than he actually does—he seizes honor that, by right, should have been distributed among other group members. If, for example, a member falsely pretends to be heroically patriotic (or a generous host or gift giver) and fools the group into awarding him honor based on this pretense, he holds on to honor that he does not deserve, honor that should have been otherwise distributed among other members. If an honor whistle-blower calls the pretender's bluff, daring and exposing him, he *releases* the honor that was unduly possessed by the pretender.

The honor whistle-blower brings back honor chips into the group's honor bank, while also cleansing the integrity of the group's honor structure. The social task that person performs is an important and risky one: failure on his part might compromise his reputation and perhaps endanger his well-being or even life itself. The whistle-blower is therefore appropriately rewarded for the service with the honor that he rescued from the fraudulent pretender. In the process, it is as if the person *sheds* shame, which the exposed pretender is now forced to own. At the end of the exchange, the exposing member exchanged some of his shame for honor, forcing the exposed member to exchange the same amount of his honor for shame. Vigilantism is appreciated and rewarded with the honor seized from its wrongful holder.

EXPOSURE: A MEANS OF SHAMING

Exposure is a key component in honor-based social interactions. A player seeking opportunities to seize honor and move up in the social hierarchy must develop skills of detecting discrepancies, cracks in façades, which might indicate the possibility of exposure and honor windfall. Anyone trying to guard his honor must learn to avoid self-exposure and prevent it at all costs. A sharp sensitivity for fraud on the one hand, and a poker face on the other, are both highly valuable assets in an honor society.

Let me demonstrate how this works in everyday life. Say your business (or marriage) is on the rocks, but you try to disguise your distress and concern, keeping up appearances and maintaining credibility and decorum. Asked how things are going, you utter that all is just great. Yet an involuntary flinch of your facial muscles gives away a hint of distress, anxiety, uncertainty. The gap between the firm front you presented and the shaky interior you unwittingly revealed is your Achilles' heel in an honor world: it is the terrain in which exposure might take place. An observant peer detects the discrepancy between the "business as usual, I am in control of my life" façade you are trying to keep up, warranting honor, and the more fragile (hence shameful) reality that you try to conceal. The viewer suspects, sniffs, asks around, and discovers that your business is about to collapse or that your spouse has run off with someone else. The fraud is made public; you have been found out. The exposure reveals that you sought to hold on to more honor than you rightly deserved: you are far less competent than you pretended to be. You are shamed, losing face, honor, and status. Your exposer gains the honor you lost.

Exposure is a strategy so central to honor societies, that almost any exposure may become honor stripping. In fact, exposure may be considered shaming per se. Any secret—or information—about you that is disclosed, any part of your body that is unclothed, may compromise your honor. Yet not any exposure is legitimate or beneficial for the exposer. At times, it may blow up in the exposer's face and shame him instead of buying him honor. For example, exposure that involves betrayal of confidence is shameful, as is exposure—or any shaming—of someone who is considered inferior to or weaker than the exposer. You may only gain honor if you pick on someone at least as big as yourself and refrain from hitting below the belt.

The exposure dynamic explains why control over one's own and one's family members' bodies, gestures, and utterances is crucial to the maintenance of honor. It is why silence is golden, and keeping your cards close to your chest is wise; the less you share with others, the safer. It is why showing weakness or admitting to vulnerability is risky and may be used against you. Why the more attuned one is to social cues, the more one is likely to preserve honor and detect opportunities to seize it from others. It is why people in honor societies live in constant fear of being found out, always looking over their shoulders.[28]

HONOR CONFLICTS: RETALIATION, DETERRENCE, FEUDING, AND DUELING

Taking honor away from peers—or at least outshining them—is the essence of participation in an honor society. Moving up in the world of honor means that you threaten all your surrounding peers, necessarily bringing one or more of them down. If you manage to accumulate enough honor chips to attain for yourself a better slot in the hierarchy, whoever occupied that slot before you must now move down in the hierarchy. The honor chips you gained were held or at least desired by someone else. More simply: when someone goes up, someone else must come down. And the person forced down harbors resentment and bears a grudge. He will seek to retaliate and to reestablish his honor by *payback* for the shame you bestowed on him. Until he exposes you and brings you down, he carries a chip of shame on his shoulder. In fact, until he retaliates, he is in a vulnerable position: everyone has seen that his honor and status may be successfully robbed, and are thus tempted to similarly benefit from his weakness. Unless he sends out a clear message that robbing him of honor is costly, he is seen as inviting all peers to usurp his honor goods.

This is why in an honor society, tolerance of trespasses against you is not a virtue; forgive and forget is not divine, but suicidal. Let alone turning the other cheek . . . If you wish to stay in the game, you find a way to regain the honor you lost. This involves a whole set of retaliatory rules that determine what you may and may not do in the course of retaliation, how you may and may not act, and how soon and toward whom. Honor societies differ in their retaliatory rules. For example, some sets of rules allow retaliation to be imposed on the offender's family members; others mandate targeting only the offender himself. What they typically all share is the understanding that retaliation must be harsher than the initial offense.

The gap between the original honor offense and the retaliation it requires may be seen as the *interest* the offender is made to pay for having taken away the avenger's honor and *used* it as his own. Collecting interest is thus an act of deterrence, announcing not merely to the offender but to the whole group: "beware, for if, attempting to move up in the world, you take chips of honor that belong to me, you will be made to pay them back with an interest."

According to this logic, once such honor debt was collected with interest and the original offender was stripped of more honor than he sought to gain, an enlarged chip of shame is placed on his shoulder, together with the obligation to make the retaliator pay an even higher honor price. In every such round, each party must shame the other more than he himself was shamed. Reciprocal honor fighting of this sort is called a feud. By its nature, the feud does not resolve honor disputes, but merely manages them. In so doing, it plays a major role in the psychological economy of honor societies.

The feud dynamic explains why an honor conflict is an escalating one. A feud may start over a belittling glance or a sneer, and then snowball into burning down each other's homes, raping each other's women, and/or stabbing each other to death. If you call me a liar (exposing my shame), I must call you gutless (exposing your greater shame); you will have to call me a traitor, to which I will have to respond by burning down your barn (which exposes your shameful vulnerability). The specifics of what may be smeared or burned down and what is a reasonable *interest* rate differ from one honor society to the next; but the underlying logic is endemic. Once a feud is under way, it must escalate until one or both parties are completely depleted. Any attempt to settle a feud necessarily leaves at least one of the parties feeling unsatisfied and honor bound to *settle the score*, rendering the settlement unstable.

Because people may acquire or lose honor through association, feuds tend to spread beyond the original combatants to friends, families, clans, tribes, and even nations. The result may be a perpetual blood-taking conflict. Or, the end may take the form of atomic bombs (say, on Hiroshima and Nagasaki). As a rule, societies with norms that promote feuds internally seem particularly likely to develop feuding relations with neighbors or other opponents.

In certain European societies, for several centuries, and in the Americas too, the duel served as a means of constraining honor disputes.[29] Within certain classes, when a man felt insulted by another, he challenged the offender to a duel, proving himself courageous and honorable. Duels were highly ritualized forms of combat, and could only take place if both parties performed their roles honorably. This focus on the honorable conduct of the two antagonists allowed the original honor conflict to be resolved without expansion to kin and clansmen. Moreover, duels did not necessarily have winners and losers. As long as they were fought fairly and courageously, they could cleanse both participants of inflicted shame. They allowed both participants to exhibit courage, skill, and honor, an exhibition often more important than the technicality of who prevailed, if anyone did.

The duel was thus an effective resolution mechanism for honor disputes; it was, however, reserved, in those societies where it flourished, for the small group of men who defined themselves as men of honor. A person who did not possess sufficient social status to be recognized as a man of honor (e.g., a woman, a foreigner, or a servant) could not challenge a person of honor to a duel. The duel, therefore, also served to conserve the existing social hierarchy by precluding those not recognized as men of honor from earning that status through dueling.

The reciprocal, escalating nature of honor warfare dynamics explains the tendency of honor societies to be militant and militaristic, and to harbor and nurture aggression and violence, both within their social boundaries and in interactions with outsiders. When two honor societies share territory or occupy adjacent territories, warfare is a frequent outcome. When an honor society encounters weaker or less honor-driven societies, predation is a frequent outcome.

COMPETITIVE, ZERO-SUM GAME

The world of honor, then, is one in which a man's honor, manifesting both his value and comparative rank, is his prized possession; it must constantly be accumulated, exhibited, guarded, and cleansed. To achieve these goals, players frequently challenge each other's honor, and must survive and prevail in ever-erupting honor conflicts. The world of honor is one of intense competition, driven by the logic of a zero-sum game, or as Miller succinctly puts it: "for the most part, people acted as if the mechanics of honor had the structure of a zero-sum or less-than-zero-sum game."[30]

A zero-sum game is one in which every player's every move effects every other player. A player's acquisition of a new position necessarily entails another player's surrendering of his, which, in turn, involves everyone's repositioning of themselves. Think of musical chairs: When the music stops and someone sits in the chair that you previously occupied, you quickly seize the best seat available, which was previously occupied by someone else. Even if no one is actively seeking to push others down and out, every player's self-interested attempt to secure the best possible seat for himself necessarily creates a competition in which any player's achievement threatens everyone else, and must come at someone's expense.

In a pyramid structured hierarchy, the race to the top must be a zero-sum game. Your legitimate interest to move up—or at least maintain your standing and not lose ground—necessarily clashes with other players' interests. Caution and suspicion are thus the logical emotional responses toward other players.

In such a game, treaties, pacts, and coalitions among players are, by definition, utilitarian: they are contracted when they serve all parties' best interests, and last only as long as they do. When circumstances change and a pact ceases to serve its members' purposes—each party is likely to seek new, useful alliances. Nevertheless, in traditional honor societies, primordial relationships are considered binding. Abandoning a clan member to whom one owes loyalty is considered shameful.

PERPETUAL SOCIAL SELF-REGULATION

Honor and shame dwell and thrive in the open, communal realm. The competition for honor takes place in the public sphere, where every move may be seen, supervised, estimated, and valued by all players and their clan members. Honor is gained and lost exclusively through publicly observed and carefully monitored social interactions. This implies that concealed emotions, worthy aspirations, cowardly thoughts, or obscured actions do not come into play in the social accounting of honor and shame. It means that a fraud that goes unobserved and unexposed does not materialize in shame. If appearances are publicly kept, then potentially dishonorable feelings or actions go unsanctioned.

This further suggests that, to minimize fraudulent pretense, all group members must actively participate in constant monitoring of their comembers. Indeed, spying on neighbors and peers and reporting their actions to the community is an essential tool of social control that all must endorse. *Gossip* is a vital means, commonly used to police and evaluate each player's every move, ranking him, accordingly, in comparison with his rivals. Social pressure is used to compel individuals to comply with social codes.

An important reason for the enduring power and success of the honor structure is that it recruits its members to partake in executing its social functions and enforcing social norms. An honor society does not require official institutions, such as legislative, judicial, and enforcement bodies: group members fill all these functions through close observation of each other, intense gossip, and social pressure. These ancient informal social institutions regulated prestate honor societies, and in many—perhaps all—parts of the world they continue to mobilize people to this day.

Traditional honor codes typically celebrate expressions of individuality and the capacity for leadership and self-rule. At the same time, honor societies demand conformity: obedience to honor codes, compliance with social pressure, and apprehension of gossip. This paradox places members of honor societies in the inescapable psychological bind of having to excel both in individuality and in conformity. This double bind can be viewed as securing an equilibrium: the contrary requirements balance each other out.

SOCIAL DYNAMICS OF PERPETUAL CHANGE

The process of honor-based ranking is dynamic, evolving, and perpetual. At any given point in time, performances of group members are measured against those of all other relevant competitors. Any honor-and-shame ranking is only valid for an instant, since everyone's next moves will reshuffle all cards. A champion who delivered the best performance and received the highest honors and most esteemed standing will have to defend his hard earned status at every following moment against anyone who chooses (and is entitled) to play, challenge, and compete.

Think of a successful western gunfighter: establishing himself as the fastest draw in Bottle Neck or Whiskey Town—he immediately becomes the mecca for aspiring young gunfighters, all eager to challenge him and make a name for themselves by outdrawing him. His hard earned championship will be challenged up to the moment of his defeat and replacement. The minute he becomes the fastest gun, the clock starts ticking, and it is only a matter of time until he is stripped of his status and rank. The same logic holds true for smaller fish in the Wild West: there are always smaller fish yet, eager to challenge and replace them.

The world of honor is, therefore, versatile, not to say volatile. It involves never-ending fierce challenge and competition. Peaceful rest is inconceivable. This motivates and drives members of honor societies to strive, invest, achieve progress, and improve their scores. To be in the race means to always do your very best and reach for the moon. It also means living with inherent uncertainty, tension, suspicion, and perhaps stress and anxiety.

DOWN AND OUT

If, you may wonder, honor competition is so stress inducing, why do people choose to partake in it? Well, in some social contexts, and in some people's deep-seated feeling, there is no alternative: it is the only game in town. And if you are not a player—you are a goner. From an honor society's perspective, the only thing that is worse than losing (some) honor and moving down in the hierarchy is having no honor at all and being situated outside the hierarchy. The only movement worse than down, is away, and the only place less desirable than the bottom, is out. This is why banishing or outcasting a member is not necessarily kinder than imposing death.

Indeed, in traditional honor societies in olden days, being banished from your group and its hierarchy often meant both social and physical death. Life outside the group and its honor structure meant not merely that you had no honor, but that you did not exist. Rules did not apply to you, and no one owed you assistance, hospitality, or loyalty. Worse still: coming in contact with you was poisonous, contaminating to group members. You became untouchable. Alone in the desert, with no law or social ties to protect you, you would only survive as long as you were young, healthy, and self-sufficient. Much like a babbler. It is little wonder that stressing over exposure or shame, or losing honor and occupying a lower slot in the hierarchy seemed preferable in comparison.

An honor society's strong hold on its members is rooted in their deeply internalized sense that there is no life outside the group hierarchy. That social death *is* death. This psychology may be powerful even among contemporary group members who never use the word "honor" and who have no conception of honor societies and their mechanisms. Think of a law professor whose law school constitutes (completely unconsciously) a harsh, competitive honor-driven environment. She might tire of the unceasing, futile, stressful competition, but feel that there is no alternative; no life outside the school. Much like a fish probably feels regarding its school.

This leads us to the self-perception of honor society members, or: how honor societies construct selves and their emotions.

SELF-PERCEPTION

So far, this chapter mostly considered the interpersonal mechanisms of honor, not its intradynamics. Indeed, honor and shame societies were initially thought to be invested mostly in interpersonal mechanisms, in contrast with guilt cultures, said to be mostly invested in intradynamics.

Traditionally, honor and shame cultures were defined in opposition to *guilt cultures*, in which individuals are indoctrinated to internalize moral notions of sin, and monitor their own social conduct in fear of sinning and experiencing guilt. Honor cultures were said to be extroverted, whereas guilt cultures were depicted as introverted. Ancient Greek and Roman civilizations, samurai Japan, saga Iceland, and Bedouin tribes are all archetypal examples of honor societies and cultures. Judeo-Christian cultures, on the other hand, are commonly cited examples of guilt cultures. Although this polar, binary definition has been criticized by many, it still offers a meaningful, basic distinction between cultural tendencies and social inclinations. In Miller's words, "The well-known distinction between shame and guilt cultures, though rightly and roundly criticized, still captures a fundamental difference between the world of the sagas and ours, between a culture in which reputation is all and one in which conscience, confession and forgiveness play a central role."[31]

Members of honor societies might not experience and judge themselves with the concepts and emotions of guilt and sin; they do, however, internalize profoundly their societies' percepts of honor and of shame, feeling them acutely. So much so, that group members' honor, value, and status are considered hard facts; that many people feel more strongly about their honor and shame than about anything else; that they can suffer tremendously over the loss of honor; and that they are even willing to kill and to die to redeem honor or prevent shame. In fact, Miller defines honor and the world of honor through the emotions and sensitivities that define people inhabiting them:

> Honor is above all the keen sensitivity to the experience of humiliation and shame, a sensitivity manifested by the desire to be envied by others and the propensity to envy the successes of others. To simplify greatly, honor is that disposition which makes one act to shame others who have shamed oneself, to humiliate others who have humiliated oneself. The honorable person is one whose self-esteem and social standing is intimately dependent on the esteem or the envy he or she actually elicits in others. At root honor means "don't tread on me." But to show someone you were not to be trod upon often meant that you had to hold yourself out as one who was willing to tread on others. . . .
> In the culture of honor, the prospect of violence inhered in virtually every social interaction between free men. . . . For shame and envy are quickly reprocessed as anger, and anger often is a prelude to aggression.[32]

Honor cultures tend thus to cultivate emotions such as envy and anger that depend on relative standing in a community, rather than more internally oriented, individualistic emotions such as guilt, remorse, angst, and ennui. Nonetheless, honor-based emotions run deep. Think, for example, of the fear of being found out. The profound anxiety of being exposed as fake torments some people to psychosis. Their dread of display as phony may drive them to despair—even if it is completely unreasonable (as friends try to persuade them). The feeling is very real, even if merely a leftover of deeply internalized, completely unconscious, honor norms.

Another familiar example is people's habitual evaluation of themselves based on their relative ranking. Many students, even as they know that an exam grade is merely that, still feel that having received a B− they have become a B− person; that a B− person is worth less than an A person, although more than a C person. The strong hold such a feeling has over some people testifies to the depth of their honor-based intuitions, often completely unacknowledged.

Or, to describe another example: Who does not remember the overwhelming feeling of devastation at being jilted, rejected, or let go of? It is no coincidence that so many forsaken lovers *lose their heads* and find themselves reacting in ways they would never have expected: their acute sense of dishonor plagues and afflicts them, leading to what seems to be madness. No matter how friends rationalize the situation, their sense of self-worth is destroyed, and the urge to *get back at* the offender and *get even* is burning. Revenge, infliction of even more pain than was inflicted on the offended, feels like the only possible venue to soothe the tormenting sting. In the meantime, they cannot eat properly, sleep properly or, indeed, think properly; that is, "properly" discounting the (often unwarranted) honor-based emotions and impulses that possess them.

J. K. Campbell reminds us that the emotional economy of an honor-based world tends to suppress tender feelings, which might be interpreted as expressions of weakness, thus boosting more aggressive sentiments: "Self regard forbids any action which may be interpreted as weakness. Normally this would include any altruistic behavior to an unrelated man. Co-operation, tolerance, love, must give way to autarky, arrogance, hostility."[33]

Pitt-Rivers stresses another crucial aspect of the emotional economy of honor: a person is only entitled to feel and demonstrate emotions that correspond with the honor that he has rightly secured for himself in the eyes of his society. Similarly, one must feel the shame his surrounding ascribes to him. This reciprocity between social acknowledgment and an individual's subjective feeling underlies the harmony of an honor society. It testifies to the "rule of honor norms" (which, in an honor society, *is* the rule of law).

> [Honor is] the value of a person in his own eyes, but also in the eyes of his society. It is his estimation of his own worth, his *claim* to pride, but it is also the acknowledgment of that claim, his excellence recognized by society, his *right* to pride. . . . The sentiment of honor inspires conduct which is honorable, the conduct receives recognition and established reputation, and reputation is finally sanctified by the bestowal of honors. Honor felt becomes honor claimed and honor claimed becomes honor paid.[34]

If scoring a bad grade in an exam, or having been fired, or divorced, is coded by one's group as shaming and shameful, one must internalize the feeling of shame that corresponds with the group's judgment. Similarly, if performing well in a competition bestows a certain amount of honor—one is entitled and expected to feel that honor and act on it.

The correlation between social judgment of one's honor and rank and that person's self-perception is crucial; the social structure's stability depends on it. If not for this correlation, every member might feel more honorable than the honor norms permit, and endless honor disputes would erupt, threatening the peace.

This is why, in many honor societies, self-perception that does not accord with the group's is grounds for loss of face. Unless, of course, you are bold, powerful, and stubborn enough to persuade the entire group to accept your self-perception as more reliable and eventually overriding the common assessment. Such an achievement testifies to one's great strength and strong social position, that is, to one's value and worth, justifying the added value the individual demanded—and received.

THE GENDERED POLITICS OF HONOR

Honor societies ascribe very different meanings to men's and women's honor and shame. Of honor societies' many characteristics, the gender distinction may be the one best studied and researched. One of the founding fathers of honor-and-shame studies, Pitt-Rivers, defines the gender difference in Mediterranean societies as follows:

> The honor of a man and of a woman . . . imply quite different modes of conduct. . . . A woman is dishonored . . . with the tainting of her sexual purity, but a man [is] not. While certain conduct is honorable for both sexes, honor = shame requires conduct in other spheres, which is exclusively a virtue of one sex or the other. It obliges a man to defend his honor and that of his family, a woman to conserve her purity . . . restraint is the natural basis of sexual purity, just as masculinity is the natural basis of authority and the defense of familial honor. . . . Masculinity means courage whether it is employed for moral or immoral ends. . . . The honor of a man is involved . . . in the sexual purity of his mother, wife and daughters, and sisters, not in his own. . . . The honorable woman: locked in the house with a broken leg. [35]

As this description demonstrates, traditional honor societies are deeply gendered. In most (perhaps all), honor is closely linked with the ideal of manhood. Typically, only men are players in any group's honor game. Many such societies offer men two routes to earn honor and status: one is accomplishment in the competition against other men (one's peers) in *manly* activities (such as warfare, sports, accumulation of wealth); the other is conquering and maintaining sexual and familial control over women. The first route includes everything presented and discussed in this chapter: adherence to the group's honor code, accurate reading of social situations, appropriate exposure of other men, public expression of firm deterrence, and bold redress of shame-inducing insults. The other route includes avoidance of shame through firm domination, restraint, and disciplining of one's womenfolk.

Traditional honor societies differ in the specific ways in which women are thought to cause shame, but many (perhaps all) define women as inherently containing potential shame. Women are shame accidents waiting to happen. Only firm manly supervision may keep this potential shame from exploding and staining the family honor. A man's success in preventing feminine shame from erupting is a source of honor (or at least prevents dishonor).

Women, in traditional honor societies, are thus a means by which men may lose honor and gain shame. Sometimes women may increase their men's honor: a bride (say, a princess) may bring, as an honor dowry, her father's prestige; a daughter may bring her father honor by attracting an honorable man for a husband; a wife may evoke other men's envy by manifesting submission to her husband, expressing proper modesty, bearing many sons, running the household economically, or simply being young or attractive. But more typically, a woman is a potential source of dishonor, and is expected, above all else, to submit to her man and obey him, to prevent honor mishaps.

At the heart of women's potential shame lies feminine sexuality. It must be concealed and veiled, protected for the use of its rightful male owner: the woman's husband. The duty to keep female sexuality guarded and concealed lies with her father, brothers, uncles, husband, or sons, depending on circumstances and the specifics of differing honor codes. The degree of required concealment varies as well. But in most traditional honor societies the failure to hide and protect female sexuality brings immeasurable shame on the unsuccessful man and his family. Exposure of female sexuality, though it may take different forms in different societies, is in many the most shameful of all forms of exposure. It is proof that the male guardian is not man enough, that is, honorable enough, to prevent the exposure of the honor asset that requires concealment more than any other. In many traditional honor societies such exposure justifies—and even requires—bloodshed.

In this context, men are literally subjects, players, whereas women are objects: currency of honor and shame. Nevertheless, they are objects that bear responsibility to the shame they might cause. They are obliged to prevent such shame at all costs—even at the cost of their lives. To prevent shaming, they are expected to conceal themselves from men, and alert their husbands or fathers to any potential threat to their honor (e.g., unwarranted attention).

In traditional Mediterranean and Middle Eastern societies, the shame attributed to female sexuality was (and often still is) associated foremost with feminine virginity. Virginity was (and frequently still is) viewed as physical embodiment of shame-about-to-happen. A father's duty (together with his sons and brothers) was to ensure that the shame happened only after the woman was properly handed over to her next rightful owner: the husband. If the shame happened otherwise, that is, if a woman lost her virginity outside of wedlock, the father's honor was stained so badly that only the offender's blood could somewhat redeem it. If the father guarded the woman's virginity properly until wedlock—the shame that did not erupt became a source of honor.

When the woman's shame was exposed by her rightful owner, the husband, it was simultaneously properly concealed by his own honor. It was as though he drew his manly honor over her bloody wound of shame that he uncovered. She lost her natural potential shame, gaining his shielding honor. From now on, it was not only her duty—but also in her self-interest—to ensure, guard, and enhance his honor, because it was the honor roof over her head. As a daughter, her duty was to uphold her father's honor by preserving her virginity; as a wife, her duty was to uphold her husband's honor by manifesting his domination over her, and by making sure that her sexuality was accessible exclusively to him.

As mentioned earlier, in honor societies, honor and shame are experienced as real facts. A woman who loses her virginity improperly is seen—and often feels herself to be—full of shame; damaged goods.

This is why in a typical traditional Mediterranean or Middle Eastern honor society, it did not matter whether a woman committed adultery or was raped: if her virginity was *taken* by a man who was not her husband—the honor of her father and/or husband (or perhaps fiancé) was tarnished, and she was spoiled. By the same token, this is why if a father committed incest, it was a crime he committed against himself and his own honor, not one of social interest. If a husband forcefully penetrated his wife—no one's honor was injured, and hence no offense committed. If a woman exposed her father or husband, reporting such conduct and publicizing it, she merely made herself look bad. Her attempt to shame them disclosed her traitorous character, manifesting a lack of loyalty. Further, if a woman was sexually assaulted but had no male relatives, no harm was done, since no one's honor was damaged. Usually, a woman's best interest was to maintain her marital status at all costs: it provided her with her husband's honor, which was her only shield from shameful existence or death.

In many honor societies, therefore, honor did not merely prescribe different conduct for men and women: it defined men and women, masculinity and femininity, constituting them as distinct categories in contrasting, binary opposition. Honor underlies, forms, and organizes much of what we think of as sexual differences. Honor molds manhood as active, assertive, aggressive, conquering, and superior, and femininity as passive, submissive, servile, vulnerable, and inferior. It constructs men as agents and women as playthings to be dominated and kept from other men. [36]

INTERGROUP HONOR DYNAMICS: THE SUMMIT OF HONOR IN MODERN EUROPEAN NATIONALISM AND THE NEED FOR AN ALTERNATIVE

Honor societies around the world perfected their understanding of honor and shame, hierarchy, honor codes, zero-sum competition, exposure, feuds, and gender politics. It seemed only natural that they would apply these same logic, economy, structures, and dynamics to the intergroup sphere. Just as individual men challenged each other within an honor society—so did groups in their mutual relations. Just as exposure of an individual shamed him—so did exposure of a group. Just as feuds escalated within groups—so did wars among groups. Such groups could be clans, tribes, cities, city-states, regions, religious groups, nations, nation-states, or corporations. Groups of babblers, too, compete for status and rank against other groups, just like their members do among themselves.

Let me narrate the modern history of Europe through this lens. It is a story of escalating honor conflicts between ever-growing groups. It culminates in two world wars, leading to a dramatic moment of acute realization that the international honor game must be replaced with an ideology and social infrastructure that are more likely to secure universal peace and the survival of the species. This historic moment, in the aftermath of World War II, gave birth to the conceptualization of human dignity as the foundation of the world order based on human rights.

Let me begin the story in the distant past: once upon a time . . .

The division between the Guelphs and Ghibellines characterized the politics of northern Italian city-states in the twelfth and thirteenth centuries. These two parties represented, respectively, pope supporters and supporters of the German, Holy Roman emperor. The political division tended to overlap with additional local schisms, often based on class, occupation, and regional interests. In the city-state of Florence, this division is said to have been launched in connection with an event that took place in 1216.

In the course of a lavish banquet, the house jester snatched one of the guests' platter of meats. The enraged guest, who felt that his honor was stained, responded harshly and was reproached by another participant, a particularly distinguished knight. In the ensuing course of events, a platter of meats was turned upside down on some participants, and the squabble culminated in the severe stabbing of the distinguished knight. The resulting tension threatened to trigger mutual retaliation that would lead to a blood feud between two powerful Florentine families. In a peacemaking effort, the two parties agreed to settle the dispute through marriage. The aggressor was to marry the young niece of the distinguished knight. "Accordingly the marriage contract was drawn up and the peace arranged; on the following day the wedding was to be celebrated."[37] But, as Pseudo Brunetto Latini tells us, one of the city's matrons (of the Donati family) shamed the groom-to-be:

"Knight, you are forever disgraced by taking a wife out of fear of the [opposing families]; leave her you have taken and take this other [that is, the matron's own daughter] and your honor as knight will be restored." As soon as he had heard, he resolved to do as he was told without taking counsel with any of his kin. And when on the following day, the morning of Thursday February 11 [1216], the guests of both parties had assembled, [the groom-to-be] passed through the gate of Santa Maria [Church] and went to pledge his troth with the girl of the Donati family, and left the [niece of the distinguished knight] waiting at the church door.

This insult enraged [the distinguished knight] greatly and he held a meeting with all his friends. . . . When all were assembled he complained in strong terms of the disgrace put upon him. . . . They then decided that the vendetta was to be carried out at the very place where the injury had been done, when the parties had gathered for the exchange of the marriage vows.[38]

The plan was fully executed and the newlywed was slain by the statue of Mars at Ponte Vecchio.[39] This killing divided Florentine society, with families offering allegiance to one or the other adversary camps. This division metamorphosed into a rift between Guelphs and Ghibellines, rival camps that tore the city-state for almost two centuries. In the course of the conflict, incessant warring, exiles, property confiscation and destruction, bloodshed, beheadings, and great suffering became inseparable from Florentines' lives. In the words of fourteenth-century Giovanni Villani:

As a result, the city was thrown into strife and disorder, for Buondelmonte's death was the cause and beginning of the cursed Guelf and Ghibelline parties in Florence. To be sure, there were already divisions among the noble citizens, and these parties already existed because of the quarrels and disputes between church and empire; yet it was because of Buondelmonte's death that all the noble families and other Florentine citizens were divided into factions, some siding with the Buondelmonte, leaders of the Guelf party, and others with the Uberti, leaders of the Ghibellines.[40]

Colorful history, urban legend, or a creative mixture of both—this anecdote exemplifies much of Europe's history. To be sure, competing economic interests, rivaling social classes, political ambitions, untampered temperaments, and heated passions—all played their important roles. Yet the logic of the game was that of honor and shame. Honor was the fundamental value and attitude that underlay the codes of conduct dictating and facilitating the parties' responses and moves. Relative precedence, esteem, status, and manly superiority determined the rhetoric and goals. Insult, shaming, exposure, goading, saving face, revenge, and deterrence composed participants' moves and strategies. Pride, determination, boldness, and fearlessness were the features extravagantly exhibited, in line with accepted honor codes.

The result was an effective, well-coordinated social game, played with collective enthusiasm and excitement. Among the collateral damages were many lives lost, social upheaval and mayhem, much property ruined, much pain inflicted, and many lives disrupted through exile and other forms of punishment and retribution.

The scale of Europe's honor maneuvers grew dramatically when city-states, princely states, and feudal structures evolved into nations and nation-states that adopted the honor-based game. Evolving nations and their states appropriated the logic of honor and shame, recruiting this powerful mechanism to erect and reinforce their own existence and power. In the process, they perpetuated the honor-based game and strengthened it. Enlisting the immense sway of honor, they harnessed it to their ends—endowing it with their own growing authority. Modeling national and nation-state honor on more traditional, localized formations (such as clan and regional honor), the new nations and states erected their honor as both natural and supreme. Personal status, precedence, prestige, and manliness were now associated with, derived from, and embellished with national honor.

In the nineteenth-century consolidation movement known as *Risorgimento* (Resurgence), Florence joined forces with its traditional rivals, such as Milan, Rome, and Naples, to form the Italian nation-state. The emerging modern entity utilized the newly invented notion of collective Italian honor to strengthen the fragile unity and inspire identification and loyalty on the part of individuals, cities, and regions. Italian national honor, adorned with symbols of antique splendor, was designed to overcome traditional regional commitments, and was hence constructed as promising greater distinction than any of them. It was also, of course, established in reference and opposition to, as well as competition with, any and every other national honor.

Similarly, German national honor soared in the long process of establishing German nationalism and unification. As in Italy, here too, the new national honor, modeled on localized traditional forerunners, appropriated popular sentiments to enhance national loyalty. The process legitimated and enhanced nationalism, while conferring brilliant new national grandeur on the long-standing logic and psychology of honor. Also in the heart of Europe, for many Poles, national honor was a source of comfort, solidarity, empowerment, and hope as they grieved Polish division and struggled to reunite the severed parts of their once free kingdom. French, English, Spanish, and other samples of European national honor may have been slightly less dramatic, but no less influential and effective.

Fusing honor mentality with nationalism, European nationalism broadened the scope of honor mechanisms, expanding and enhancing the honor mentality to full bloom. This development peaked in World War I. The assassination in Sarajevo, in June 1914, of Archduke Franz Ferdinand of Austria, triggered an Austro-Hungarian honor-bound response, which included a belligerent ultimatum delivered to the Kingdom of Serbia, followed by a declaration of war and subsequent invasion. This invoked the mobilization of an entangled web of international alliances that had been building up in Europe in the previous decades. Based on these preexisting treaties, reflecting complicated local interests, European nation-states and empires each offered allegiance to one or the other adversary camps, and Europe was divided between the Central and Allied powers. This honor-bound allegiance-based division differed mostly in scope from the 1216 divide of Florentine society, and many other schisms throughout European history. It prompted an unprecedented, global-scale blood feud.

Four and a half years later, in the winter of 1918, the Austro-Hungarian, German, Russian, and Ottoman Empires were all dissolved, and many new nation-states were founded. The collateral damage included more than *thirty million human casualties*, and a far greater number of lives ruined in diverse ways. The new nation-states (such as Poland) utilized national honor to confirm their existence and evoke loyalty. Concomitantly, the new German nation-state was struggling with an overwhelming sense of humiliation. This shame was felt to have been inflicted by the victorious Allied powers in the Treaty of Versailles, signed June 28, 1919. The brewing sentiment of dishonor in Germany, as well as the looming national honor in new nation-states, consequently played into the eruption of World War II, the deadliest conflict in human history, which resulted in approximately seventy million casualties, countless injured, and enduring universal trauma.

The two world wars can be jointly viewed as the climax of European culture's long-standing honor-based mind-set and politics. Chapter 4 suggests that in the aftermath of this climax, representatives of the world's nations realized that the honor game threatened not merely world peace but also the mere survival of the species. This generated the conceptualization of human dignity as the foundation of a new world order, focused on universal human rights.

EPILOGUE: CONTEMPORARY CONFUSION OF HONOR AND DIGNITY

In the first section of this chapter I introduced you to the complaints, voiced by scholars of honor, that the concept has become so politically incorrect and disgraceful that it is mostly shunned by just about everyone.[41] Interestingly, some brave scholars who do refer to honor, do so disguising it under a different name: that of dignity. Consider, for example, the following description of "meritocratic dignity," by Josiah Ober in *The Cambridge Handbook on Human Dignity*, published in 2014:

> In a system of meritocratic dignity, my dignity or lack thereof is determined by the place I hold in a hierarchy of merit, and on other's acknowledgment that I am worthy of that place. . . . Those beneath me in the hierarchy offer me their deference: they recognize my superiority, as I offer deference to and recognize the superiority of those above me. Cooperative relations among persons of similarly high rank (for example, Agamemnon and Achilles) are always threatened by ongoing contests seeking to establish who is best.
>
> Meritocratic dignity is a scarce social resource and it is distributed by high-stakes contest. . . . I must be ready to protect my dignity against any hint of presumed superiority from those I regard as my peers. As a result, social interaction among elites in Homeric society was marked by incessant feuding, dueling and flyting.[42]

In the Latin that was used in the Roman Empire, the word *dignitas* was a synonym for honor, both referring to the type of social value described in this chapter.[43] In English, as well, the terms "honor" and "dignity" were often used synonymously. Long-standing anthropological terminology contributed to the association of "honor" with social status, much as the UDHR dignity-and-rights talk contributed to the association of "dignity" with the humanitarian, universal, egalitarian value. This is a useful distinction between two different values and worldviews that generate distinct types of social orders.

The context that invites and encourages the contemporary linguistic reference to honor as dignity is the overwhelming popularity of the term "dignity," and the ostracism of the term "honor." It seems that since honor is no longer in favor and dignity is very much so, those who wish to refer to honor refer to it as dignity. This leads to the confusion of honor and dignity, expanding the outstretched meaning of dignity and contributing to its dilution. It might also invoke criticism of dignity on the part of those who have reservations regarding honor. This is why I believe that it is crucially important to distinguish honor from dignity. Only clear, narrow definitions of both honor and dignity enable meaningful discussion, analysis, and dialogue.

NOTES

1. Amotz Zahavi and Avishag Zahavi, *The Handicap Principle: A Missing Piece of Darwin's Puzzle*, trans. Naama Zahavi-Ely and Melvin Patrick Ely (New York: Oxford University Press, 1997). In the following paragraphs I do not quote the Zahavis' work, but rather paraphrase some of their insights as I understand them based on the book and on the information gained during guided tours to babbler-land in the Arava desert, near Eilat, Israel (in 2013, 2014, 2015, and 2019).

2. It is no coincidence that the Hebrew term that the Hebrew-speaking Zahavis chose for the handicap principle is *ikron ha-hakvada*, which in Hebrew means "the burdening principal," as well as "the honoring principle" (*kavod*, meaning honor).

3. See, for example John G. Péristiany, ed., *Honor and Shame: The Values of Mediterranean Society* (Chicago: Chicago University Press, 1966); Julian Pitt-Rivers, *The Fate of Shechem, or the Politics of Sex: Essays in the Anthropology of the Mediterranean* (Cambridge: Cambridge University Press, 1977); J. K. Campbell, *Honor, Family and Patronage: A Study of Institutions and Moral Values in a Greek Mountain Community* (Oxford: Clarendon, 1964); and Juliet Du Boulay, *Portrait of a Greek Mountain Village* (Oxford: Clarendon, 1979).

4. See David D. Gilmore, ed., *Honor and Shame and the Unity of the Mediterranean* (Washington, DC: American Anthropological Association, 1987); and Peregrine Horden and Nicholas Purcell, *The Corrupting Sea: A Study of Mediterranean History* (Oxford: Blackwell, 2000).

5. Frank Henderson Stewart, *Honor* (Chicago: University of Chicago Press, 1994); Lila Abu-Lughod, *Veiled Sentiments: Honor and Poetry in a Bedouin Society* (Berkeley: University of California Press, 1986); Jan Goodwin, *Price of Honor: Muslim Women Lift the Veil of Silence on the Islamic World*, rev. ed. (New York: Plume, 2003); Nicole Pope, *Honor Killings in the Twenty-First Century* (New York: Palgrave Macmillan, 2012); and Asma Afsaruddin, ed., *Hermeneutics and Honor: Negotiating Female "Public" Space in Islamic/ate Societies* (Cambridge, MA: Harvard University Press, 1999).

6. David G. Mandelbaum, *Women's Seclusion and Men's Honor: Sex Roles in North India, Bangladesh, and Pakistan* (Tucson: University of Arizona Press, 1993).

7. Oleg Benesch, *Inventing the Way of the Samurai: Nationalism, Internationalism, and Bushidō in Modern Japan* (Oxford: Oxford University Press, 2014).

8. Lyman L. Johnson and Sonya Lipsett-Rivera, eds., *The Faces of Honor: Sex, Shame, and Violence in Colonial Latin America* (Albuquerque: University of New Mexico Press, 1998); Ann Twinam, *Public Lives, Private Secrets: Gender, Honor, Sexuality, and Illegitimacy in Colonial Spanish America* (Stanford, CA: Stanford University Press, 1999); Sueann Caulfield, Sarah C. Chambers, and Lara Putnam, eds., *Honor, Status, and Law in Modern Latin America* (Durham, NC: Duke University Press, 2005); and Osvaldo F. Pardo, *Honor and Personhood in Early Modern Mexico* (Ann Arbor: University of Michigan Press, 2015).

9. Bertram Wyatt-Brown, *Southern Honor: Ethics and Behavior in the Old South* (New York: Oxford University Press, 1982), and *Honor and Violence in the Old South* (New York: Oxford University Press, 1986); Kenneth S. Greenberg, *Honor and Slavery: Lies, Duels, Noses, Masks, Dressing as a Woman, Gifts, Strangers, Humanitarianism, Death, Slave Rebellions, the Pro-slavery Argument, Baseball, Hunting, and Gambling in the Old South* (Princeton, NJ: Princeton University Press, 1996); and Richard E. Nisbett and Dov Cohen, *Culture of Honor: The Psychology of Violence in the South* (Boulder, CO: Westview, 1996).

10. Pieter Spierenburg, ed., *Men and Violence: Gender, Honor, and Ritual in Modern Europe and America* (Columbus: Ohio State University Press, 1998); and James Bowman, *Honor: A History* (New York: Encounter Books, 2006).

11. William Ian Miller, *Bloodtaking and Peacemaking: Feud, Law, and Society in Saga Iceland* (Chicago: Chicago University Press, 1990).

12. Robert A. Nye, *Masculinity and Male Codes of Honor in Modern France*, new ed. (Berkeley: University of California Press, 1998).

13. Ute Frevert, "The Taming of the Noble Ruffian: Male Violence and Dueling in Early Modern and Modern Germany," in *Men and Violence: Gender, Honor, and Ritual in Modern*

Europe and America, ed. Pieter Spierenburg (Columbus: Ohio State University Press, 1998), 37–63.

14. By making the analogy to Arabian babblers, I do *not* take a stand on the question whether honor is an instinct that dictates human conduct just as the handicap principle mobilizes in birds and other mammals. Having no expertise in social biology, I remain agnostic.

15. Numerous readers of this chapter had difficulty understanding how and why honor was a value. I realize that for readers who are no longer familiar with honor mentality and terminology, this may be bewildering. Nevertheless, a member of an honor society will proudly declare that honor is a value that they adhere to. Many specific values, such as generosity, loyalty, and hospitality, are seen to derive from honor. In a way, honor is a value in the same way that for many people family is a value, and there is a whole set of specific derivative family values. Additionally, the principle of honor accords every member of an honor society their value within the group and its norms. Being honorable is being valuable. If you cannot digest my use of the term "value" in the context of honor, please replace it with attitude, mentality, or any other term that feels right.

16. Charles Taylor, "The Politics of Recognition," in *Multiculturalism: Examining the Politics of Recognition*, ed. Amy Gutmann (Princeton, NJ: Princeton University Press, 1994), 25–74; Pierre Bourdieu, "The Sentiment of Honor on Kabyle Society," in *Honor and Shame: The Values of Mediterranean Society*, ed. John G. Peristiany (Chicago: Chicago University Press, 1966), 191–241; and Peter L. Berger, "On the Obsolescence of the Concept of Honor," in *Revisions: Changing Perspectives in Moral Philosophy*, ed. Stanley Hauerwas and Alasdair MacIntyre (Notre Dame, IN: University of Notre Dame Press, 1983), 172–81.

17. Bourdieu, "Sentiment of Honor," 228.

18. Berger, "Obsolescence of the Concept of Honor," 177.

19. Taylor, "Politics of Recognition," 27, 37.

20. Kwame Anthony Appiah, *The Honor Code: How Moral Revolutions Happen* (New York: Norton, 2010), ix.

21. Robert L. Oprisko, *Honor: A Phenomenology* (New York: Routledge, 2012), 3.

22. See particularly William Ian Miller's books: *Bloodtaking and Peacemaking* (1990); *Humiliation: And Other Essays on Honor, Social Discomfort, and Violence* (Ithaca, NY: Cornell University Press, 1993; and *Eye for an Eye: Justice Anatomized* (New York: Cambridge University Press, 2005).

23. Oprisko constructs a consistent theoretical definition of honor, which resembles the one suggested in this chapter. Yet he highlights slightly different elements. Compare his definition to the one you have been reading:

> Because honoring is the process whereby a group confers a value upon the individual, it represents nothing less than the means by which individuals and groups bind themselves, and it incorporates the assumption and divesting of sovereignty. Through the action of conferral, the honoring agent is claiming sovereignty over the individual, granting a distinction of, it nothing else, exceptionalism, typically referred to as excellence. The individual divests him- or herself of personal sovereignty in order to gain and maintain social value according to rules and rituals that represent the sacred and bind the parties together. This is not always a happy and unchallenged process.
>
> This valuation becomes real for the members of the designating group. More appropriately, the individual members of the group accept the particular value designation as a fact. . . . The process of honoring is continuous; it is the manner in which reality is socially constructed because it is the means by which value is conferred by the sovereign and accepted by the group. Oprisko, *Honor*, 4–5

24. Oprisko does not distinguish glory and dignity from honor, as I do. For his discussion of the term "glory," see, for example, *Honor*, 100–109; for his discussion of the term "dignity," see, *Honor*, 121–24.

25. The following sections rely on the ample anthropological research mentioned in previous endnotes; on Miller's conception of honor, as it appears in his many publications and in his

courses that I attended in the early 1990s; and on my own countless observations of social situations and readings of cultural texts—ancient, old, and contemporary.

26. Instead of or in addition to the three-dimensional pyramid metaphor, you may think of such a social structure as a two-dimensional circle, in which the most important and worthy members are situated in the very center. The further away from the center one is situated—the lower his honor, prestige, and status, and the greater his shame. The race to the top is in this metaphor a race to the center. The pyramid-inspired fear of hitting rock bottom is the fear of finding yourself outside the circle. I am grateful to Steve Kaplan who suggested this metaphor to me.

27. The very top was often allotted to just one person, who was often perceived as both at the top of the structure—and outside it. Usual rules did not apply to him. That person was beyond shaming. Pitt-Rivers, *Fate of Shechem*, 37.

28. For a thorough analysis, see William Ian Miller, *Faking It* (Cambridge: Cambridge University Press, 2003).

29. Frevert, "Taming of the Noble Ruffian," 37–63.

30. Miller, *Humiliation*, 116.

31. Miller, *Humiliation*, 116.

32. Miller, *Humiliation*, 84.

33. Campbell, *Honor, Family and Patronage*, 151.

34. Pitt-Rivers, *Fate of Shechem*, 21–22; emphasis in the original.

35. Pitt-Rivers, *Fate of Shechem*, 42–45.

36. For feminist honor-sensitive critique, see Orit Kamir, *Framed: Women in Law and Film* (Durham, NC: Duke University Press, 2006), and "The Dignitarian Feminist Jurisprudence with Applications to Rape, Sexual Harassment, and Honor Codes," in *Research Handbook on Feminist Jurisprudence*, ed. Robin West and Cynthia Grant Brown (Northampton, MA: Edward Elgar, 2019), 303–20.

37. An anonymous Chronicle account from Pseudo Brunetto Latini, Cronica (late 13th century), in Ferdinand Schevill, *Medieval and Renaissance Florence* (New York: Harper & Row, 1961), 1: 106–7; inhttp://courses.washington.edu/hsteu401/Buondelmonte.htm, Fordham University online Medieval Source Book (https://sourcebooks.fordham.edu/search.asp). I am grateful to Anna Kocharov for introducing me to this juicy narrative and its sources.

38. Anon. Brunetto Latini, centuryin Schevill, *Medieval and Renaissance Florence*, 1:106–7.

39. Excerpt:

And so it came about that on Easter morning, with his bride at his side, Messer Buondelmonte came riding over the bridge in a doublet of silk and mantle, with a wreath around his brow. No sooner had he arrived at the statue of Mars [at Ponte Vecchio], than Messer Schiatta degli Uberti rushed upon him and, striking him on the crown with his mace, brought him to earth. At once Messer Oddo Arrighi was on top of him and opened his veins with a knife. And having killed him, they fled. The ambush had occurred at the houses of Amidei, who lived at the head of the bridge. Immediately there was a tremendous tumult. The body of the murdered man was placed on a bier, and the bride took her seat next to him, holding his head in her lap and weeping aloud. In this manner the procession moved through all Florence. And on this day, for the first time, new names were heard, those of the Guelf party and the Ghibelline party. Anon. Brunetto Latini, in Schevill, *Medieval and Renaissance Florence*, 1:106–7.

40. Giovanni Villani, *Nuova Cronica* [New chronicles] (ca. 1300–1337), in *Florentine Chronicle*, trans. David Burr, Fordham University, Internet Medieval Sourcebook,http://www.fordham.edu/halsall/source/villani.html.

41. See Appiah, *Honor Code*; and Oprisko, *Honor*.

42. Josiah Ober, "Meritocratic and Civic Dignity in Greco-Roman Antiquity," in *The Cambridge Handbook of Human Dignity: Interdisciplinary Perspectives*, ed. Marcus Düwell, Jens

Braarvig, Roger Brownsword, and Dietmar Mieth (Cambridge: Cambridge University Press, 2014), 54–55.

43. For further exposition of this, see chap. 3.

Chapter Three

Divine Human Glory

In the Image of God

In his popular 1941 sermon and essay "The Weight of Glory," Christian theologian, author, and scholar C. S. Lewis referred to glory in the following manner:

> The promise of *glory* is the promise, almost incredible and only possible by the work of Christ, that some of us . . . shall find approval, shall please God. To please God . . . to be a real ingredient in the divine happiness . . . to be loved by God, not merely pitied, but delighted in as an artist delights in his work or a father in a son—it seems impossible, a weight or burden of *glory* which our thoughts can hardly sustain. But so it is. . . . For *glory* meant good report with God, acceptance by God, response, acknowledgment, and welcome into the heart of things. The door on which we have been knocking all our lives will open at last. [1]

Written seven years before the United Nations Universal Declaration of Human Rights (UDHR), this theological essay is unapologetic in its use of the term "glory." It seems to assume that readers are familiar and comfortable with both the concept and terminology. Dignity, either divine or human, is never mentioned and glory is not associated with it.

In 2013, the prolific Christian theologian Ron Highfield seems to be referring to the same concept of glory in his monograph *God, Freedom and Human Dignity*. But now, sixty-five years after the UDHR and well into the era of dignity talk, Highfield seems to offer a reflexive translation of the earlier Christian glory talk into dignity talk. Please note not merely the content of his claims, but also his terminology (which I highlighted by using italics).

Thinking about God's *dignity* likely brings to mind God's power, majesty, holiness and *glory*. We think of such passages as Isaiah 6:3: "Holy, Holy, Holy, is the Lord Almighty; / the whole earth is full of his *glory*." . . . God's *glory* is the "manifestation and perception of the greatness, splendor and excellence of God's being and actions." Karl Barth speaks of divine *glory* as "the self-revealing sum of all divine perfections. It is the fullness of God's deity, the emerging, self-expressing and self-manifesting reality of all that God is. It is God's being in so far as this is in itself a being which declares itself." In speaking of God's *glory* Edward Leigh makes a distinction that also applies to God's *dignity*. God's *glory* may be understood as "the inward excellence and worth whereby he deserves to be esteemed and praised" or as "the actual acknowledging of it, for *glory* is defined as clear and manifest knowledge of another's excellence; therefore the *glory* of God is two-fold." Understood exclusively in these ways, God's *dignity* puts God at a distance from us, transcendent and exalted. . . . Yet in the darkness and shame of the cross God revealed a *glory* and *dignity* far deeper than the superficial *glory* and *dignity* the world seeks. . . . God's *dignity*, then, is the power, wisdom and *glory* of his love and is manifested most fully in the self-giving of Jesus on the Cross. The *glory* and *dignity* of a human being follows the same pattern. . . . Our *dignity* consists in being loved by the Father of our Lord Jesus Christ. God's love makes us *worthy*.[2]

In this theological rhetoric, glory appears to be the essence and merit of God's divinity, which he bestows on humankind through his love for us and through the mediation of Jesus Christ, his divine human son.[3] This divine glory is also God's dignity, and hence also the derivative human dignity. As Highfield puts it in the passage above: "The glory and dignity of a human being . . . consists in being loved by the Father of our Lord Jesus Christ. God's love makes us worthy." Glory is, therefore, divine human dignity; it is our human value, worth, conferred by God. This dignity-glory put forth by Lewis and Highfield is the metaphysical, spiritual, theological, Judeo-Christian glory that this chapter presents and explores.

Lewis's popular twentieth-century sermon and essay suggest that "glory" seems to have been a familiar, common term that did not require explanation or justification. Quite distinctly, Highfield's twenty-first-century text uses "dignity" to mediate, explain, and justify the use of glory. Joining the prevailing dignity talk, Christian theologians seem to be translating glory into the more popular discourse of dignity, thus making their traditional *glory talk* more timely and accessible in an era dominated by *dignity talk*. This has made the term "glory" almost distinct, and may explain the widespread unease of colleagues and friends at my usage of this dated term.

Yet it is precisely the distinction between human dignity and glory that I wish to pinpoint in order to unpack the condensed, expanded, overburdened concept of dignity. To distinguish glory from dignity I must employ the term "glory," which I believe to be the most accurate term for the theological,

Judeo-Christian notion I tackle. I therefore ask my readers to tolerate my usage of the word—until it, hopefully, begins to "sound right" (as it once did).

This chapter does not feign to be either a theological treatise or academic theological scholarship. Nor does it pretend or aim to be a linguistic study. Based on both theology and theological scholarship, it attempts to sketch a theological concept that, I claim, presented a Judeo-Christian supplement—or even alternative—to honor as a fundamental value and attitude underlying social institutions and determining people's worth. As the presentation refers to a historical period of two millennia, it is, of course, no more than a sketch. Further, addressing a readership that, like myself, is not necessarily theologically informed, I deliberately avoid awe-inspiring technical terminology, the manifold contradictory views on each and every point, and enriching—yet often bewildering—scholarly footnotes. Readers seeking more exact theological rhetoric are encouraged to turn to my primary sources such as Highfield's many publications.

In order to link this chapter's analysis of glory with the discussion of honor in the previous chapter and with the discussion of dignity in the next one, I present the discussion in narrative form. The resulting linearity and simplification are meant to render the abstract analysis more accessible.

GOING BACK: ANCIENT GODS, GODDESSES, AND HONOR

Ancient pantheons, much like the human societies that worshipped them, manifested the logic and structure of honor, as presented in chapter 2. Honor underlay the informal institutions that deities lived by. Gods and goddess—on the Olympus as in any Near Eastern Garden of Eden—were preoccupied with their relative rank and prestige in their divine pyramid-shaped hierarchies. Much of their routine, lifestyle, warfare, competition, and aggression revolved around obtaining, securing, and avenging their honor and manifesting their respective status and esteem in their divine pecking orders.

Whether the pantheon was Egyptian, Mesopotamian, Canaanite, or Greek, the deity of the Netherlands might feel scorned by deities ruling more elevated realms, such as fertility, and might avenge its hurt honor by kidnapping and/or slaughtering a superior deity's beloved, young, beautiful, divine son, daughter, or lover (recall—or look up—Osiris, Dumuzi, Tammuz, Ba'al, Adonis, Persephone). This could start a passionate world war, urging gods and goddesses to align with the combatants according to their honor duties and interests. The war would disrupt fertility and climate, causing turbulence and disaster in the universe. Its settlement would require lengthy, delicate, honor-bound negotiations and peacemaking mechanisms.

Often, the mythical kidnapping or killing, lament, negotiation, and settlement would be a cyclic, repetitive, seasonal event in human life. But sometimes a ruthless competition for honor among the deities would lead to a war enfolding the destruction of an entire city-state and its culture (this, of course, in the eyes and narration of believers). Such was the famous case when Aphrodite, Hera, and Athena each demanded to be declared the fairest of the Olympian goddesses, and Paris, prince of Troy, was chosen to judge among them. Taken with beauty and love, Paris chose Aphrodite. As his judgment humiliated and infuriated Athena and Hera, his city, Troy, was eventually burned to the ground by these goddesses' devotees; the city-state's culture was erased and its citizens killed or enslaved. Interestingly, the myth begins with a minor goddess, Eris. Not invited to a wedding party, humiliated Eris chose to avenge her wounded honor by introducing the Olympian goddesses with the famous golden apple bearing the fateful scripture "for the fairest."

Humans were acutely aware of their gods' and goddesses' incessant hunger and thirst for honor. They spent much of their time, energy, and fortune ensuring, increasing, and displaying their deities' honor. Cult members would dedicate statues bearing their divinity's image, build ornate shrines and temples, and offer expensive sacrifices to honor their deity above all others. They knew all too well that hell has no fury like a deity scorned.

DIVINE HONOR AND THE HEBREW BIBLE'S MONOTHEISM

Enlil was lord of the storm, king of heaven and earth, father of the gods. His name and image appear in Sumer, Akkad, Assyria, Babylon, Hatti, Canaan, and other Mesopotamian-culture lands. The Canaanites addressed their version of this father of gods as El and El Elyon, meaning "most elevated patriarch god." He was no different from other supreme patriarch deities, such as Zeus or Jupiter: mostly busy ruling the world and all other members of his pantheon (the Elohim), and appeasing his wife. His honor was, of course, sacred and important. Disobedience on the part of other gods offended his supreme, divine honor, and he would avenge, retaliate, and deter, as the logic of honor dictates. When the jealous Mot (Canaanite deity of death and the Netherlands) killed El's beloved Ba'al (god of fertility), Anat (virgin goddess of love and war) expressed her loyalty and devotion to El by avenging him on Mot and bringing Ba'al back from the dead.

This ancient, familiar logic of honor among the divine was disrupted when the Hebrew-speaking Semites who lived in the land of Canaan, the Israelites, established that their El, El Elyon (God and God Almighty in Hebrew as in Canaanite), was not merely a supreme deity, but also the one and only. This exclusivity, which we call monotheism, eradicated the entire pantheon, deleting the whole divine community. Furthermore, according to the Hebrew Bible (the Old Testament), the Israelites' version of El refused to be visible to humans and was strictly averse to material iconization. After some wandering, he established his invisible residence in one single temple in Jerusalem, firmly prohibiting worship and the adoration of any idols anywhere.

The monotheistic eradication of the entire pantheon obstructed the hierarchical structure of the divine sphere, and with it—the underlying logic of divine honor. Honor is a team game, not one to be played by a solitary player, human or divine. In the absence of a group and a hierarchy, how can honor manifest each participant's relative standing, status, esteem? In the absence of competitors—as well as coveted, prestigious positions—what would it mean to *gain* or *lose* honor? Whose honor could this single god's honor surpass in a single-participant honor-based competition? Further still: If the Hebrew Bible's single divine player was invisible, how could he be exposed? Exposure is a central move in any honor game and the means of shaming. In the absence of exposure, how would honor be taken, and shame installed?

Clearly, the shift to monotheism entailed rethinking of the whole underlying honor-based infrastructure. One plausible option was that with monotheism, the Israelites would abandon the honor structure altogether, replacing it with an alternative centerpiece that underlies a radically different informal institution. The Hebrew Bible refutes this possibility. According to biblical narratives, Israelite and Judean kings, judges, and patriarchs sought honor, fought to accumulate and maintain it, and avenged its infringement. The Hebrew word for honor, *kavod*, is very prevalent in the Hebrew Bible narratives, connoting weight, significance, and distinction.

So, perhaps honor, *kavod*, was relegated by the monotheistic Israelites to the human sphere alone? Perhaps only human kings and patriarchs were honorable, whereas the divine was absolved of such dimension? The Hebrew Bible precludes this option as well. The Hebrew God is defined as king of *kavod*, as he whose *kavod* fills the whole world. In fact, the word *kavod* is assigned to him more often than to humans. But as a solo deity, what could God's *kavod* possibly mean?

THE MEANING OF GOD'S GLORY

Much like honor, God's glory testifies to his value and worth, manifesting his supreme greatness—yet it cannot and must not carry with it connotation of hierarchy, competition, rivals, adherence to conduct code, rank, or relative standing. Those elements, inherent to the logic of honor, would undermine the exclusivity of the single God and his unique value. Glory, God's "honor substitute," must, therefore, feature the opposite of honor's relativistic attributes. It must be an innate, unchanging, absolute manifestation of inherent divine worth. Based on the Hebrew Bible references, glory must also be an awesome, shining demonstration of the presence of God's incomparable, all-encompassing, unlimited holiness. In the words of the prophet Ezekiel: "the earth shined with his glory" (Ezekiel 43:2).[4]

GOD'S GLORY IN THE KING JAMES TRANSLATION OF THE HEBREW BIBLE

The exact meaning of God's *kavod* must have (consciously or unconsciously) troubled many of the Hebrew Bible's translators, including the seventeenth-century English composers of the King James Bible.[5] Composing the definitive English version of the Bible, they often translated human *kavod* into the English word "honor,"[6] but chose the English word "glory"[7] to translate biblical references to the *kavod* of God. In so doing, they suggested that the biblical God's *kavod* must be distinct from honor.[8]

Perhaps most clearly indicative of this is their translation of a Proverb phrase in which the Hebrew word *kavod* appears twice: once referring to God and once to flesh-and-blood kings. In the King James translation, the divine *kavod* is translated into glory, whereas the human *kavod*—into honor: "It is the *glory of God* to conceal a thing: but the *honor of kings* is to search out a matter" (Proverbs 25:2).

The English word "glory," from the Latin *gloria*, is a synonym for honor. At the same time, it also connotes radiant light and a halo. The translational choice to refer to God's *kavod* as glory rather than honor emphasized ancient biblical imagery and turned it into a fundamental, deep-seated Jewish-Christian paradigm.

The Hebrew Bible had already suggested that God's *kavod* was luminous; the translation of this shining *kavod* into the glowing glory successfully sealed this imagery and stamped it in our minds. Think of the radiant honor that shines in familiar verses such as "and the sight of the glory of the lord was like devouring fire" (Exodus 24:17), or "the earth shined with his glory" (Ezekiel 43:2). Thanks to the choice of the term "glory" to denote the divine *kavod*, we intuitively see this radiant divine honor in countless other verses and contexts; some that invite this gleaming image more readily,[9] and others that take it on merely because the brilliance of glory requires it.[10]

GOD'S IMAGE IN HUMAN FORM

Throughout most of the twentieth century, most Bible scholars believed—as many still do—that the book of Genesis (together with Exodus, Leviticus,

Numbers, and Deuteronomy) is compiled of excerpts from four distinct literary sources, referred to as the J (Jahwist) source, the Priestly source, the Elohist source, and the Deuteronomist source. In accordance with this, scholars distinguish between two different biblical accounts of the creation of humanity. One includes the creation story of the first man, Adam, from earth, and the first woman, Eve, from Adam's rib; it contains the prohibition to eat from the tree of knowledge in the Garden of Eden, the serpent's luring of Eve, and her seduction of Adam. It culminates in the fall, curse, and exile from Eden; leading to the birth of the first siblings, Cain and Abel, and the slaying of Abel by his brother Cain. This version is attributed to the J source.

The other, less sensational account is attributed to the Priestly source. It narrates the simultaneous creation of the first man and woman in the image of God (Genesis 1:26–27). The name "Adam" in this account refers to both of them together, to the human couple (Genesis 5:2). This narration presents the first human procreation, the birthing of Seth, as re-creation (duplication) of the divine image of God in human form (Genesis 5:3). Next, it derives the prohibition of manslaughter—as well as the compulsory death penalty for such crime—from the divine image embedded in the human person: "Whoso sheddeth man's blood, by man shall his blood be shed: *for in the image of God made he man*" (Genesis 9:6; emphasis mine).

I believe that the notion that all humans bear the image of the divine is one of the Hebrew Bible's greatest assets and contributions to civilization. It is the source of the idea that all human beings are born with innate worth.

Creation in God's image is often referred to as the bestowing of God's glory on humanity. The endowment of Adam with the image of God is interpreted as God "crown[ing] him with glory" (Psalm 8:5). Apparently, God found Adam, the human couple, worthy of his glory, and thus created man and woman in God's image, which contains his divine glory. And this attribute Adam bequeathed to human offspring through re-creation. All human beings bear the divine, shining glory, because they all inherit from their ancestors the image of God.

HALAKHIC (JEWISH LEGAL) SIGNIFICANCE OF GOD'S RESIDENCE IN THE HUMAN IMAGE

Professor of jurisprudence and Judaic studies Yair Lorberbaum composed a meticulous, exhaustive study titled *In God's Image: Myth, Theology, and Law in Classical Judaism* (law and fiction). Lorberbaum argues that in the era of the Second Temple some Jewish rabbis interpreted the Hebrew Bible to mean that Adam's creation in the image of God meant that there was divine presence in the human person. This interpretation was ardently adopted by later, post-Temple generations of rabbinical scholars. After the destruction of the Temple (ca. 70 CE), rabbis were all too keen to declare that the demolition of God's house did not necessarily mean his departure from Israel, because, in fact, he resided in each and every one.[11] Lorberbaum goes on to state that this theological paradigm plays a key role in Jewish jurisprudence and law.[12] In fact, Lorberbaum goes on to argue that this theological paradigm became a legal principle that influenced the formation of many *halakhic* (legal) spheres.[13]

The notion of God's presence or residence in the human being carries with it the attribution of God's divine glory to Adam (man and woman combined). So the divine human glory became a legal principle that generated significant parts of Jewish law.

This section fleshes out the outline of Lorberbaum's argument for readers who wish to delve deeper into this ancient Jewish history and law. In antiquity, particularly in the Hellenistic and Roman worlds, gods were believed to reside and be present in the idols that bore their images. This meant that the icon was literally an extension of the essence it represented and the two (essence and extension) were inherently drawn to each other.[14] This iconic worldview was reformulated by the main strand of rabbinical scholars. They determined that the creation of Adam in God's image meant that God made the human to be his icon, and that it was in us that he resides.[15] To strengthen its hold, rabbinical scholarship attributes this view to one of its greatest, earliest, and most esteemed rabbis, Sanhedrin president Old Hillel and to his revered successor, the *tannah*[16] Rabbi Akiva.[17]

Regarding human creation in the image of God, Hillel is quoted as emphasizing that even when using the lavatory or the bathhouse, he worships God, since maintenance of the human body is devout preservation of God's image.[18]

Rabbi Akiva, perhaps the most revered and cited of rabbis, a first-century CE *tannah*, that is said (by Talmudic sources) to have developed this Hillelic worldview, established it as a fundamental legal principle and based *halakhic* law on it.[19] Lorberbaum suggests that this development was initiated in the shadow of the Roman destruction of the Jewish Temple.[20]

> The idea of Imago Dei [image of God], whose seeds first budded among the Pharisees during the Temple period (in Hillel and Hillel's school) gained tremendous momentum in wake of the Destruction. The timing of these developments was apparently not coincidental. Tannaitic speculation regarding the *zelem* conception, the manner of its development and the significance attached to it, may be understood as a response to God's departure from His sanctuary. The idea of creation in *zelem Elohim* in the iconic-theurgic sense provided an effective (albeit not exclusive) solution to the profound religious crisis caused by the Destruction. God has left his dwelling, but has not abandoned the Land. To the contrary, in certain senses He was far closer, because of His presence in humanity created in His image.[21]

Lorberbaum claims that this *tannaic* worldview generated binding *halakhic* legal regulations.[22] Much of this *halakhic* discussion revolves around the death penalty and procreation. Half of Lorberbaum's monograph is dedicated to close reading of rabbinical (mostly *tannaic*) texts engaging with execution and reproduction.[23]

Horrified at raising a human hand on God's image and abode (that is, on the human being), the *tannaim* made every conceivable effort to reduce—perhaps preclude altogether—the death penalty,[24] and to regulate that if ever inflicted—it would cherish and preserve bodily unity and integrity.[25] They insisted that execution must leave no traces on the dead body.[26] Accordingly, they interpreted the biblical execution-by-stoning as requiring that the convicted felon be pushed to his death from a second floor, in a manner that would not compromise bodily integrity.[27]

Hanging, which in antiquity often included leaving the body to rot and be devoured by animals, was considered particularly humiliating.[28] The Hebrew Bible demands that a hanged body be buried on the day of the hanging (Deuteronomy 21:23). The *tannaim* interpreted this biblical command as requiring *immediate* letting down of the hanged body, since the sight of God's image hanging is offensive to God.[29] Rabbi Meir is quoted as narrating a fable about a king who sentenced his gangster twin brother to death. Seeing the gangster crucified, passersby remarked that the king himself seems to be humiliated (*Tosefta, Sanhedrin* 9:7).[30]

Cherishing the dead human body, *tannaim* were even more reluctant to harm the living person. This principle led them to interpret the Bible's physical punishments such as "eye for an eye and tooth for a tooth" as imposing strictly and exclusively *monetary* damages.[31] If a murderer remains an icon/image of God and the integrity of his body must not be harmed—all the more so a felon convicted of a lesser felony, such as gouging an eye or breaking a tooth.

Concurrently, Rabbi Akiva's determination that shedding human blood diminishes God's image was interpreted by his students to mean that abstaining from procreation is equivalent to blood shedding, and is hence diminutive of the divine image.[32] Simply put: celibacy diminishes the image of God (in human form).

God's creation of Adam as a male-female human entity indicates a divine wish that humanity procreate and extend the divine presence in the world.[33] If "God implanted the procreative mechanism in His *demut*,"[34] it must mean that he contemplated its multiplication. An *amoraic* (post-*tannaic*) saying states explicitly that the essence of humanity is in combining God's image with reproduction. Human purpose must therefore be to procreate and extend God's image.[35] This principle informs the detailed *tannaic* directives on and regulation of procreation.[36]

As demonstrated by their reference to human bodies, the *tannaim*'s concept of the human being did not favor the mind or soul over body. Lorberbaum claims that for the *tannaim*, humanity included all components of the concrete person, including body and emotions:

> In their view, the term comprises all components of a human being—consciousness, personality, and body—all of which are organic elements of the flesh-and-blood person. This understanding of *zelem* differs from other approaches (those of Philo and Maimonides, for example), that detach the term from the realm of the physical and the concrete, confining it exclusively to the rational faculty, the soul, the conscience, or the like. These approaches are deficient in two ways: they restrict the "image" to a particular, partial aspect of the human being, and they premise it on an abstract foundation. [37]

As this is not a theological treatise, I will not trace the development of the notion of divine human glory in the following millennia of Jewish culture. Suffice it to say that the conceptual-legal development described here is the foundation of mainstream Jewish culture and law to this day. The image of God was continuously interpreted as more and more abstract, and the reference to Adam as God's flesh-and-blood icon and abode lost its sway. But man's divine image remained the source of the special affinity between God and man, and the *halakhic* rules that derive from the legal implications attributed to the notion of God's image were never abolished.

DIVINE HUMAN GLORY IN EARLY CHRISTIANITY

If the rabbinic development of the divine human glory began with Old Hillel (first century BCE) and peaked after the destruction of the Second Temple (first and second centuries CE), it is very likely that the first Christians, who began to form their theology at that very time, were familiar with the rabbinical conceptualization and perhaps influenced by it.

Alon Goshen-Gottstein traces in rabbinical scholarship two types of reference to Adam's creation in the image of God. The first is the *tannaic* conceptualization described by Lorberbaum. The second conceives God's image as a body of light that Adam initially had—yet forfeited through the sin, fall, and banishment from Eden. [38] Whereas mainstream rabbinic Judaism seems to have preferred the first view, it would appear that the first Christians were among those who opted for the second.

In most Christian interpretation, Adam's fall lost humanity the divine image and glory; only in the coming of the second Adam, Jesus Christ, God once again materialized in human image: that of his son. The divine image and glory (the radiant body of light) were, therefore, not inherited through procreation from the first days of Adam; they were exclusively embedded in the Christ, and distributed through Christianity and its holy mass.[39] A Christian who partakes in the ritualistic communion, a symbolic/partaking of Christ's body and drinking of his blood—embodies the divine image and glory. This conceptualization is manifest in St. Paul's phrase "the light of the glorious gospel of Christ, who is the image of God" (2 Corinthians 4:4). Christ is the image of God and his gospel is glorious light, that is, divine glory that shines unto the believers. Those who receive Christ, therefore, receive the image of God and its shining glory.

Consider some additional references to glory in the New Testament:

- I have glorified thee on the earth: I have finished the work which thou gavest me to do. And now, O Father, glorify thou me with thine own self with the glory which I had with thee before the world was (John 17:4–5);
- And the glory which thou gavest me I have given them; that they may be one, even as we are one (John 17:22);
- Father, I will that they also, whom thou hast given me, be with me where I am; that they may behold my glory, which thou hast given me: for thou lovedst me before the foundation of the world (John 17:24);
- Wherefore receive ye one another, as Christ also received us to the glory of God (Romans 15:7);
- For a man indeed ought not to cover his head, forasmuch as he is the image and glory of God: but the woman is the glory of the man (1 Corinthians 11:7);
- But we all, with open face beholding as in a glass the glory of the Lord, are changed into the same image from glory to glory, even as by the Spirit of the Lord (2 Corinthians 3:18);
- For God, who commanded the light to shine out of darkness, hath shined in our hearts, to give the light of the knowledge of the glory of God in the face of Jesus Christ (2 Corinthians 4:6);
- And that every tongue should confess that Jesus Christ *is* Lord, to the glory of God the Father (Philippians 2:11);
- But we see Jesus, who was made a little lower than the angels for the suffering of death, crowned with glory and honour (Hebrews 2:9);
- And the city had no need of the sun, neither of the moon, to shine in it: for the glory of God did lighten it, and the Lamb *is* the light thereof (Revelation 21:23).

These early Christian references to glory create the strong impression that whereas Jewish rabbinical texts derive divine human glory from the creation of Adam (that is, the first human couple) in the image of God, the New Testament links divine human glory with Jesus Christ, God's beloved son who took on human form. Christ is God's presence in a human body; he is the image of God and God's extension. It is not through genetic lineage to

Adam that God's glory is accessible to humans, but through Jesus Christ, God's human icon, and his gospel.

Simply put: glory is not hereditary; it resided in Jesus, and must be chosen and embraced together with Christianity. Nevertheless, it is accessible to any human being: all one needs to do is accept Jesus Christ; this choice secures God's image and glory in man. Even if not innate to the human being as such, glory is within reach, and any person, rich or poor, young or old, may acquire it through Christianity. This *imago dei* of early Christianity was later integrated with the other notion, of the divine image as innate to humankind.

GLORY AS AN ALTERNATIVE SOURCE OF HUMAN WORTH

This presentation of the origins of both ancient Jewish and early Christian divine human glory is clearly much too concise to be accurate or nuanced. Yet my goal is not to delve into numerous theological sources and their countless interpretations, but to present the claim that in the ancient world of honor, the Judeo-Christian idea of divine human glory offered an alternative source of human worth. In a world in which a person's worth—in his own estimation as much as in his social group's—was solidly determined by the honor he inherited, accumulated, and preserved within his social group, divine human glory offered a subversively alternate value system and fundamental attitude that defined human worth applying completely different standards and parameters.

Glory opened up the possibility to imagine human value outside the honor-based social system. It challenged the honor system by suggesting that any person might have value—without regard to their status in the hegemonic social order. This alternative human value was indifferent to social rank, standing, prestige, and esteem; it derived from a source that was exterior and far superior to society and its rules. It did not depend on visible, acknowledged social success or failure; on comparative, competitive distinction according to prevailing social standards. It sprang directly from each person's deep, intrinsic connection with the absolute, ultimate source of this value: God almighty himself. This connection ensured each person of—at least potential—innate value, which was perhaps invisible, yet holy, unlimited, and eternal.

In the ancient world, society was built on its collective honor-bound hierarchy and every member's personal relative standing. Glory's transcendence of any specific social order made it both universal and innately personal. It was universal since, unlike honor, it did not belong to a particular social order (be it of a small village or of the whole Roman Empire). The value that it ascribed transcended borders, languages, rulers, and social groups. It was inherently transcendental. At the same time, the value assigned by glory was not attached to a person's social standing, to their roles or functions, but to themselves, whether or not they even had a social affiliation. Honor is inseparable from standing within a particular social order; if you fail to gain standing, or lose it, you fail to gain or you lose your honor value (and have, in its stead, shame). Very differently, glory is embedded in you and me, without regard to any social standing you or I may or may not possess. In this sense, although the concept that all human beings possess glory identically is abstract and impersonal, glory is personal in that it is intrinsically attached to the person, and not to their relative, tentative social position, roles, and identities.

It is easy to see how such an alternative source of value would be comforting and reassuring for individuals who did not possess much honor within their social systems, for those who lost their standing, for those who were weary of the constant, all-consuming competition for honor, or for those seeking a more spiritual, uplifting, metaphysical, and enduring sense of self-worth.

GLORY'S APPEAL WITHIN HISTORICAL JUDAISM AND CHRISTIANITY

The historical narration reveals why the concept of glory was so timely, useful, and therefore attractive for post-Temple Jews as well as for the postulating early Christians. Historical context explains why the idea of glory caught on in the first century CE, in both Judaism and Christianity.

According to Lorberbaum's analysis, it was the post-Temple rabbis (*tannaim*) who fully developed the Jewish concept of divine human glory. With the destruction of their Temple and the loss of national sovereignty and autonomy, Jews of the *tannaic* era clearly lost honor by the Roman conquest, destruction, exile, and rule. Losing their independence, freedom, and political self-determination, Jews lost their worth and value in the eyes of the world—and surely in their own eyes as well. It is not surprising that their spiritual leaders developed an alternative concept, ensuring Jews of their value even in the absence of the lost honor.

Lorberbaum suggests that, losing God's presence in his Jerusalem Temple, the rabbinic construction reassured Jews that God dwelled in each one of them. I suggest further that the newly developed divine human glory guaranteed Jews not only of God's presence, but also a transcendental sense of worth and meaning in the face of colossal, collective loss of honor.

Almost simultaneously, developing the Christian concept of glory, the first Christians offered it to the citizens of the Roman Empire as an alternative basis for self-evaluation. It was a way of gaining self-appreciation,

meaning, and even divinity—independently of one's social roles and acknowledged honor within the hegemonic social order. Anyone feeling disenfranchised, marginalized, oppressed, or underappreciated within the hegemonic social structure under the Roman rule could find refuge and redemption in attaining divine human glory through Christ. It is little wonder that
slaves, women, and many among the poor and disillusioned were grateful to
accept the generous offer to substitute their shame in the conventional social
order with glory in the Christian community. It is similarly clear why the
hegemonic Roman culture did not look kindly on the subversive value system and its novel foundation for self-evaluation.

For Romans who accepted Jesus Christ and the Christian divine human
glory, this new foundation for self-evaluation challenged their absolute adherence and loyalty to the Roman honor-bound social order. Deriving from a
completely different worldview, glory threatened to weaken and subvert Roman honor-based social order. If one received God's image and glory
through Christ and his gospel—one could no longer fully believe that the
Roman emperor, be it Nero or Caligula, was the divine lord of honor, and
that everyone else was only entitled to the honor value bestowed on them by
the emperor's will and honor-bound codes of conduct. Christian glory was,
therefore, potentially subversive and revolutionary in the context of Roman
society.

MERGER AND CONFUSION OF GLORY AND HONOR WITH
LATIN *DIGNITAS* AND ENGLISH *DIGNITY*

It is the dramatic juxtaposition of the Judeo-Christian notion of glory, the
Roman honor and the Latin term *dignitas* that gave rise to the confusion of
dignity, honor, and glory that obscures the discourse to this day.

In his theological discussion of dignity, *Imago Dei: Human Dignity in
Ecumenical Perspective*, Thomas Albert Howard rightly states that

> in the Roman world *dignitas* was the amount of personal clout that a male
> citizen acquired throughout his life—a concept we might today associate more
> with "esteem" or "prestige." It possesses a hierarchical, aristocratic connota-
> tion that does not sit easily in our democratic age.[40]

Similarly, other scholars of dignity often point out the historical meaning
of the Latin *dignitas* in ancient Rome. Michael Rosen says that "Cicero uses
dignitas as a conventional status term. . . . *Dignitas* here evidently just means
something like 'honor.'"[41] Jeremy Waldron notes that "in Roman usage,
dignitas embodied the idea of the honor, the privileges, and the deference
due to rank or office."[42]

Indeed, in the days of early Christianity, in the Roman world, the term *dignitas*, like *gloria*, conveyed the notion that I have presented in chapter 2 as honor. It denoted the value underlying the informal social institutions that structured Roman society and empire, and from which Romans derived their sense of worth. As the previous sections show, the idea of intrinsic, absolute, God-given divine human worth, which the Hebrew Bible calls *kavod*, the Vulgate sometimes referred to as *gloria*, and the King James Bible later labeled "glory," was a revolutionary, subversive Christian supplement—or even alternative, substitute, replacement for the Roman honor-*dignitas*. Romans accepting Christ would no longer derive their worth exclusively from the hegemonic Roman social hierarchy, structured by its honor/*dignitas* value system, but rather, primarily from their divine human glory.

The fateful encounter of Roman honor, the Latin term *dignitas*, and the Judeo-Christian idea of divine human glory marked the beginning of a lasting relationship, fraught with mutual enrichment and much confusion. Through this encounter, the term *dignitas* and its English descendant "dignity," initially denoting what I refer to as honor, became forever entangled with the idea that I refer to as glory: that every human being, disregarding social position or any other circumstance external to themselves, has absolute worth deriving from a transcendental source. It is with this historical encounter that honor, the social status–based human worth, was forever intertwined with glory, the universal-yet-personal human worth, and together they coalesced in the term *dignitas* and the English "dignity." Whereas Hebrew Bible–based monotheism conceptually (even if not linguistically) distinguished *kavod* (divine) glory from *kavod* (social) honor, *dignitas* reunited them in one multifaceted term.

Thirteenth-century Dominican theologian Thomas Aquinas played a particularly important role in Christening *dignitas*/dignity to mean glory rather than honor. As Rosen summarizes: "For Aquinas, 'dignity' is a term for . . . something's intrinsic value—the value that it has by occupying its appropriate place within God's creation."[43] Aquinas was immensely influential within the church as well as throughout the European world. His reconstruction of *dignitas*/dignity demonstrates how some Christian theology subtly disarmed—even deconstructed—the honor character of *dignitas*/dignity, while simultaneously linking this very notion with the idea of divine human glory.

Whereas *dignitas*-honor indicated that a person's worth corresponded with his standing in the hegemonic social hierarchy, Aquinas's *dignitas* replaced "hegemonic social hierarchy" with "God's creation." This baptized *dignitas* acknowledges each creature's worth as corresponding with his standing in a divine structured universe. In this framework, man's worth corresponds with his nature, which is having been created in the image of God. Humankind's *dignitas* is, therefore, not honor, but rather their divine human glory.[44]

The unison of honor and glory in *dignitas*/dignity gradually engraved glory-bound features onto European notions of honor. So, for example, in European societies, love of God, piety, charity, and compassion for other humans made in the image of God often contributed to a person's honor; their absence could inflict shame. Yet the marriage (of honor and glory) was never smooth; the history of Christian Europe is rife with tension between the competing values. So much so that one way of portraying this history is through the constant mediation of the honor-glory bipolar pull.

Officially, the pope, Vatican, churches, and their teachings represented divine glory, whereas feudal hierarchies and the social structures they entailed manifested honor-based social institutions. European kings and aristocrats symbolized the pinnacles of honor pyramids, as the churches symbolized God and his divine glory. Yet Christian kings and other leaders claimed to be appointed by God, hence exhibiting and responsible for the preservation, maintenance, and expansion of his divine glory. English, French, Spanish, and other European monarchs, just like Italian, German, and other princes and dukes, demanded their subjects' obedience and fought each other in the name of God's glory, even as they were pursuing their own honor. So doing, they recharacterized their honor institutions and drives using glory-imbued rhetoric (even if not always the terms comparable to glory).

Concurrently, the pope and many clergymen intertwined the divine glory that they represented with more mundane, human honor: in the name of divine glory they demanded honor, accumulated it, exhibited it, bestowed it, fought for it, and upheld its logic and psychology. The discord between the two distinct types of motivation was just as blunt, the camouflage being just as manipulative, disturbing, and costly in human life.

The medieval Crusades are an extreme example of the tension inherent in the merger of honor and glory. In the name of God's glory they boosted Europe's honor culture, nurturing honor-bound military orders that thrived on honor-driven combat among themselves—no less than on the wars they waged on their non-Christian rivals. God's glory was a banner under which crusading armies fought for honor. In the name of glory and honor, European crusaders inflicted horrific, inhuman abuse on "heathens"—as well as on other Christians. So did also European armies that invaded other continents, using the name of God and his glory as they competed for leaders' and empires' honor.

Over the course of this history, the Latin *dignitas* and the derivative English "dignity" combined aspects of both social honor and Judeo-Christian religious glory. This fusion, or *confusion*, can be found everywhere, including in theology.[45]

As mentioned in the beginning of this chapter, since 1948, in the wake of international dignity talk, more and more Christian reference to the idea of glory has been presented in dignity terms.[46] In fact, in recent decades the term "glory" all but disappeared, giving way to discussion of the Judeo-Christian concept almost exclusively in dignity terms. In their discussions of divine human worth and creation in the image of God, theologians—including those quoted in the following section—refer almost exclusively to "dignity," often with no mention of "glory" (except when referring to older sources). Just as in antiquity, Christians claimed the Latin *dignitas* to infuse Roman honor with the idea of divine human glory, so since the mid-twentieth century, churches claim the term "human dignity" to infuse this modern foundation of universal human rights–based social order with the image of God-inspired divine human glory.

The obvious downside of this phenomenon is that as the Christian glory became "dignity," dignity now means different things to different people; encountering the term we cannot foresee with certainty what it is meant to convey. People who would adhere to the universal, humanistic dignity of the UDHR (presented in the next chapter) might refrain from using the term, fearing that it entails religious and perhaps conservative undertones (such as antiabortion and/or anti-LGBT).

STANDARDIZATION OF DIGNITY-GLORY IN CONTEMPORARY CHRISTIAN THOUGHT

Christian reference to human dignity-glory is immense and surely beyond survey here. I find very telling the observation, made by political philosopher Rosen, that since World War II Catholic discourse of human dignity has become largely humanistic, egalitarian, and universal: "At what point did Catholicism lose its ambivalence about liberalism and democracy and accept the idea of human dignity as entailing social and political equality? It is very hard to say for sure. . . . My own belief is that the Second World War was a watershed."[47]

I suggest that perhaps the watershed was the 1948 UDHR, and that this is true not merely of Catholic but of most Christian reference to dignity-glory. In fact, contemporary Christian reference to dignity-glory sounds like mostly egalitarian, universal, liberal talk, ornate with references to *imago Dei* and Jesus Christ. Differences seem to be in subtle nuance.

Howard's edited collection *Imago Dei* presents three references to dignity-glory: an Eastern Orthodox, a Catholic, and a Baptist.

Father John Behr of the Eastern Orthodox Church believes that

> although all human beings have a certain baseline dignity, which ought to be respected as such, Christ alone "is the image of the invisible God, the first born of all creation" and all Christians are enjoined to accept a path of *theosis*, literally becoming godlike—something Orthodox Christians regard as distinctive to their tradition.[48]

On behalf of Catholicism, Russell Hittinger notes that

> it is commonly taught that *imago* pertains in an unqualified sense to Christ, who is *the* (eternal and consubstantial) image of the Father . . . the created human person . . . is an imperfect likeness. . . .
>
> It is also commonly taught that although human reason untutored by faith can detect within itself and in other human persons something divine-like in the operations of knowledge and love, the notion that the created person is an analogue of a trinity of divine persons can be grasped only by faith, and by sight only in glory. [49]

The third contributor to the volume is the Baptist scholar C. Ben Mitchell. Regarding early Christianity, Mitchell quotes D. J. A. Clines, stating:

> All mankind, without distinction, are the image of God. The image is to be understood not so much ontologically as existentially: it comes to expression not in the nature of man so much as in his activity and function . . . to be human and to be the image of God are not separable. [50]

Mitchell deduces that

> we would do well . . . not to locate the *imago Dei* in some component of our identity, but in the created whole. [51]

As for Protestant teachings, he shows that

> John Calvin's views echoed those of Luther. In his reading of Scripture, the French Reformer thought that humanity had been the image, yet because of the fall, humanity had lost the image, or at least some of it. . . . Calvin seemed to believe that the image was restored in human creatures through regeneration . . . we learn on the one hand, what is the end of our regeneration, that is, that we may be made like God, and that his glory may shine forth in us; and on the other hand, what is the image of God, . . . the rectitude and integrity of the whole soul, so that man reflects, like a mirror, the wisdom, righteousness, and goodness of God. [52]

Finally, he states that "Baptist Faith and Message" declared in 1925 and 1963 that

> the sacredness of human personality is evident in that God created man in his own image, and in that Christ died for man; therefore every man possesses dignity and is worthy of respect and Christian love. [53]

In the year 2000, this Baptist declaration was amended to state that "every person of every race possesses full dignity." It further states that "husband

and wife are of equal worth before God, since both are created in God's image."[54]

Particularly interesting is Martin Luther King Jr.'s conceptualization of human dignity and rights in the context of his Christian personalism. Presenting personalism in his *God and Human Dignity*, Rufus Burrow Jr. claims that "in God, qualities such as self-consciousness, intellect and will reach a perfection that far surpasses that of human persons, who are but faint images of essential personhood."[55]

Nevertheless, humankind is wholly precious. Bringing King's words, Burrows writes: "'Man is a child of God, made in His image, and therefore must be respected as such.' For King, persons have infinite dignity and worth precisely because they are created and sustained by God, who is the source of human dignity."[56] King, a social activist, translated his philosophy into practice. He was concerned with the question:

> What does the dignity or sacredness of persons mean in the most concrete sense of day to day living for those with their backs pressed against the wall, that is, those among the disinherited? . . . [E]ach person, regardless of gender and race, is inherently precious to God, and therefore should be treated as such under actual living conditions.[57]

King, thus, equated "human dignity" with "sacredness," and both these notions with fundamental rights to the most disenfranchised and disinherited among us.

Jürgen Moltmann (Protestant) offers an interesting Christian connection of human dignity and rights:

> Human rights mirror the right of the coming God and the future of humanity. The destiny of the human being to be the image of God indicates the indivisible right of God to the human being and, therefore, the irreducible dignity of the human being.[58]

I think what this means is that God has a right to his human image, that is, to human dignity. This divine right bestows on humans the basic rights (to life, freedom, and so forth) that are required to sustain them as proper mirrors and images of God, to maintain their human dignity. In this way, dis right to them as his human images and dignity endow them with human rights.

Robert Spaemann (Catholic) also derives human rights from a Christian human dignity, stressing the religious and the moral aspects of dignity:

> Dignity signals something sacred. The concept is a fundamentally religious-metaphysical one. . . . For one reason and one reason only human beings possess what we call "dignity," because as moral beings they represent the Absolute.[59]

Spaemann's line of thought seems to be, in some respects, more traditional, or conservative. From the very outset, he associates human dignity not just with rights but also with duties, stating that "dignity is the transcendental ground for the fact that human beings have rights and duties. They have rights, because they have duties." He defines dignity as "inviolable," states that it "is not subject to compromises," and declares that "human dignity can never be in conflict with human dignity." Yet he determines that a person may forfeit his or her own dignity through immoral conduct.[60] His treatise on human dignity and rights opposes state recognition of divorce and assisted suicide. Nevertheless, even this human dignity is universal, absolute, and the source of some human rights.

DIGNITY-GLORY AND THE RADIUS METAPHOR: "EQUIDISTANT FROM GOD"

Let me close this chapter with an image suggested by Gilbert Meilaender in his theological discussion of human dignity. "All people," he writes, "whatever their respective talents or accomplishments, are equal because equidistant from God."[61]

The term "equidistant," used here metaphorically, suggests a circle. God is the center of the circle, and every point on the circle is one of us. The radius of the circle is the distance between each of us and God. The radius distance from God is identical for every human being, since we are all God's icons, his human images. It is in this radius that we are all equal. Our equality does not mean similar characteristics, but identical distance from the center, God, whom we all mirror, or represent, or manifest, or embody. In this framework, our equality is not established vis-à-vis each other, but vis-à-vis him, who is the focal point of the system. It is in reference to him that we each and all acquire value; and since that "reference" is an identical "radius"—it renders us equal in value.

The image I suggested for the world of honor is a pyramid: within it, each of us is located in a spot that is higher than some and lower than others. Our value is derived from and measured by our position within the pyramid. Since there is constant movement within the pyramid, our value is necessarily tentative, relative to the value of our neighbors in the hierarchy. Very differently, in the world of glory, we are permanently positioned on a circle drawn around a transcendental center. We are all similarly close to the center, and this similar closeness establishes our equal value.[62]

The two worldviews, one represented by a pyramid and the other by a circle, differ greatly. They are not easily reconcilable. One way of reconciling them harmoniously is by thinking of glory as marking a floor, that is, an innate, fixed, transcendental, absolute human worth, that every one of us should always be presumed to possess unconditionally. Honor, an accumulative, tentative, relative human worth, acquired through dynamic, ever-ongoing social interactions, may be sought and amassed as an addendum. This way, the versatile, adaptable honor may complement the static, uncompromising glory. The two combined secure a solid minimum while also envisioning an ambitious, unlimited horizon.

THE BALL: A WORD ON SPIRITUAL DIMENSIONS OF GLORY

Since I am neither a Jewish nor a Christian theologian, I attempted to tell the story of glory refraining from presumptuous spiritual undertakings. Yet, devoid of any spiritual reference, the discussion of a notion laden with spiritual overtones may seem dry, technical, and disconnected. Exploring diverse theological references to glory, I therefore strived to grasp a glimpse of its spirit. Let me curb the detached, academic nature of this chapter's exposé by sharing an insight and adding a perceptual layer to the circle imagery presented in the previous section. This is an attempt to touch on and to convey a spiritual meaning of this chapter's deeply spiritual subject matter.

I presented Meilaender's metaphorical use of "radius" to instill the image of a circle drawn around God, on which we are all situated. To communicate a more spiritual sense of this image, I suggest that we add a dimension and turn the circle into a ball. In this image, each one of us is located on the surface of the three-dimensional, round orb.

The surface of the ball is our social world. It is carefully charted and divided into distinct locations, all loaded with symbolic meaning and status-bearing ranking. Our honor value is defined by our relative position within this mapped matrix, by our comparative standing in relation to all other occupiers of locations that together make up the charted surface of the ball.

Glory is our value in reference to the ball's invisible center. Each person is intensely connected to this core, which is called God. This beating heart of all existence is the absolute and eternal depth of our being. It is the center of my being just as much as it is yours and that of every other human. Not a physical place but a transcendental dimension, it is the unity of profound gravity,[63] wholeness, centeredness, and totality. Each and all of us reflect it and exhibit something of its perfection. Glory is the supreme value of every person's intense and inviolable oneness with this center. It is the absolute value of the image of that perfection that is stamped in every one of us.

Focused on looking sideways, at the social honor game on the charted face of the universe, we lose sight of the center. Focusing on dynamic competition on the face level, we may not experience our connection to the center of gravity; our centeredness. Only by silencing the sounds of our surface existence and turning inward, toward the center, we may delve into this profound dimension and experience our intense attachment to it and the vitality it implies. In so doing, we realize how innately drawn we are to the infinite center of the ball. The peace this realization instills in us is love, flowing to and from our core. In this serene feeling of unqualified oneness we recognize our glory.

The center, our inherent union with it and divine human glory are always there, intrinsic to our human nature; yet we are conscious of them only when we open up to feel the additional dimension that transforms the circle into a ball, only when we direct our energy inward, which is then revealed to also be upward.

In this context, a balanced combination of honor and glory would be the peaceful, proportionate unification of two feelings: the horizontal (surface-bound), outward-sideways-looking ambition, with the perpendicular (depth-oriented) in-and-upward-bent elation and enlightenment. When these distinctly diverse perspectives, each pulling in a different direction, curb each other, they create a healthy, fruitful, intense tension. This nourishing pull sustains us tranquil but on our toes; it inspires internal peace with the sensation of human vitality.

Words are, of course, inappropriate to capture the spiritual. I hope that the suggested image conveys something of the sense that I believe divine human glory inspires in Judeo-Christian traditions.

NOTES

1. C. S. Lewis, "The Weight of Glory," *Theology* 43, no. 257 (1941): 263–74; repr. London: Society for Promoting Christian Knowledge, 1942, preached originally as a sermon in the Church of St. Mary the Virgin, Oxford, on June 8, 1941; seehttp://www.verber.com/mark/xian/weight-of-glory.pdf, 6–7; emphasis mine.

2. Ron Highfield, *God, Freedom and Human Dignity: Embracing a God-Centered Identity in a Me-Centered Culture* (Downers Grove, IL: IVP Academic, 2013), 122–23; emphasis mine.

3. As I address conventional Judaism and Christianity, I refer to God using male linguistic terms.

4. For all references to biblical verses from both the Hebrew Bible and the New Testament, see Hebrew Bible (HB), 2019; and the King James Bible (KJV), 2019, both available athttps://biblehub.com/.

5. The King James Version of the Bible is, of course, not necessarily more important than any other translation. I refer to it and quote it since this analysis is written in English, and the King James Version has been the most authoritative source of Bible talk in the English-speaking world.

6. The English choice of "honor" often corresponds with the Latin choice of *honora* in the Vulgate translation from the fourth century AD. Interestingly, in only four instances does the Vulgate translate the Hebrew *kavod* into the Latin word *dignitas*, which also meant honor (Proverbs 14:28; Proverbs 20:29; Esther 10:2; and Esther 9:3). For reference, see Latin Vulgate Bible (VUL), 2019,https://www.biblestudytools.com/vul/.

7. The English "glory" sometimes corresponds with the Latin *gloria* of the Vulgate translation from the fourth century AD.

8. The King James Version translation is by no means "scientific" in its translation of human *kavod* into honor and divine *kavod* into glory. Sometimes the English "glory" stands for

a different Hebrew word, such as *hod* or *hadar*. In other instances *kavod* is juxtaposed to *busha*, shame, and should have been thus translated as honor; it was nevertheless translated as glory. See for example in the HB, "As they were increased, so they sinned against me: therefore will I change their glory into shame" (Hosea 4:7); "Thou art filled with shame for glory . . . shameful spewing *shall be* on thy glory" (Habakkuk 2:16); "The wise shall inherit glory: but shame shall be the promotion of fools" (Proverbs 3:35). Nevertheless, in the overwhelming majority of many dozens of cases the KJV's translation seems to follow the rule.

9. Think of "the glory of the Lord appeared in the cloud" (Exodus 16:10); "The heavens declare the glory of God" (Psalm 19:1); "all the earth shall be filled with the glory of the Lord" (Numbers 14:21); and "the glory of the Lord had filled the house of the Lord" (1 Kings 8:11).

10. Think of verses such as "Declare his glory among the heathens" (1 Chronicles 16:24); "Give unto the Lord the glory due unto his name" (1 Chronicles 16:29); "Who is this King of glory? The Lord strong and mighty, the Lord mighty in battle" (Psalm 24:8); "Help us, O God of our salvation, for the glory of thy name" (Psalm 79:9); and "The glory of the Lord shall endure forever" (Psalm 104:31).

11. Yair Lorberbaum, *In God's Image: Myth, Theology, and Law in Classical Judaism* (New York: Cambridge University Press, 2015), 2.

12. Lorberbaum, *In God's Image*, 76.

13. Lorberbaum, *In God's Image*, 86.

14. Lorberbaum, *In God's Image*, 51, 166–70.

15. Lorberbaum, *In God's Image*, 2.

16. The *tannaim* were rabbis in the first two centuries AD, who created, most famously, the *halakhic* discussions compiled as the *Mishnah*.

17. Lorberbaum, *In God's Image*, 173–84.

18. *Avot D'rabbi Nathan*, chap. 30, 66, in Lorberbaum, *In God's Image*, 173–74.

19. Lorberbaum, *In God's Image*, 266.

20. Lorberbaum, *In God's Image*, 267.

21. Lorberbaum, *In God's Image*, 276–77.

22. Lorberbaum, *In God's Image*, 2–3.

23. Lorberbaum, *In God's Image*, 100–251.

24. Lorberbaum, *In God's Image*, 199–200, 213.

25. Lorberbaum, *In God's Image*, 102.

26. Lorberbaum, *In God's Image*, 121.

27. Lorberbaum, *In God's Image*, 140.

28. Lorberbaum, *In God's Image*, 141–43.

29. Lorberbaum, *In God's Image*, 153.

30. *Tosefta, Sanhedrin* 9:7; in Lorberbaum, *In God's Image*, 161. Plainly, "The tannaim regarded the execution of the criminal, including that of the murderer, as a form of negative theurgy because it damages God, who is present within the criminal just as He is in every human being" (197).

31. Lorberbaum, *In God's Image*, 219.

32. Lorberbaum, *In God's Image*, 225.

33. Lorberbaum, *In God's Image*, 227.

34. Lorberbaum, *In God's Image*, 233.

35. Lorberbaum, *In God's Image*, 229–30.

36. Lorberbaum, *In God's Image*, 245–51.

37. Lorberbaum, *In God's Image*, 4.

38. Alon Goshen-Gottstein, "The Body as Image of God in Rabbinic Literature," *Harvard Theological Review* 87, no. 2 (1994): 171–95.

39. Lorberbaum, *In God's Image*, 242.

40. Thomas Albert Howard, ed., *Imago Dei: Human Dignity in Ecumenical Perspective* (Washington, DC: Catholic University of America Press, 2013), 3.

41. Michael Rosen, *Dignity: Its History and Meaning* (Cambridge, MA: Harvard University Press, 2012), 12.

42. Jeremy Waldron, *Dignity. Rank, and Rights*, ed. Meir Dan-Cohen (Oxford: Oxford University Press, 2012), 30. See also reference to Josiah Ober (*Cambridge Handbook*, 2014), at the end of chap. 2.

43. Rosen, *Dignity*, 16–17.

44. For additional reference, see chap. 4. Aquinas's Aristotelian *imago dei* stresses every human's innate divine image, forsaking the earlier Christian view that only the Christian choice of Jesus and his gospel gives rise to a person's image of God.

45. When Rosen repeatedly stresses that "in the nineteenth century the Catholic Church used the term 'dignity' as part of a fiercely anti-egalitarian discourse" (*Dignity*, 8), this means that a conservative nineteenth-century church used the term *dignitas* and its derivatives in their honor-bound sense to support nonegalitarian hegemonic honor structures, which were claimed to be ordained by God. If today the same church "pursues its fight against secular conceptions of human dignity in socially egalitarian terms" (*Dignity*, 51), this means that the church uses the term *dignitas* and its derivatives in their glory-bound sense to challenge the secular dignity rhetoric. The Catholic Church now uses *dignitas*/"dignity" to denote its (relatively) egalitarian idea of divine human glory, pitting it against the modern, secular idea of dignity.

46. Mary Ann Glendon attributes the change to Pope John XXII. "Finding [the UDHR's] principles compatible with Catholic social teaching, he adopted (to the surprise of many) its dignitarian language of rights in his 1963 encyclical *Pacen in Terris*." Mary Ann Glendon, *A World Made New: Eleanor Roosevelt and the Universal Declaration of Human Rights* (New York: Random House, 2001), 217.

47. Rosen, *Dignity*, 53.

48. Howard, *Imago Dei*, 9.

49. Russell Hittinger, "Toward an Adequate Anthropology: Social Aspects of *Imago Dei* in Catholic Theology," in Howard, *Imago Dei*, 46.

50. C. Ben Mitchell quoting D. J. A. Clines, "The Audacity of the *Imago Dei*: The Legacy and Uncertain Future of Human Dignity," in Howard, *Imago Dei*, 90–91.

51. Mitchell, "Audacity of the *Imago Dei*," in Howard, *Imago Dei*, 92.

52. Mitchell, "Audacity of the *Imago Dei*," in Howard, *Imago Dei*, 95, 97, 98–99.

53. Mitchell, "Audacity of the *Imago Dei*," in Howard, *Imago Dei*, 106.

54. Mitchell, "Audacity of the *Imago Dei*," in Howard, *Imago Dei*, 107, 108.

55. Rufus Burrow Jr., *God and Human Dignity: The Personalism, Theology, and Ethics of Martin Luther King, Jr.* (Notre Dame, IN: University of Notre Dame Press, 2006), 75.

56. Martin Luther King Jr., quoted in Burrow, *God and Human Dignity*, 74.

57. Burrow, *God and Human Dignity*, 70.

58. Jürgen Moltmann, *On Human Dignity: Political Theology and Ethics*, trans. with intro. M. Douglas Meeks (Minneapolis, MN: Fortress, 2007), 16–17.

59. Robert Spaemann, "Human Dignity and Human Nature," in *Love and the Dignity of Human Life: On Nature and Natural Law* (Grand Rapids, MI: Eerdmans, 2012), 42, 44.

60. Spaemann, "Human Dignity and Human Nature," 27, 29, 42, 43, 30.

61. Gilbert Meilaender, *Neither Beast nor God: The Dignity of the Human Person* (New York: Encounter Books, 2009), 44.

62. In chap. 2, n26, I suggested that we may think of the honor-based social structure as a circle, in which the honored, prestigious member is in the very center, and our closeness to the center indicates our honor and status. In contrast, in Meilaender's metaphoric circle the center is occupied by God, and we are all equally distant from him.

63. Gravity connotes heaviness, which is implied by the Hebrew *kavod*.

Chapter Four

The Concept of Dignity That Underlies Human Rights

Unlike many—perhaps most—writers on dignity, I am *not* interested in the English term, but in the moral concept that underlies the ideology of human rights. The United Nations Universal Declaration on Human Rights (UDHR) chose to refer to this concept as "dignity," and therefore I do too.[1] This chapter on dignity does not attempt to reveal, trace, and discuss all the historical and contemporary usages of the English word "dignity," nor to construct a concept that would somehow acknowledge and contain all these (contradicting) meanings, doing them all some historical justice.[2] Instead, this chapter focuses on a single meaning of the term "dignity": the meaning that was established by the UDHR and underlies the universal ideology of human rights.

Surely, the English word "dignity" has been used to mean what I refer to as honor, glory, and respect. This has been shown vividly by philosophers such as Michael Rosen and Jeremy Waldron. It is an interesting historical anecdote, but it cannot help us understand, review, and develop the concept that inspires the ideology of human rights. The ideological project of focusing on the foundation of human rights requires careful distinction of the concept that generates human rights from other concepts that determine human worth based on status, divinity, or individualistic self-expression. It requires the carving of a narrow definition of human dignity that distinguishes this concept from the concepts of honor, glory, and respect.

Jeremy Waldron's criticism of this perspective would surely be such: "I do not understand why 'dignity'—with it distinctive connotations—is a good term to use to do work that might be done as well by 'worth' or 'sacred worth.'"[3] My answer is simple: a rose by any other name would smell as sweet to me. Had the UDHR chosen "worth," I would have been content to explore and construct the meaning of the value-idea in reference to that term. Yet it was "dignity" that was chosen to be the declaration's fourth pillar, together with liberty, equality, and fraternity, marking the value of humanity and constituting the foundation of universal human rights. This choice was neither arbitrary nor a whim. "Dignity" was chosen, in an excruciatingly deliberate process, for the universal appeal of *some* of its heritage for the task of uniting humanity around innate human worth and rights. It is this strand of dignity's heritage that I wish to single out, focus on, understand, and develop as coherently and usefully as possible.

This chapter suggests that the UDHR's human dignity grew out of the age-old Judeo-Christian idea of divine human glory, and must, therefore, be compared with—yet carefully distinguished from—this theological predecessor. The chapter further proposes that the UDHR's concept of human dignity was intended to serve as an alternative to honor as an underlying fundamental value, and to generate alternative norms and patterns of conduct. Human dignity must therefore be compared to—and contrasted with—honor and the mind-set that it implies. Since the UDHR's concept of human dignity was affected by Kantian philosophy, this source of influence must be examined, and since the UDHR is the founding document that established dignity as the basis of human rights ideology, it is important to revisit this historical text. Last but not least, as the UDHR establishes human dignity as the foundation of human rights, this connection between dignity and rights must be presented. This chapter addresses these five points. It begins with a narrative suggesting how the accelerating use of honor as a fundamental value and attitude led the United Nations to offer an alternative that would enable peace and survival: a worldview based on human dignity.

THE ESCALATION OF HONOR CONFLICTS AND THE CONSEQUENT CONCEPTUALIZATION OF DIGNITY

Chapter 2 suggests that in antiquity and for many centuries following, honor was the name of the international game—as much as the logic of personal life. In the ancient world, Israelites, Philistines, Canaanites, Phoenicians, and many others competed for honor, as did the Athenians and the Spartans, the Macedonians and the Persians. They did so between clan or city groups—as their respective members did among themselves.

Centuries later, King Arthur of Camelot and the Knights of the Round Table slayed dragons and saved damsels in their ceaseless quest for honor. As these legends were being told, the English navy fought the Spanish Armada and the French fleet in its quest for honor. For centuries Florence, Siena, Venice, Naples, and Rome fought each other for honor—much like the aristocratic families within each of these city-states. The Christian crusaders contested for honor among themselves—and against the Muslims. Japan's samurais lived by the *bushidō* code of honor—and their society imposed its honor perception on its neighbors. European empires conquered territory in Africa, Asia, and the New World competing among themselves for honor.

In the final section of chapter 2, I suggest that the two World Wars can be jointly viewed as the climax of European culture's long-standing honor-based mind-set and politics. Let me pick up where I left off.

Nazi ideology was committed to pure, unmediated (Aryan) honor,[4] with absolutely no regard to divine human glory or any other sense of inherent human value. In fact, while clearly denying the enlightenment notions of human liberty and equality, Nazi ideology most vehemently rejected the tenet that all human beings have innate, inviolable worth and merit. The industrial annihilation of human populations and the enslavement of many others bluntly defied the ideal of intrinsic human value.

For a brief moment in the aftermath of World War II, world thinkers and leaders realized that upholding the honor-based mentality is likely to result in self-destruction. In that brief moment, these thinkers and leaders joined forces to establish the foundation of an alternative world order. As a vital part of this foundation they erected the dignity-based, human rights–centered universalistic ideology and ethos.

Representatives and leaders of the Allied nations were deeply shaken and horrified by the atrocities deliberately and systematically inflicted by Nazi Germany and its allies on tens of millions. They realized the danger of ideological inhumanity, and responded by seeking and founding a shared new universalistic ideology, professing the absolute value of every human life.

As stated by the editors of a 1999 edited volume on the UDHR, *The Universal Declaration of Human Rights: A Common Standard of Achievement*, Gudmundur Alfredsson and Asbjørn Eide:

> The atrocities of WWII, with its intensive and unbelievable repression and brutality, provide the immediate background for the drafting and adoption of the UDHR. The conscience of human beings worldwide was shocked by Mussolini's fascist government of Italy, the Spanish civil war and the Franco regime, Japanese militarism and cruel occupation politics, and, above all, Nazi expansion and extermination practices under Hitler, coinciding with Stalin's reign of terror in the Soviet Union. These developments laid the groundwork for a broad consensus that a new humanistic legal order would have to be established.[5]

Similarly, the editors of the 2014 *Cambridge Handbook of Human Dignity*, Marcus Düwell, Jens Braarvig, Roger Brownsword, and Dietmar Mieth, declare that:

> Choosing human dignity immediately after the Second World War was a state-
> ment against the Shoah, against totalitarianism, and against the atrocities of the
> war.[6]

In the terms put forth by this book, I suggest that Nazism, which manifested extreme (almost ideal-type) honor-based doctrine, exposed this doctrine's sinister aspect. Post–World War II world thinkers and leaders were
repelled by this sight, and opted for an alternative, humanitarian, universalistic ideology, rooted in the age-old acknowledgment of divine human glory.
Since it has always suggested an alternative to honor-based social order, this
competing worldview now seemed hopeful and promising. Modern thinkers
and leaders were familiar with glory-based worldview in its enlightenment
and Kantian configuration, which was less theological and more humanistic.
It now seemed an attractive, available, reasonable replacement for the ruthless honor-based framework.

Glory-based dogma (presented in chapter 3) was, therefore, translated by
the United Nations into a universal, nonreligious principle, which was
promptly formulated in the 1948 UDHR as a humanistic, liberal, nonreligious basis of the universalistic human rights culture. This new culture was
designed to be internationally implemented, cherished, and upheld unconditionally. In this new configuration, it was encapsulated in the term "human
dignity." It is this and only this post–World War II formulated, humanistic,
universalistic, human rights–oriented, Kantian-espoused notion that I refer to
as *human dignity*. It is this specific, modern notion that this chapter addresses.

KANTIAN DIGNITY (STANDING ON THE SHOULDERS OF AQUINAS AND MIRANDOLA)

Immanuel Kant, the eighteenth-century Prussian Enlightenment philosopher,
has left such an eminent mark on the concept of human dignity that it is hard
to imagine it without him. Nevertheless, no idea has ever been born fully
grown and fledged out of any one person's forehead (as did the goddess
Athena out of Zeus's forehead). Count Pico della Mirandola, the fifteenth-
century Florentine Renaissance classist and humanist, is an important fore-
runner whose publications must have contributed to Kant's formulation of
human dignity. Since political philosopher Michael Rosen, in his *Dignity: Its
History and Meaning*, has recently composed an eloquent exposition of both
Mirandola's and Kant's philosophical contributions, this section will be in
dialogue with it.

Two centuries before Mirandola, the thirteenth-century Dominican philosopher, theologian, and jurist St. Thomas Aquinas revived the Aristotelian
notion that every organism in this world has an intrinsic purpose. According

to this line of thought, the pursuit of this purpose contains the organism's innate value.[7] Aquinas famously linked this innate value with the Latin term *dignitas*, which had initially meant what I call here honor. At the same time, he linked this innate value not merely with the pursuit of an organism's nature (as did Aristotle), but with the pursuit of its "place within God's creation." As Rosen puts it: "The important question becomes: What kind of dignity does any particular thing that has dignity have and in virtue of what does it have it?"[8] For Aquinas, the innate value of humans lay in their pursuit of their purpose as the image of God. He called it *dignitas*. I call this notion glory.

To recap more simply, Aquinas linked the Aristotelian notion that humans have innate value with the concept of glory and with the terminology of dignity, which previously connoted honor. His theology crafted a human dignity that means innate human value embedded in the pursuit of glory. As Thomist theology-philosophy was at the very heart of mainstream European medieval culture, it influenced and inspired all European intellectuals.

Pico della Mirandola's celebrated 1486 "Oration on the Dignity of Man" has been dubbed the "Manifesto of the Renaissance." He adopted the Thomist construction of human dignity, but suggested a crucial twist: the purpose of humans was not to pursue their role within the divine order, but *to choose their own destinies*.[9]

Mirandola did not explicitly confront religious dogma; he merely stated that God created man as an autonomous intellect. In Aristotle's vision, man was, above all else, a creature of reason. For Mirandola, this creature of reason was above all else free to choose and determine itself. Free reason was man's nature, essence, purpose, and hence also value, dignity. In the terms of this book, Mirandola transformed *human dignity* from *glory* to *dignity*.

It was this Aristotelian-Mirandola "autonomous intellect human nature" that, centuries later, Kant famously linked with human capacity for morality. For Kant, "the moral law" was the only thing endowed with "dignity": innate, categorical, positive value. Every human being is an autonomous intellect, and therefore each one of us equally embodies this moral law, and hence also its dignity.[10] "Human dignity," then, is the intrinsic value of the moral law, embedded in the liberty of every human being. Our innate, equal autonomy and morality are the basis of our human dignity. And since only we, humans, possess autonomy and morality, there is no other dignity beside human dignity. "Dignity" and "human dignity" are one and the same.[11] Neither one of them is explicitly linked with God, the divine order of things, or any theological context.[12] So Kant's dignity is a secular notion that attributes absolute value equally to every human being, because we are all free and therefore moral.

Kant's most popular and influential references to dignity are in the context of humanity. In the *Groundwork of the Metaphysics of Morals* he writes:

> In the kingdom of ends everything has either a price or a dignity. What has a
> price can be replaced by something else as its equivalent; what, on the other
> hand, is raised above all price and therefore admits of no equivalent has a
> dignity. Now, morality is the condition under which alone a rational being can
> be an end in itself . . . hence morality, and humanity insofar as it is capable of
> morality, is that which alone has dignity. [13]

Kant continues:

> Humanity itself is a dignity; for a man cannot be used merely as a means by
> any man (either by others or even by himself) but must always be used at the
> same time as an end. It is just in this that his dignity (personhood) consists, by
> which he raises himself above all other beings in the world that are not men
> and yet can be used, and so, over all things. [14]

Most famously, his fourth articulation of the "categorical imperative" (the
formula of humanity) commands: "So act that you treat humanity, whether in
your own person or in the person of any other, always at the same time as an
end, never merely as a means." [15]

Let me simplify. In Kant's categorical imperative, humans are *subjects*,
and as such—they are *not objects*. Objects, in this binary dichotomy, are
things that have a price and may be used as mere means to a subject's ends.
Subjects, on the other hand, are priceless, but have intrinsic value, dignity,
and may therefore never be treated as mere objects, that is, as means to ends
other than themselves. The moral obligation to recognize human subjects as
such (as priceless nonobjects), means that one must never treat a human
subject merely as a means; a human subject must always be acknowledged as
an end in its own right.

We may treat ourselves and each other as means to other ends, but we
must never treat humans *exclusively* as means, as most of us treat the chair
that we sit on. We must always treat every human being *also* as an end, a
purpose, in his or her own right. We may *use* another person to achieve
sexual gratification, but never do so as if that other person were merely a
sexual object, completely ignoring their well-being, needs, wants, and desires. [16] Kant's categorical imperative defends human dignity by prohibiting
the objectification of humans.

Seminal as Aquinas's and Pico della Mirandola's contributions have been
to the development of dignity, it is Kant's categorical imperative that has
made this human dignity a central and inseparable part of modern (or at least
modern Western) culture. Treating humanity as an end and never as merely a
means, together with the binary subject-object distinction it implies and the
innate, priceless quality of human worth have all become undisputed hall-
marks of the notion of human dignity.

Noting that Kant developed his moral philosophy using the German term *Würde*, Waldron claims that "there is a well-established practice of translating *Würde* as 'dignity.' But the two words have slightly different connotations. *Würde* is much closer to 'worth' than our term 'dignity' is."[17] Perhaps the specific history of the English word "dignity" associates it with the concept of honor. Yet the "well-established practice" of associating that English word with Kant's *Würde* justifies the use of "dignity" to mean the Kantian idea of *Würde*.

Further, Waldron is surely correct in claiming that Kant's philosophical writings include sayings that "associate dignity with rank."[18] A member of an honor-bound society, Kant—not surprisingly—sometimes indeed conflated honor and dignity. This by no means justifies or necessitates a systematic conjoining of the two distinct notions (as Waldron proposes). It merely illustrates that the age-old confusion of honor and dignity runs deep in European cultures and languages, requiring vigorous efforts to clearly distinguish the two concepts that they denote from each other. Kantian honor-bound *slips* do not jeopardize the integrity and coherence of the colossal task of constituting human dignity as a distinct fundamental value.[19] This task was advanced, above all else, by the United Nations UDHR.

THE UDHR'S FORMULATION OF DIGNITY

The UDHR established the secular, Kantian-bound human dignity as a conceptual pillar of the post–World Wars vision of global social order and as the foundation of international human rights. This was by no means an oversight; it was a carefully considered choice, closely scrutinized, and repeatedly confirmed and upheld by several international forums in lengthy and thorough discussions and votes. Although neither the drafters nor the delegates consciously declared that the declaration's human dignity was meant to replace the traditional, militant honor as a cornerstone of universal social order, I believe that this purpose can be found in the subtext, or between the lines. Not only European states, but also the United States, third-world countries, and Arab states were consenting and leading partners in this communal mission. Since this important development is not readily familiar to readers, I address it in some detail, highlighting elements most relevant to this discussion.

On June 1945, immediately after the conclusion of World War II, fifty nations signed the United Nations Charter featuring the following preamble:

> We the peoples of the United Nations, determined to save succeeding generations from the scourge of war, which twice in our lifetime has brought untold sorrow to mankind, and to regain faith in fundamental *human rights*, in *the dignity and worth of the human person*, in the equal rights of men and women

and of nations large and small, and to establish conditions under which justice and respect for the obligations arising from treaties and other sources of international law can be maintained, and to promote social progress and better standards of life in larger freedom, and for these ends to practice tolerance and live together in peace with one another as good neighbors, and to unite our strength to maintain international peace and security, and to ensure, by the acceptance of principles and the institution of methods, that armed force shall not be used, save in the common interest, and to employ international machinery for the promotion of the economic and social advancement of all peoples, have resolved to combine our efforts to accomplish these aims.

Accordingly, our respective Governments, through representatives assembled in the city of San Francisco, who have exhibited their full powers found to be in good and due form, have agreed to the present Charter of the United Nations and do hereby establish an international organization to be known as the United Nations. [20]

The UN Charter echoed the famous beginning of the American Declaration of Independence ("We the People"), and was strongly supported by American president Franklin D. Roosevelt (who, in 1942, coined the term "United Nations"). The UN Charter declares that all signatory nations are determined to prevent future war and to regain faith, above all else, in "fundamental human rights" and "in the dignity and worth of the human person." [21] The world war that just ended, together with the one that had preceded it, "brought untold sorrow to mankind," threatening to deprive humanity of faith in both fundamental human rights and human dignity and worth. The UN Charter vows that fifty nations will combine their efforts to prevent reoccurrence of these sorrows or materialization of this threat. The charter further provides for the creation of the Commission on Human Rights, entrusted with the responsibility to draft a universal bill of rights.

It is worth noting that the horrors of both world wars are associated in the UN Charter, not with infringement of liberty, equality, and fraternity, but with the threat of annihilating even the basic faith in human rights and human dignity. It was, therefore, *faith in human dignity and rights* that the UN Charter pledged to reestablish and safeguard. I daresay that a vibrant vision of liberty, equality, and fraternity was far too optimistic for the international assembly gathered in San Francisco in 1945; re-creating faith in the basic, minimal, kernel notion of human dignity and in fundamental human rights seemed daunting and ambitious enough.

In light of Nazi-inflicted inhuman atrocities, the aspiration was modest and minimalistic: to regain and ensure *the ability to believe* in fundamental human worth/dignity and rights. This grave task was to be pursued through "the acceptance of principles and the institution of methods." The Human Rights Commission was instructed to formulate such principles and methods in the shape of a bill of rights, to be ratified by the United Nations General

Assembly and finally called the Universal Declaration of Human Rights, UDHR.

The leading characters and most influential participants in this epic endeavor were the commission's American chair, Eleanor Roosevelt, deeply committed to a progressive, liberal, human rights–centered worldview; the French law professor René Cassin, who, despite his orthodox Jewish upbringing and lifelong dealings with anti-Semitism, held uncompromising secular, liberal, universalist convictions—severely wounded as a combatant in World War I, he served as General Charles De Gaulle's leading jurist in World War II; the Lebanese professor of philosophy Charles Malik, a deeply religious Greek Orthodox who served as a spokesperson of the Arab League; Dr. John Humphrey, Canadian professor of law and a human rights advocate, director of the United Nations Division of Human Rights within the United Nations Secretariat. P. C. Chang, a Nanking University professor from China; the feminist activist Hausa Mehta from India; General Carlos P. Romulo of the Philippines; Herman Santa Cruz from Chile; and Alexander E. Bogomolov of the Soviet Union were also highly effective committee members. [22]

The construction of human dignity as the foundation of an international human rights–based social order is inseparable from the drama of the UDHR's crafting, formulation, and delivery. The incredible story of this political enterprise has been recently narrated lucidly and with great vigor by law professor Mary Ann Glendon, in her *A World Made New*. I usurp bits of her account to outline the process in which human dignity was affixed at the heart of the UDHR.

Glendon documents that the first draft of a universal bill of rights was written by John Humphrey. This draft included the political and civil rights that were formulated in the seventeenth and eighteenth centuries and are usually called first-generation rights. But it also contained the second-generation economic and social rights defined in constitutions that were composed in late nineteenth and early twentieth centuries. "The UN proudly announced in its *Weekly Bulletin* that it had produced 'the most exhaustive documentation on the subject of human rights ever assembled.'" [23]

Humphrey's draft did not include a preamble, nor any mention of human dignity. It was the French Jewish jurist René Cassin, steadfastly committed to the spirit of the UN Charter, who affixed human dignity in the UDHR's preamble and first article, establishing it as the source and raison d'être of fundamental human rights. This raison d'être survived the many changes the document underwent over the next year and a half. [24]

It was this contribution that awarded Cassin "his later reputation as the 'father of the Declaration'" [25] and a 1968 Nobel Prize.

The next essential stage was the surveying, by a United Nations Educational, Scientific and Cultural Organization (UNESCO) committee, of cultural conceptions of human rights and their sources.

> [The UNESCO philosophers' committee] had received about seventy responses to their questionnaire asking for reflections on human rights from Chinese, Islamic, Hindu, and customary law perspectives, as well as from American, European, and socialist points of view. . . .
>
> Several respondents from non-Western backgrounds noted that the sources of human rights were present in their traditions, even though the language of rights was a relatively modern European development. . . .
>
> All in all, the results of the UNESCO survey were encouraging: they indicated that the principles underlying the draft Declaration were present in many cultural and religious traditions, though not always expressed in terms of rights. Somewhat to the UNESCO group's surprise, the list of basic rights and values submitted by their far-flung correspondents were broadly similar. . . .
>
> Finding that several practical concepts constituted "a sort of common denominator" among widely separated ideologies, the philosophers pronounced themselves "convinced that the members of the United Nations share common convictions on which human rights depend."[26]

Simply put: based on seventy responses from philosophers and theologists worldwide, UNESCO's committee of philosophers established that despite a multitude of diverse languages, ideologies, and beliefs, most cultures, societies, and religions view the human person as endowed with worth and fundamental rights. Whatever their affiliations and conceptual frameworks, most people around the world subscribe to the idea of human dignity and rights—even if they refer to it in very different ways.

Crafting the exact phrasing of the preamble and Article 1, the commission was initially divided on whether fundamental human rights derived from divine human glory (as presented in chapter 3), or from a secular, enlightenment-inspired concept. Whereas Cassin and Romulo suggested the formula "All men are . . . born equal in dignity and rights," Malik cited the American Declaration of Independence and suggested to add the words "by their Creator." Cassin opposed "on the ground that references to God would undermine the universality of the document."[27]

Strongly supported by China's representative Chang, Cassin's view prevailed. After consideration and debate the commission was unanimously convinced and decided that the UDHR's human dignity and rights should not be in any way connected to any notion of divinity. When, on June 11, 1948, Charles Malik was asked by Eleanor Roosevelt to make good use of the coming weekend and prepare the next version of the UDHR's preamble, he maintained human dignity as a secular raison d'être of human rights.[28]

The UDHR was now submitted to the General Assembly's Third Committee on Social, Humanitarian, and Cultural Affairs. The committee closely scrutinized and debated every concept and word.[29]

One of the points the Third Committee revisited was the secular nature of human dignity.

> A Brazilian amendment would have added that "all human beings are created in the image and likeness of God." It was Chang, again, who carried the majority by reminding everyone that the Declaration was designed to be universally applicable. . . . The first line of the article, therefore, should refer neither to nature nor to God.[30]

Cassin, Chang, Roosevelt, and their colleagues thwarted the Brazilian attempt to replace the secular dignity with a glory-oriented one. Shortly later, the drafters once again succeeded in convincing the Third Committee to defy a similar Dutch proposal.[31]

The General Assembly's Third Committee accepted that *human dignity was the source of fundamental human rights and the reason for their universal enactment.* In the words of Ashild Samnøy:

> That an agreement on the Declaration finally was reached was due largely to the rejection of any reference to religious or philosophical justifications of human rights. The most persistent attempt to include the source of human rights in the UDHR came from those who supported a reference to God as the creator. . . . [Yet] references to both God and to nature were omitted. The text of article 1 was the lowest common denominator of human rights philosophy among members of the United Nations.[32]

Martti Koskenniemi similarly emphasizes that "the preamble to the UDHR situates the text of the Declaration within the ideological atmosphere of the liberal Enlightenment."[33] And Tore Lindholm reiterates:

> A justification for human rights along the classic lines, that is, by recourse to God, nature, reason or self-evidence, was rejected by the mothers and fathers of international human rights. . . . For this reason, article 1 of UDHR exemplifies a more complex, a more context-sensitive, and a politically more realistic mode of rights justification than do its classical predecessors.[34]

On December 9 and 10, 1948, the General Assembly discussed, debated, and voted on each article of the UDHR. This was followed by a vote on the document as a whole. Thirty-four delegates participated in the discussion; forty-eight nations voted in favor of the declaration, none voted against it, and eight abstained; twenty-three articles (of thirty) were accepted unanimously.

The final version of the UDHR opens with the following preamble statements:

> Whereas recognition of the inherent dignity and of the equal and inalienable rights of all members of the human family is the foundation of freedom, justice and peace in the world.
>
> Whereas disregard and contempt for human rights have resulted in barbarous acts which have outraged the conscience of mankind, and the advent of a world in which human beings shall enjoy freedom of speech and belief and freedom from fear and want has been proclaimed as the highest aspiration of the common people.

Article 1 asserts that:

> All human beings are born free and equal in dignity and rights. They are endowed with reason and conscience and should act towards one another in a spirit of brotherhood.

One of the delegates, Haiti's Mr. Saint-Lot, said the following things:

> After the war . . . the United Nations representatives had sought out, among old-established or recent political, economic, social and cultural rights, formulas which might be acceptable to men from the four corners of the earth. The text of the draft declaration represented a kind of common denominator for those various ideas. It was perhaps not perfect, but it was the greatest effort yet made by mankind to give society new legal and moral foundations; it thus marked a decisive stage in the process of uniting a divided world. [35]

Historians, philosophers and jurists who study the UDHR are typically unanimous in referring to it as a monumental achievement; as a threshold, envisioning and pointing the way to a new universal social order. Some of these references emphasis the central role of human dignity in this new vision of social order. For example, Glendon states that "when read as it was meant to be, namely as a whole, it is an integrated document that *rests on a concept of the dignity of the human person* within the human family. . . . The starting point was the simple fact of the *common humanity* shared by every man, woman and child on earth." [36]

THE DECLARATION'S DIGNITY VIS-À-VIS HIERARCHICAL HONOR

In most traditional societies around the world, many families' most valuable symbolic possession is their honor. Like a banner, honor marks a family's relative value, rank, and distinction, endowing it—and its members—with the acknowledged right to feel and demonstrate self-esteem. Slight to a family's honor can be expressed through degrading reference (in speech or deed) to any of the family's members; the offense is collective, as must the response be. It stands to reason that the UDHR's reference to "inherent dignity of all members of the human family" invokes this almost universally traditional prototype. This may help make the UDHR's concept of dignity intuitively familiar, accessible, and acceptable to large parts of the world's population. Nonetheless, while invoking universal familiarity with honor, the UDHR distinguishes its human dignity from this traditional notion, presenting us with a value system built exclusively on innate, equal human merit and unconditional worth. This section spells out three of the main points on which the declaration's human dignity differs entirely from the notion of honor.

Equality

First, in an honor society, honor is anything but egalitarian: family members do not all enjoy identical honor. Although their family membership constitutes some entitlement to the family's honor, some members *possess* a lot more of it than others. In fact, a major function that honor serves is the determining, embodying, manifesting, and ensuring of each individual's rank in the group's pecking order. In honor societies, honor is inseparable from the hierarchy that it embodies. So, for example, in most patriarchal honor societies, the male *head of the family* manifests and possesses much of the family's honor, while all other members must honor him accordingly. Typically, in such societies the patriarch's firstborn son enjoys a more honorable status than his siblings. Often the patriarch's first wife is entitled to more honor than other wives or concubines, even though a wife's honor may also be derived from that of her birth family's (pedigree), or from features she possesses and are highly ranked (fertility, beauty, certain body mass).

In short, family honor is a cherished symbolic possession, but different family members are entitled to different shares of it. The UDHR's human dignity replaces the inherently hierarchical idea of honor with a concept that implies intrinsic identity of merit, which it calls "equal dignity." In place of honor that establishes and sustains entrenched social order within the family, the UDHR proposes a communal symbolic asset that negates such hierarchy and replaces it with total, inherent sameness/equality of value among all family members.

Innate Value

Second, in most honor societies, honor incarnates hard earned rank and privilege. A man's honor is largely dependent on his every observable gesture, every bit of which is constantly measured and evaluated by the watchful community. The group's collective consciousness is constantly moderating: Did he show sufficient courage? Did he exhibit adequate generosity? Did he display satisfactory grandiosity? How much self-assuredness did he demonstrate, on a commonly approved scale? In such societies, a woman—and more importantly her menfolk—are continuously honor-rated by observant neighbors based on her every display of modesty, servitude, obedience, fertility, homemaking, and beauty.

The standards and norms according to which honor is bestowed, withheld, or lost within a defined group are applied uniformly: all men (of a given social circle) are expected to display specific *manly audacity*, and all women—typical *feminine humility and deference*. Manly audacity in a certain class may be particularly appreciated in battle, whereas another class may prefer to see it manifested in business, or in scholarship, wit, politics, or religious piety. Yet whatever the specific content of a group's honor norm, it is unanimously applied to all group members who are considered players and *competitors* within the specified honor game. The hierarchical ranking conferred through compliance with an honor norm is uniformly applied to them all. In this sense, they all enjoy equal standards and opportunity within the competitive honor game and are thus likely to consider it fair and unbiased.

Nevertheless, some people (outsiders) are barred from participating in the honor game altogether, and there is nothing they can do to enter the game and gain honor (in Europe, "Gypsies" and Jews were the two most obvious groups of people who were widely considered incapable of participating in honor games). At the same time, some players gain so much honor that the regular rules no longer apply to them; their honor places them above the game.

The UDHR's idea of human dignity lacks—and negates—every one of these components entirely: dignity follows no norms of conduct and is measured against no standards of achievement. *In fact, it requires no conduct whatsoever*; it is indifferent to people's actions. This human dignity is *earned* universally, by everyone, thanks to a single passive, uncontrollable occurrence in their lives: that of being born to human parents and thus to our universal human family. Brave or cowardly, modest or flamboyant, manly, feminine, or neither, conformist or rebel, pleasing or belligerent, *high* or *low*—all human beings alike earn their identical share of human dignity at birth; none of their actions or inactions has any bearing on it.

Permanent Stability

Third, honor-based ranking is a dynamic, evolving, ongoing process. Members of honor groups are continuously observed and judged, and at any given point in time their performances are measured against those of all other players. As explained in chapter 2, any honor-and-esteem ranking is valid but for an instant, since everyone's next moves will reshuffle all cards. A champion who delivered the best performance and received the highest honors and most esteemed standing will have to defend this hard earned status at every following moment against whoever chooses (and is entitled) to play and compete.

The world of honor is, therefore, versatile, not to say volatile. It involves never-ending challenge and competition. Every player is, by definition, always facing every other player's potential challenge and rivalry; one's gain or progress is necessarily others' loss, or at least their setback. The stakes are high, as are the inherent uncertainty and tension.

Unlike honor, the UDHR's human dignity is not embedded in a dynamic process, nor does it constitute a game of any sort. It involves no competition and no rivalry. It is indifferent to the dynamics of human action: nothing a person does or refrains from doing can enhance or endanger their human dignity. No normative social conformity can win a person human dignity points, and no failure or eccentricity can negatively impact human dignity ranking or status. In fact, the UDHR's logic of human dignity does not contain notions such as "failure," "eccentricity," or "points" to speak of. Similarly, it is not conceptually possible to accumulate human dignity, to strip a competitor of it, or to gain any amount of it at the expense of an "adversary." Competitors and adversaries do not exist in the UDHR's world of human dignity, nor do quantities or accumulation.

This human dignity is all about static, permanent certainty and security among siblings who have nothing to compete for, since their innate sharing of the communal merit is permanently identical. The single cautionary tenet is that every member of the human family, as such, is as valuable as any other, and this principle must always be unconditionally acknowledged, upheld, and followed by all.

This brief comparison reveals that even if intuitively evoking and recruiting the familiar, traditional notion of (family) honor, the UDHR's human dignity replaces it with a basic value that is *diametrically antithetical to it*. On most important points, this human dignity implies the exact *opposite* of what traditional honor would involve. Indeed, it appears that the most precise way of defining the UDHR's fundamental human dignity is through binary opposition to honor societies' underlying traditional honor.

Other Scholars' Views

Some dignity scholars aspire and attempt to interpret the human dignity at the heart of contemporary human rights culture in light of a concept they call *dignity*, which is similar—or identical—to what I call *honor*. In other words, they endeavor to synthesize the two ideas that I strive to present here as distinct and incompatible. Waldron seems to be the most openly self-conscious of them:

> It might be thought that the old connection between dignity and rank was superseded by a Judeo-Christian notion of the dignity of humanity as such, and that this Judeo-Christian notion is really quite different in character. I am not convinced. I don't want to underestimate the breach between Roman-Greek and Judeo-Christian idea, but I believe that as far as dignity is concerned the connotation of ranking status remained, and that what happened was that it was transvalued rather than superseded. So let us explore some ways in which the idea of noble rank may be made compatible with an egalitarian conception of dignity. . . .
>
> So that is my hypothesis: the modern notion of *human* dignity involves an upward equalization of rank, so that we now try to accord to every human being something of the dignity, rank and expectation of respect that was formerly accorded to nobility. . . .
>
> We are not like a society that has eschewed all talk of caste; we are like a caste society with just one caste (and a very high caste at that). Every man a Brahmin. Every man a duke, every woman a queen, everyone entitled to the sort of deference and consideration, everyone's person and body sacrosanct, in the easy that nobles were entitled to deference or in the way that an assault upon the body or the person of a king was regarded as a sacrilege. [37]

On this point, Rosen declares:

> I am with Waldron. I see nothing incoherent in the idea that we should all be of high rank. . . . The story that Waldron tells is principally one of "levelling up"—that we should all be accorded the treatment previously reserved for those with the highest status—and this is, I think, generally true. [38]

In his monograph on the history and meaning of human dignity Rosen elaborates:

> One very common way in which writers present the history of dignity is as part of what I call an "expanding circle" narrative. From this perspective, the quality of dignity, once the property of a social elite, has, like the idea of rights, been extended outward and downward until it has come to apply to all human beings. This is all part of the great, long process by which the fundamental equality of human beings has come to be generally accepted. There is something right (and appealing) about this picture, yet what it leaves out is also important. [39]

I agree with Waldron and Rosen that the vision of everyone treated like a queen or a duke may be considered appealing (although personally I prefer the vision of everyone treated according to their self-determined needs). I completely agree with Rosen that what this picture leaves out is important. And here is what it leaves out: that everyone being a queen, a duke, or a

Brahmin is a nonsensical contradiction in terms. Because being a queen, a duke, or a Brahmin is exactly about being superior to many others. Being a queen, a duke, or a Brahmin (to use Waldron's words) does not mean "being treated well"; it means "being treated with due deference, as befitting only those occupying high positions in the social pyramid."

A queen is not a conservatively dressed elderly woman; it is, by definition, a woman positioned as close to the top of a social hierarchy as possible. To be a queen means to outplay any number or jack—yet be outplayed by king, ace, or joker.[40] Because being a queen is an integral component of a coherent world, it is a building block in an honor system. It is only meaningful within a hierarchical, multiple-class system. It is only meaningful precisely because it is a building block; precisely because it defines some people as belonging to an upper class, and others as belonging to lower ones; because it confers the *us/privileged/elevated* status on some—but not on others; because it demands certain conduct of the privileged, if they are to maintain the privilege of being one of us/elevated. Strip the title duke, queen, or Brahmin of its status symbols, remove it from the honor game in which it belongs, which it manifests and upholds—and you render it meaningless.

Waldron wants the perks and benefits of the honor/class/hierarchy game—with no honor/class/hierarchy. He wants the dynamics and excitement of a zero-sum game—with no unpleasant consequences (of status differences, that is, discrimination, domination, and depravation). He would like to have his cake and eat it too; inhale and exhale at the same time. Common sense teaches us how unlikely that is.

The honor/class/hierarchy social game assumes hierarchically distinct classes, relies on them and reinforces them, allowing, prohibiting, and prescribing certain modes of action within each caste and others between them. A "one-caste system" is no longer a caste system at all and does not constitute a game. It does not inspire, motivate, or mobilize the participants.[41]

If we are in a single-class world in which all members are human beings of equal value, we can no longer attempt to play using tools (such as rank and title) that are indistinguishable from a hierarchical, competition game. If we insisted on using such tools, we would be like the medieval crusaders, claiming they revere divine glory—while using the deadly tools of honor wars. Even if unconsciously, we would be co-opted by our powerful tools to play disguised honor games, necessarily inventing ever new enemies and frontiers, creating ever-new nonclass classes. We would be waging disguised holy wars; jihad by any other name. We would be escaping dignity and stepping into honor traps.

If we truly wish to erect and inhabit a single-class world in which all members are human beings of equal value, a world devoid of queens, dukes, or Brahmins, we must consider, develop, and promote the logic of this New Atlantis and construct new, appropriate tools that could and would serve it.

This is, indeed, the heroic mission undertaken by the UDHR, and which this book attempts to frame.

An argument preceding Waldron's was put forth by legal historian James Q. Whitman in his "Nazi 'Honor' and New European 'Dignity.'" Due to its nuance and force, let me quote it in some length:

> The New Europe is founded on a forthright rejection of the fascist past. . . . In the wake of World War II, "human dignity" was sanctified in a number of constitutions—most significantly in those of post-Fascist Italy and post-Nazi Germany. . . . Indeed, if we were looking for one phrase to capture the last fifty years of [continental] European legal history . . . we might call it the high era of "dignity". . . we should credit the triumph of the values of "dignity" precisely to the widespread disgust Europeans have felt for the practices of the era of Mussolini and Hitler.
>
> But . . . the truth is that important threads of continuity connect the fascist era, horrific as it was, with the subsequent era of dignity. . . .
>
> [T]he right way to understand the connection between the Nazi period and the high era of "dignity" that followed it, is to focus on the connection between contemporary values of "dignity" and older values of "honor." And those values are indeed connected: *modern "dignity," as we see it in continental legal cultures, is in fact often best understood, from the sociological point of view, as a generalization of old norms of social honor.* . . .
>
> Everybody who counted as a member of the *Volk*-community was a person of "honor," in Nazi ideology; and, repulsive as that ideology was, it established some of the doctrinal framework for the broad extension of a claim to "dignity" that characterizes contemporary Germany. . . .
>
> When ordinary Germans believe they have been criminally insulted today [and that their dignity has been offended], they are, in fact, acting in a way that dueling aristocrats and military officers once acted: over the course of the last couple of centuries, the *right to take offence* has slowly been generalized throughout German society . . . the Nazi chapter was central to the long-term tale of *levelling up*, the tale of the extension of high-status dueling norms of behavior to the lower orders of German society.
>
> The Nazis extended the claim to honor to the lowest-status "Aryans": they pushed honor down toward the bottom of the social hierarchy. Contemporary jurisprudence has simply continued to push the claim to honor down, reaching at last what were formerly the most despised sectors of the population. In both eras, we see the twentieth century culmination of a process of social change that extends back to the eighteenth century in Germany, and to the seventeenth century in France.[42]

Whitman's poignant, provocative argument is challenging and sinister indeed. Yet it does not necessitate the confusion of dignity with honor. Fully conscious of the claimed conceptual distinction between the two concepts, Whitman points to the fact that both honor and dignity serve the societies that embrace them as foundations of value systems and sources of human worth. He correctly points out that societies may construct social norms, standards of conduct, and legal rights that seem very similar on their face, but derive from either honor or dignity. The right not to be slandered may be similarly drafted in laws that derive it from honor, and those that sanction human dignity. Whitman claims that this is the case with "old, honor-bound Germany" and "new, dignity-revering Germany."[43]

I suggest that as disturbing as they may be, Whitman's findings and conclusion, read carefully, do not compel the conflation of dignity with honor. On the contrary, they offer important cautionary insight. When Nazi nationalism extended honor to "all Germans" ("levelling-up"), it constructed "all Germans" as a class superior to "all others." "All Germans" became the elite group, the high caste, and hence, according to the logic of honor, other, inferior groups had to be created, defined as such, and placed beneath it. In the case of Nazi Germany, these groups were instituted on racist foundations, but they could have just as well been founded on any other ideology. "Jews," "Gypsies," "Slavs" could have otherwise been constructed as "heretics," "bourgeois," "Reds," or "untouchables"—so long as these categories were defined as lower classes, undeserving of honor.

As long as an honor-based structure is uncritically preserved—the expansion of the *honorable people* class merely means that a new *honorless* class must be erected. Any "levelling-up" that does not acknowledge and confront the deep structure, logic, and psychology of an honor-based system is likely to trigger a similar course of events. This, of course, does not necessarily mean enslavement or extermination. But it does mean reenacting and perpetuating hierarchy, class distinction, and the honor-based structure at large. And these do lead, as history teaches us, at least to some domination, exploitation, and discrimination.

If, as Whitman's argument implies, contemporary Germany does, in fact, adhere to the honor-based logic, having merely dubbed "German honor" as "human dignity," then there is cause for caution. Even if all humans are currently awarded high status, as members of the new upper class defined by the new value (human dignity), perhaps nonhumans, such as animals, or in the future cyborgs (cybernetic organisms) do or will serve as "the honorless other." This may imply inhuman treatment of such creatures.[44] Further, the perpetuation of an honor-based system (even if by another name) means that society may, at any time, revert back and restrict its definition of the boundaries of the upper class, hence also of the *outsider* groups.

But Whitman's interpretation is not exclusive; there is another way of looking at this. It may well be that contemporary Germans—and Europeans at large—appreciate and enjoy legal rights that resemble those once founded on honor. Nevertheless, it may be that these contemporary rights are now genuinely derived from a distinct dignity foundation. If this is the case, then the fact that contemporary rights may seem to resemble older ones does not mean that they manifest and reinforce an honor-based social system. It may well be the case that New Germany's norms, standards, and rights are elements of a completely different social order.[45]

Whitman's article does not address these concerns. It does not contend with the exact meaning of a dignity-based social order and its underlying structure, logic, and psychology. This book does. It proposes that we must explore dignity, in clear distinction from honor, so that we can accurately assess whether New Germany and Europe have indeed broken with their honor-bound heritage; so that we can define and develop dignity, its structure, logic, and psychology, to yield a coherent system that inspires, instructs, and supports the social order that we envision.

If, as this section shows, dignity is incompatible with the logic and tools of honor, then perhaps we should adopt the logic of glory, as it too, much like the UDHR's dignity, denies classes and hierarchy, prescribing equal worth to all. The next section examines this proposition.

THE UDHR'S DIGNITY VIS-À-VIS DIVINE HUMAN GLORY

Chapter 3 attempts to visualize the distinction between the systemic logics of honor and of glory through the geometrical images of a triangle and a circle. Honor constitutes a pyramid-shaped social order; within it, at any given moment, each of us is located in a spot that is higher than some and lower than others. Our value, at every instance, is derived from and measured by our position within the pyramid. Our comparative conduct constantly determines our ever-changing position and value. Very differently, in the world based on glory, we are permanently positioned on a circle drawn around a transcendental center. We are all similarly close to the center, and this similar closeness establishes our equal value. The center is God, whose image we all reflect.

In terms of this visual metaphor, the logic of the UDHR's human dignity is, indeed, very similar to that of glory. In fact, the image of the circle is even better suited to capture the logic of dignity that that of glory. All it requires is that we affix, at the center of the circle, human instead of God. In the world of the UDHR's human dignity, we are all permanently positioned on a circle drawn around the *idea* of humanity. This idea embodies absolute value. We are all equally close to that center, and this identical, inherent closeness establishes our universal, absolute, and equal value. In the world of glory, some claim that sin distances us from the transcendental center, decreasing our divine human value. In the world of the UDHR's human dignity, nothing can affect our position in reference to the center; our equal proximity to the *notion of human* is permanent, it is intrinsic to each and every one of us from womb to tomb.

Like the world of glory, the world of human dignity enables no competition, advance, decline, or other mobility. Like glory, dignity can neither be accumulated nor lost, hence requiring no action. All it demands is mutual recognition and due reverence.

Yet, some differences are critical. In the world of glory, each of us is a mirror, inherently reflecting the image of God. The value ascribed to us is that of the image that we reflect. Our reflecting nature is intrinsic, yet the value-laden image is not ours; both image and its inherent value are God's. We must, therefore, cherish them as we would a precious valuable that was lent to us by its owner. In other words, *imago Dei* and glory confer on us *duties of due care*; we must treat them as God, their powerful owner, commands. If he determines that his image and glory require us to refrain from certain sexual conduct (such as masturbation or homosexual conduct)—we must obey, as it is his image and value that we merely reflect and enjoy.

Since God's glory commands adoration, we, its bearers, enjoy this benefit. But these rights, which we enjoy vicariously, are secondary to and derivative of the duties toward the divine glory in us. In his book *Love and the Dignity of Human Life*, Robert Spaemann puts it very clearly: "[Humans] have rights because they have duties."[46]

Quite distinctly, human dignity is the value inherent in our own humanity. The value-laden spark that each of us contains does not belong to a metaphysical entity that is inherently distinct from us (God); it is the kernel of our own essence. True, the stamp of humanity and its value that are branded in me are not *mine* but *ours*. Both humanity and its value belong to the family that we are members of, the human family—much like a family name belongs to the family it denotes. So, although I am not an exclusive owner, I do belong, by birthright, to the family that *owns* humanity.

The metaphor of manifesting another entity's image imposes duties owed that entity. In contrast, metaphoric co-ownership of the human image confers predominantly rights. That is, whereas a glory-based system entails duties, a human dignity–based one bestows rights. As co-owner, I have the right to participate in the ongoing collective determination of the meaning and scope accorded to the notion of humanity. This includes the right to participate in the collective, universal determination of rights derived from such co-ownership. So, as co-owner of humanity, I am entitled, among many other things, to participate in the continual collective deliberation whether humanity necessarily implies *heterosexuality*, and whether all co-owners are entitled, as such, to choose sexual orientation and conduct.

Duties are also a part of this dignity-focused world: duties to enable all co-owners to equally participate in such deliberations and enjoy the rights that co-ownership confers on them. That is: a human dignity–based world imposes the duty to revere humanity and its dignity, as well as the derivative duties that protect and ensure the rights of all humans. But these duties are secondary; they are required to protect and facilitate the rights that are inseparable from membership in humanity.

The UDHR embraces and expresses this position. After much consideration and debate, it was decided and confirmed that the preamble and first articles declare only that membership in the human family gives rise to human rights.[47] The corresponding duties are only briefly mentioned in Article 29, one before the declaration's last:

1. Everyone has duties to the community in which alone the free and full development of his personality is possible.
2. In the exercise of his rights and freedoms, everyone shall be subject only to such limitations as are determined by law solely for the purpose of securing due recognition and respect for the rights and freedoms of others and of meeting the just requirements of morality, public order and the general welfare in a democratic society.

No less important is the difference between the ways glory- and human dignity–based systems define the damage caused by the denial of human worth. Within a glory-based system, denial of divine human glory is an offense against God. It is a sin. It must be punished as God ordained. Within a human dignity–oriented system, denial of human dignity is betrayal of humanity. Even if perpetrated to a single human being, it is not a damage done to them but to us, and it is up to us to amend it, remembering that the perpetrator, like the victim, is a family member, a "co-owner" of the humanity that was betrayed.

If I may take poetic license, I would conclude this section on glory and dignity by inviting you to summon Michelangelo's depiction, in the Sistine Chapel ceiling frescos, of God's creation of Adam. In this superb Renaissance visualization, which has molded our collective imagination, Adam's marvelous grace is clearly due to his creation in the image of God. His body's relaxed posture mimics that of his fierce creator's; his eyes are drawn to him, and his hand is gently sent toward God to receive his touch of life. This human image glows with divine human glory. Michelangelo's David is similarly magnificent. But it stands alone. Unlike the *imago Dei* Adam, David is intensely focused and tranquil as he faces his life's challenge. His eyes are fixed on the task ahead of him, his facial muscles tense, as his large arms carry his tools and his strong legs stand their ground. Comfortable in his human capacity, David radiates human dignity.

Whereas a glory-centered universe raises questions regarding the nature of divinity, the meaning of "bearing image of and likeness to God" (as in Genesis 1:26) and the precise content of one's duties regarding the divine image, human dignity–based culture focuses on defining humanity, *the hu-*

man, the rights embedded in it, and the means to promote and protect them. The next sections address these concerns: humanity and human rights.

THE *HUMAN* COMPONENT AND THE SYSTEMIC LOGIC IT IMPLIES

What exactly is the "human" that the UDHR's human dignity marks as valuable? The UDHR does not elaborate on this point. Its first article does, however, point us in a clear direction, stating that "all human beings are born free and equal in their dignity and rights. They are endowed with reason and conscience and should act towards one another in a spirit of brotherhood."

The article states that we, humans, are all "free," endowed with "reason" and "conscience," and capable of treating each other as "brothers." In the UDHR, therefore, being human consists of freedom, rationality, and capacity for conscientious morality and familial empathy. According to the UDHR, human existence bears no marks of sinfulness, primordial guilt, inherent wickedness, dutifulness, or servitude; nor is it endowed with divinity, metaphysical superiority, a destiny to rule the world, or the vocation to partake in its redemption. The declaration's explicit association of humanness with liberty, reason, moral responsibility, and emotional compassion points clearly to the cultural legacy that is commonly referred to as the Enlightenment. It is this modern, humanist, liberal, and secular tradition that the UDHR guides us to in our search of the human condition.

The UDHR's cryptic reference to freedom does not clearly indicate whether it is negative and/or positive liberty (as they were differentiated by Isaiah Berlin) that is the essence of humanity.[48] It does not imply whether it is freedom that requires society's "non-interference" or "non-domination" (as elaborated by Philip Pettit).[49] It does, however, clearly indicate that personal choice, self-definition and determination, and some degree of self-rule (autonomy) are at the heart of human existence, human nature, or humanness. Thus, *humanness* entails that a human being's freedom to think, dream, imagine, and believe are not be restrained, in order to allow for free choice and self-definition.

Restrictions on an individual's free *action* must enter, as John Stuart Mill explained in his 1852 *On Liberty*, merely to prevent one human being's expression of his or her freedom at the expense of the (equal) freedom of others.[50] Consequently, the notion of humanness commands that a human's mind, heart, and soul never be restricted; they must be left untouched to exercise their unlimited potential in the realms of thought, imagination, and emotion.

It is worth noticing that, breaking with the long-standing Aristotelian tradition, the UDHR's humanness is not singularly linked with reason. Since reason gave rise to modern science and its ruthless applications, perhaps in 1948 it could hardly be trusted to secure the existence and well-being of humanity. It could certainly not be trusted to cherish and uphold the value of humanness in all members of the human family. Traumatic experience has taught humanity that conscientious consideration and empathy for all human beings could not be assumed to derive from reason; they must be determined as independent, equally important components of humanness.

Humanness is, thus, the basic *human mold* that has been stamped in all of us, entailing freedom, reason, conscience, and compassion. The UDHR's human dignity is the intrinsic value ascribed to this mold. Denying a person's potential to cultivate the core components of humanness renders that person's existence less than human, and is therefore *inhuman*. Such denial of even a single individual's humanness challenges the UDHR's determination that all persons are human and that all human existence is endowed with the value of human dignity. It defies the paradigm that we are a family (of humans) and that our family trait (humanness) is valuable and must be acknowledged (as dignity).

An offense to humanness and human dignity is, therefore, not an affront to the individual person whose freedom, reason, conscience, or compassion is at stake: it is an affront to the whole family, humankind, and its self-determined collective worth. Accordingly, it is not the individual person's duty to stand up to such a challenge; the duty falls on their entire clan: humankind. When any individual person's human component (such as freedom) is unduly limited in a way that defies human dignity, it is our collective dignity that is challenged, our communal worth as human beings that is disputed, and we must all rally around it to protect it together. It should not matter to us who happened to be the individual person—victim—through whom human dignity was abused, since it is the same dignity that we assign each and all of us. Similarly, the specific victim of dehumanization must not, in this universe, feel shame, humiliation, or disgrace. Instead, we the human family, must feel outrage and compassion. All this in stark contradiction to an honor-bound world.

The UDHR's worldview postulates that denial of humanness and human dignity are absolutely and categorically prohibited, since they defy the fundamental paradigm: the worth of our family's essential human quality. The UDHR avows that we categorically denounce such defiance of our humanness and its value.

The UDHR's categorical prohibition of human dignity denial clearly echoes Kant's famous categorical imperative, presented above, which commands: "Act so that you treat humanity, whether in your own person or in that of another, always as an end and never as a means only."[51] Kant's categorical imperative defends human dignity by prohibiting the objectification of humans, that is, the denial of human subjecthood. The UDHR's bar on denial of any human being's worth is a reiteration of Kant's categorical imperative.

I am confident that many readers find all these general statements on humanness and its value easily acceptable, perhaps obvious and self-evident. The spirit of the Enlightenment has, after all, been with us for generations. The devil is, as always, in the details. If humanness, according to the UDHR, consists of freedom, reason, and the capacity of moral and empathetic choice, then what degree and what kinds of denial of these basic human features constitute such defiance of the paradigmatic human dignity that we, the human family, consider absolutely unacceptable and intolerable? Surely, a parent's restriction of a child's play with a rifle, although clearly an infringement of freedom, would not be considered an offense to human dignity. But a parent's operative determination that an offspring—child or adult—marry, refrain from marriage, conceive a child, or refrain from such conception, with disregard to the offspring's own will, would surely constitute a prohibited affront to human dignity. How and where do we draw the line between these two cases?

The UDHR's literal phrasing does not and cannot supply a definitive answer, and any interpretation must be tentative, qualified, unsatisfactory, and somewhat tautological. I believe that a reasonable interpretation of "the spirit of the law" is that the restriction or denial of a person's freedom—or other basic human features—becomes an unacceptable offense to human dignity if and when it renders a person's existence "inhuman" by the standard of prevailing sensitivities. Such judgment is, of course, contextual.

In most societies, it used to be a father's prerogative to determine whether and to whom his offspring could marry; many Shakespearian comedies thrive on this social norm. Yet in our contemporary world, we consider the choice of whether to marry and to whom as strictly personal and definitively autonomous. It has become a part of what we view as human existence, to control one's own choice of partner and/or commitment to family life. We, the people and nations of the twenty-first century, therefore, consider forcing such a choice on anyone to be inhuman. Even in traditional societies in which patriarchal customs still prevail, it is not considered advisable for parents to force children into marriage against their will.

But what about the denial of a person's choice of same-sex marriage: Would we consider such treatment inhuman? Would it constitute a severe offense to human dignity? For many of us around the world the intuitive answer is an unequivocal yes. Yet I suspect that a numerical majority of the members of our human family would vote otherwise. How, then, do we define a severe offense to human dignity? Must our determination be based on a majority's view regarding the inhumanity of the discussed condition? Do we refrain from determining that something is an offense to our human dignity if the universal jury is still out regarding a specific point? Or do we delegate the power to make such decisions to a professional tribunal? And if so, what would such a tribunal base its judgment on?

These specific questions are the ones that require much universal, public debate. It is precisely on them that the UDHR invites us to focus and deliberate. It is to them that we must channel our communal energy. Personally, I believe that, in accordance with the spirit of the UDHR, we must always err on the side of individual liberty. But even more importantly, we must frame the questions and engage in universal and rigorous discussion.

DIGNITY AS THE NORMATIVE EQUIVALENT OF SPECIFIC WEIGHT

Let me offer yet another metaphor, this time drawing on the natural sciences. The image of Archimedes leaping out of his bathtub and running naked through the streets yelling, "Eureka! Eureka!" is illustrious. In that legendary moment of enlightenment, Archimedes is said to have discovered the concept of *specific weight.*

Measuring material density, *specific weight* ascribes every material a number: that material's weight per unit volume. In simple words: if we divide the mass of any piece of pine wood (its weight) by its volume (size), we will always get the same number, which is the *specific weight* of pine wood. The same holds true for any piece of iron. Since the *specific weight* of wood is smaller than that of water—wood floats on water. Since the *specific weight* of iron is greater than that of water—iron does not float on water. *Specific weight* is, therefore, an inherent feature of a type of material. Every item made of that material contains and exhibits that feature.

I suggest that, analogously, every category of beings or things can be said to have a *specific value*, which is not an empirical, descriptive *is*, but an ethical, normative *ought*. It implies *quality* that we ascribe to that category. "Dignity" is the name of this type of value. "Human dignity" is the *specific value* of the human category; hence, every human being has the exact same human dignity as every other.

In terms of this metaphor, honor can be thought of as the value analogs of mass and volume (that is, weight and size). Just as items can be measured and determined as bigger or smaller, heavier or lighter, so people can be normatively measured as more or less honorable. Human dignity is the value equivalent of neither weight nor size, but of the permanent relation between them.

This metaphor allows us to conceive of "dignity" as a class of *specific values*, human dignity being one of them. In this framework, glory is another, distinct, *specific value*. Whereas glory is the *specific value* of the human that was made in the image of God, human dignity is the *specific value* of the human that is an autonomous, rational, emotional, and moral subject.

Let me apply this metaphor to one more dimension. Many writers on dignity follow Kant in assuming, like George Kateb in his work *Human Dignity*, that

> the human species is indeed something special, that possesses valuable, commendable uniqueness or distinctiveness that is unlike the uniqueness of any other species. It has higher dignity than all other species, or a qualitatively different dignity from all of them. The higher dignity is theoretically founded on humanity's partial discontinuity with nature. Humanity is not only natural, whereas all other species are only natural.[52]

I know of no convincing justification for such blanket singling out of humans, and prefer the Aristotelian-Thomist view that every category of living thing has its own dignity, just as every type of material has its own *specific value*. As this view is entirely compatible with the UDHR, while also inviting conceptualization of animal value and rights, I propose it over Kateb's.

HUMAN DIGNITY AND FUNDAMENTAL HUMAN RIGHTS

It is in declaring a universal, categorical connection between innate human value and fundamental human rights that the UDHR can and should be seen as the revolutionary, groundbreaking, and defining onset of our era. Human dignity is the means by which it achieves this definitive unity, establishing that "it is because humans have dignity that they have human rights."[53]

I suggest that the most coherent interpretation of the UDHR's unqualified linkage of human dignity and of fundamental human rights is a simple one: fundamental human rights are those that derive unconditionally from the mandatory acknowledgment and reverence of human dignity. This means that fundamental human rights are those that every human being must be defined as possessing in any given situation if human dignity is to be secured.

The criteria for determining whether something is a fundamental human right in a given situation must be these: Is the claimed right crucial for the preservation of human dignity in the given context? Would denial of the claimed right in the given circumstances render a human being's existence inhuman or less than human? Would such denial undercut our commitment to the value of humanness in the situation at hand?

This line of thought does not differentiate civil from cultural and economic rights, nor does it refer to people's necessities or needs, as, indeed, the UDHR deliberately does not.[54]

Let me illuminate this interpretative suggestion through illustration.

Some Roman emperors amused their populace by hurling prisoners into arenas to be devoured by wild beasts. We would all agree that this treatment of prisoners does not acknowledge human dignity, and is an intolerable offense to the value of humanness. Clearly, the fact that only some people—and not all—were subjected to beastly devouring, or even that they were convicted felons or heretics, in no way diminishes the offense to human dignity.

It is easy to agree that "not being thrown forcefully into an arena swarming with wild beasts" is a fundamental human right: it is absolutely necessary in order to maintain human dignity.

Consider a slightly different scenario. Consider a sane, reasonably intelligent and emotionally stable adult, who, after deep thought and long consideration chooses to step into the wilderness to be devoured by animals. Does this person have a fundamental human right to do with their life and body as they please, or is there, perhaps, a fundamental human right dictating that they may *not* exercise this choice? Furthermore, consider a sane, reasonably intelligent and emotionally stable adult who, based on deep conviction, asks that after their death, their body be left in the wild, to be devoured by animals. Does this person have a fundamental human right to do with their dead body as they please, or is there, perhaps, a fundamental human right dictating that they may *not* exercise their said choice?

Exploration of these questions instantly reveals important nuances that must be addressed. For example: whereas in the second scenario, acknowledgment of the individual's fundamental human right to walk into the wilderness would not require our active (positive) intervention, in the third scenario, acknowledgment of a fundamental human right would. At the same time, of course, the second scenario involves the exposure of a living person to torturous death; the third scenario involves *merely* the mutilation of a human corpse.

I suggest that in the UDHR's universe of human dignity, these considerations, like many others, are all important in the distinction between scenarios, but the overall determining criteria regarding each scenario are universally the ones presented above: Is it crucial for the preservation of human dignity in any of the given contexts that the individual's choice be recognized as a fundamental human right? Or, perhaps is it crucial for the preservation of human dignity in any of the given contexts that the *prohibition* of the person's choice be defined as deriving from a fundamental human right? In each of the scenarios presented above, would it be an intolerable offense to our collective human dignity if we granted—or categorically denied—the wishes of said individuals?

Although I chose a particularly rare and gruesome set of examples, the considerations that they raise are not different, in essence, from those raised by people's hugely varied claims that they have fundamental human rights to end their lives, to sell their body parts, to abort fetuses or sell babies, or to offer themselves as bowling balls or as prostitutes. Despite fascinating differences between such situations, from a perspective considering human dignity and fundamental human rights, each of these many scenarios poses the same difficulty: How exactly do we define human, where do we draw the line between human and inhuman (or less than human), and how, based on this, do we define fundamental human rights?

If it is inhuman to restrict a person's free choice (autonomy) regarding their corpse—then it is a fundamental human right to will one's corpse to be devoured by animals. Conversely, if it is inhuman that a human corpse be devoured by animals, then it is a fundamental human right that no human corpse be so devoured. Similarly, turning to one of the many scenarios not presented here: if it is inhuman to force a person to continue living when that person suffers intolerable pain—then it is a fundamental human right to take one's own life when one experiences intolerable pain. However, if ending a human life is categorically inhuman, then each human life possesses a fundamental human right to live.

Regarding the third scenario described above, we may well conclude that it is not inhuman to restrict certain choices regarding one's corpse, nor that it is inhuman for a human corpse to be consumed by animals. If so, then the particular issue in the third scenario does not involve human dignity, or fundamental human rights. It must be assessed in light of a different value and different rights. (In chapter 5, I suggest that this other value is what I call "respect," and that the relevant rights are "respect-based human rights." I suggest that respect and respect-based human rights are the appropriate framework for most situations, and that only very few situations actually involve human dignity and fundamental human rights.)

Extreme limitations may threaten human existence and human dignity in many diverse spheres that have nothing to do with corpses and wild animals. Education is an important case in point. Let us imagine a regime that prohibits girls and women from acquiring any kind of education and constrains them to their homes. Would we consider this policy grossly offensive to human dignity? Would we deduce that access to basic education is a fundamental human right? Surely we would agree that the answer to both questions is positive. Denying people the opportunity to foster their thinking, reasoning, and deliberating, merely because they are not men, amounts to denial of universal, equal human dignity.

And what if the regime allowed girls to attend primary schools, but not high schools or universities, or certain departments in universities? Surely, depriving a person the opportunity to enroll in a specific university department does not amount to inhuman treatment. If a region is not affluent enough to sustain in its university a philosophy department, would we consider the consequence inhuman and a breach of fundamental human rights?

Surely not. Perhaps we would not consider it inhuman even if such a region could not afford to sponsor high education altogether. Nevertheless, group (such as gender) based differentiation that denies some people—but not others—the opportunity to study philosophy constitutes intolerable offense to human dignity and breach of fundamental human rights. If high schools, universities, or even certain departments are only available to boys and men, then the exclusion of girls and women denies the concept of universal human worth, and, as such, is unacceptable offense to human dignity. The same is true for any such exclusion based on race, ethnicity, sexuality, class, religious affiliation, or any other type of grouping. Any policy that recognizes the intrinsic value of some people—but not of others—is deeply offensive to human dignity.

A fundamental human right may be breached through the use of torture, imprisonment, starvation, isolation, or rape. It may also be breached by denial of basic self-determination, which includes, among other things, free speech, choice of education, sexuality, cultural and/or religious affiliation, and participation in social, political, or cultural activity. In each case we must weigh the *extent* of the restriction or depravation together with other specific relevant circumstances to determine whether the value of humanness as such is indeed severely compromised.

If human dignity, the value of core humanness, must be universally upheld and absolutely revered, then so must human dignity–based rights. This means that they may not be *balanced* against other pressing considerations, such as policies. Fundamental human rights must always prevail. In order for this to be possible, human dignity must be narrowly defined, and human dignity–based rights must be defined so that they do not contradict or negate each other. Consequently, in order to be absolute and always prevailing, fundamental human rights must be minimalistic.

Hence, the human dignity–based right to education cannot include "any amount of any education that any person chooses freely." If this were a fundamental human right, imposing a legal duty on the state, it would be so costly that it would necessarily come at the expense of people's fundamental rights to health, nutrition, and housing. To be absolute, the human dignity–based right to education must, therefore, only include as much freely chosen education as a society can offer equally—without compromising any other fundamental human rights. This would, of course, differ in different places at different times. The *quantity* of education included in human dignity–based rights must, therefore, be determined in context. At the same time, it is perfectly possible—and reasonable—to determine that human dignity dictates an absolute right that no person's body ever be penetrated without that person's free consent. Such a fundamental human right is minimalistic enough even when phrased in absolute terms. It prohibits rape—as well as the forced feeding of striking prisoners or of patients defined as anorexic.

Thus, the UDHR's commitment to "equal dignity" gives rise to minimal human dignity–based fundamental human rights that guarantee everyone's dignified existence in any given situation. [55]

NOTES

1. United Nations General Assembly, Third Session, Universal Declaration of Human Rights (UDHR), Resolution 217A, Paris, December 10, 1948,http://www.un.org/en/universal-declaration-human-rights/. All quotes from the UDHR may be found at this online site.

2. Michael Rosen's research offers one example of such motivation. His historical exploration of the English-language "dignity" leads him to try and construct a concept that contains the four distinct strands that he has uncovered: "The first was dignity as a rank or status. . . . The second was that of intrinsic value. . . . The third was dignity as measured and self-possessed behavior. Fourthly, there was the idea that people should be treated with dignity—that is respectfully." Michael Rosen, *Dignity: Its History and Meaning* (Cambridge, MA: Harvard University Press, 2012), 114.

3. Jeremy Waldron, *Dignity, Rank, and Rights*, ed. Meir Dan-Cohen (Oxford: Oxford University Press, 2012), 28.

4. In his chapter on "On Nazi 'Honour' and New European 'Dignity,'" James Q. Whitman rightly observes that "Nazi law revolved around the value of 'honor.' This fact is hard to miss, since Nazi authors proclaimed the supreme value of 'honor' all the time; and historians of Nazi law have not failed to note it. Nevertheless, I think it is fair to say that historians have not taken Nazi talk of 'honor' quite seriously." James Q. Whitman, 2003, "On Nazi 'Honour' and New European 'Dignity,'" in *Darker Legacies of Law in Europe: the Shadow of National Socialism and Fascism over Europe and its Legal Traditions*, ed. Christian Joerges and Navraj Singh Ghaleigh (Oxford: Hart, 2003), 247.

5. Gudmundur Alfredsson and Asbjørn Eide, eds., *The Universal Declaration of Human Rights: A Common Standard of Achievement* (The Hague: Martinus Nijhoff, 1999), xvii.

6. Marcus Düwell, Jens Braarvig, Roger Brownsword, and Dietmar Mieth, eds., *The Cambridge Handbook of Human Dignity: Interdisciplinary Perspectives* (Cambridge: Cambridge University Press, 2014), xvii.

7. See also chap. 3.

8. Rosen, *Dignity*, 16–17.

9. "'Dignity' goes from being a matter of the elevated status of a few persons in a particular society to being a feature of human beings in general, closely connected with their capacity for self-determination." Rosen, *Dignity*, 15.

10. "The dignity of the moral law makes human beings—its embodiment—worthy of respect. . . . Since we are subject to the moral law and that law has its source within ourselves, human beings also embody 'autonomy' (literally: their selves are the sources of law) and are thereby 'raised above' the natural world." Rosen, *Dignity*, 30.

11. In Rosen's words: "Under the influence of Kant, it has come to be taken for granted (outside the Catholic tradition, at least), that dignity is always human dignity and that dignity and equality go together." Rosen, *Dignity*, 31.

12. For a comparison of Kant's dignity with Aquinas's see Rosen, *Dignity*, 22–24.

13. Immanuel Kant, *Groundwork of the Metaphysics of Morals (1785)*, in *Immanuel Kant: Practical Philosophy*, trans. Mary Gregor (Cambridge: Cambridge University, 1996), Ak. 4:35; referring to Preussische Akademie edition by volume and page.

14. Kant, *Metaphysics of Morals*, Ak. 6:462.

15. Kant, *Metaphysics of Morals*, Ak. 4:429.

16. I have suggested that we define the offense of rape as using another person as merely a sexual object, hence defying human dignity. See Orit Kamir, "The Dignitarian Feminist Jurisprudence with Applications to Rape, Sexual Harassment, and Honor Codes," in *Research Handbook on Feminist Jurisprudence*, ed. Robin West and Cynthia Grant Brown (Northampton, MA: Edward Elgar, 2019), 303–20.

17. Waldron, *Dignity, Rank, and Rights*, 24.

18. Waldron, *Dignity, Rank, and Rights*, 25. Ironically, this argument almost undermines Waldron's previous one: apparently *Würde*, like the English "dignity," is also prone to be linked with honor.

19. From a different direction, Rosen criticizes the Kantian conceptualization of dignity by exposing what he perceives as its inapplicability to real-life situations. Rosen argues that taking cover from the wind behind a line of people who are waiting for the bus on a cold winter day objectifies them, yet is not morally wrong: "Although your using the bus queue as a windbreak is to use the people in it as a means only, it does not seem that you are doing anything morally objectionable. After all, although you are taking advantage of them, you haven't disadvantaged them in any way." Rosen, *Dignity*, 82. I suggest that, in fact, the described conduct *is* morally objectionable, exactly because the hypothetical protagonist *does* treat fellow human beings as pieces of wood. The moral thing to do would be to offer the people in the line to take turns, so that all can enjoy each other's presence. This would be "fair usage" of everyone, acknowledging everyone's humanity. Nevertheless, the "offense" to human dignity here is so minimal and trivial that it does not warrant moral or legal reference.

20. United Nations, The Charter of the United Nations. And the Statute of the International Court of Justice, San Francisco, June 26, 1945, http://www.un.org/en/charter-united-nations/ (hereafter noted as UN Charter); emphasis mine.

21. It is hard to interpret the distinction suggested by the wording between "dignity" and "worth." It reads more as a repetition than as referring to two distinct meanings. Interestingly, the UDHR does not repeat this double phrase, suggesting, perhaps, that its drafters considered "dignity" to include "worth."

22. See, for example, Alfredsson and Eide, *Universal Declaration of Human Rights*, 28; and Mary Ann Glendon, *A World Made New: Eleanor Roosevelt and the Universal Declaration of Human Rights* (New York: Random House, 2001), 61, 124–28, 206, 225.

23. Glendon, *World Made New*, 57–58.

24. Glendon, *World Made New*, 63–64.

25. Ashild Samnøy, quoted in Alfredsson and Eide, *Universal Declaration of Human Rights*, 7.

26. Glendon, *World Made New*, 73 and 76–77.

27. René Cassin and Carlos P. Romulo, quoted in Glendon, *World Made New*, 89.

28. Glendon, *World Made New*, 117–18. Glendon documents that Malik fought and failed to include a "minority article," meant to give people belonging to well-defined linguistic, ethnic, or religious minority groups the right to establish their own educational, cultural, and religious institutions. The idea was refused by the United States and France. Glendon, *World Made New*, 119–20.

29. Glendon, *World Made New*, 143.

30. Glendon, *World Made New*, 144.

31. Glendon, *World Made New*, 161. On a somewhat different note, the South African delegation opposed the mention of human dignity since, it claimed, the UDHR was meant to state fundamental human *rights*; dignity was not a *right* and therefore had no place in the document. The South African opposition to human dignity was defeated. Glendon, *World Made New*, 144–45.

32. Samnøy, quoted in Alfredsson and Eide, *Universal Declaration of Human Rights*, 17.

33. Martti Koskenniemi, quoted in Alfredsson and Eide, *Universal Declaration of Human Rights*, 38.

34. Tore Lindholm, quoted in Alfredsson and Eide, *Universal Declaration of Human Rights*, 61, 67.

35. United Nations General Assembly, Third Session, Address by Mr. Saint-Lot (Haiti), Rapporteur of the Third Committee, 853–54, Paris, December 9, 1948, https://undocs.org/A/PV.180. See similar sentiment expressed by Herman Santa Cruz, Chilean representative, quoted in Glendon, *World Made New*, 169.

36. Glendon, *World Made New*, 174, 232, emphasis mine. See also 173–76, 232, 235; Tore Lindholm, quoted in Alfredsson and Eide, *Universal Declaration of Human Rights*, 73; and Alfredsson and Eide, *Universal Declaration of Human Rights*, 27.

37. Waldron, *Dignity, Rank, and Rights*, 31, 33, 34.

38. Michael Rosen, quoted in Waldron, *Dignity, Rank, and Rights*, 80.

39. Rosen, *Dignity*, 8.

40. The joker is the "wild card": free of and outside the honor hierarchy. It is the exception that maintains the rule. For a vivid demonstration of the joker/jester's special role, see the anecdote in chapter 2, 41.

41. This is no different from my argument in chap. 3 that within monotheism, God cannot have honor, since honor can only exist in a group-game of a pantheon.

42. Whitman, "On Nazi 'Honour,'" 243, 245–46, 250, 266; emphasis mine.

43. Whitman does seem to claim that contemporary "dignity" is simply a new name for old honor: "[Dignity] is a value that rests on the norms of hierarchical honor whose history reaches well back into the early modern period." Yet he correctly refers to honor as "honor," distinguishing the two terms. Interestingly, in his reply to Whitman's article, Gerald L. Newman suggests that the English word "dignity" carries the meanings that I attribute to "honor," whereas "human dignity" means "a dignity that is intrinsic to humanity, that is shared by every individual human being." Although practically possible, this distinction does not make coherent sense, as it implies that human dignity is a subcategory of honor, whereas I believe that this chapter shows they are distinctly different. Gerald L. Newman, "On Fascist Honor and Human Dignity: A Sceptical Response," in *Darker Legacies of Law in Europe: The Shadow of National Socialism and Fascism over Europe and Its Legal Traditions*, ed. Christian Joerges and Navraj Singh Ghaleigh (Oxford: Hart, 2003), 267.

44. As this book restricts itself to *human* dignity, I will not develop this line of thought, which is dear to my heart.

45. And, of course, it may be the case that the distinctions between honor and dignity, and the systems that they inspire are not fully and perfectly embraced, causing gray areas of confusion.

46. Robert Spaemann, "Human Dignity and Human Nature," in *Love and the Dignity of Human Life: On Nature and Natural Law* (Grand Rapids, MI: Eerdmans, 2012), 27.

47. Glendon, *World Made New*, 75.

48. Isaiah Berlin, *Four Essays on Liberty* (Oxford: Oxford University Press, 1969).

49. Philip Pettit, *Republicanism: A Theory of Freedom and Government* (Oxford: Oxford University Press, 1997).

50. John Stuart Mill, *On Liberty* (1852; repr., London: Longman, Roberts, & Green, 1869), 9.

51. Kant, *Grundlegung zur Metaphysik der Sitten* (Riga, Latvia: bey Johann Friedrich Hartknoch, 1785), Gr. 4.429.

52. George Kateb, *Human Dignity* (Cambridge, MA: Harvard University Press, 2011), 5.

53. Alan Gewirth, "Human Dignity as the Basis of Rights," in *The Constitution of Rights: Human Dignity and American Values*, ed. Michael J. Meyer and W. A. Parent (Ithaca, NY: Cornell University Press, 1991), 10.

54. For discussion of cultural and economic rights, see chap. 5.

55. The shift from "equal" (dignity) to "minimal" (dignity-based human rights) may bewilder readers trained in analytical philosophy. Yet "equality" here refers to the sameness of people's fundamental worth, whereas the "minimum" standard refers to the measure of fundamental human rights that is required to protect that universal human worth.

Chapter Five

Respect

The Value of Our Singularity

In the course of writing this chapter, as the winter holiday season set in, a dear friend presented me with a lovely bright yellow cosmetics bag, advising in bold silver letters "BE THE BEST VERSION of you." Assigned to any and every aspect of our lives, this motto is the *categorical imperative* of our time. Pythia's ancient Delphic motto "Know thyself" has been fortified with "Be true to your true self," "Express yourself," and "Make the most of yourself." But what *is* the virtue of being ourselves?

The maxim on my cosmetics bag captures and eloquently encapsulates an entire worldview. Obvious and unproblematic as it may seem to us, it is culturally specific, and would have been incomprehensible to members of traditional societies. We are creatures of the Enlightenment era, and therefore assume and believe that each of us is an individual, a unique *self*, and that each such self has the potential to develop and blossom into various versions. We hold dear John Stuart Mill's ethics of liberty, assuming that in order to be fully human, each one of us may—and indeed must—*choose* among these potential versions, and pursue the realization of their preferred one.[1] We presuppose the existence and merit of human freedom, agency, competency, power, and responsibility that underlie the creative task of self-making. We hail them as autonomy, spontaneity, and authenticity, and believe that they enable us to confront the epic task of self-determined personal creation and development. We believe that this task is good and even sacred. We further believe that its products, our diverse personalities, have moral value, worth.

This chapter focuses on the *concrete product* of the autonomous quest for authenticity, on the *version of ourselves* that we actually build. How do we evaluate the actual realization of a person's pursuit of their particular self?

What moral terms do we apply to it? Let me clarify the question through an analogy. We use inches, yards, kilometers, and miles to measure distance. It would be nonsensical to try to apply these terms to evaluate an object's weight. For this type of measurement we use pounds or kilos. But these concepts are worthless to measure an object's volume, bulk. For that purpose we must apply liters or gallons or square meters. In the sphere of moral or social evaluation, we use honor to measure the value of a person within a social hierarchy of importance, precedence, and prestige. We determine that a certain person has great honor, and another much shame in comparison with his peers. We use glory to refer to a person's priceless divine spark, and dignity to refer to her immeasurably valuable humanity. What concept, measure, value system do we use to estimate the worth of a person's self-created personality?

I use the term "respect" to express the appreciation, the moral and social value of our self-made personalities. If the term puzzles you, think of phrases such as "You have my respect for striving and achieving your goal," meaning "I value you for your self-creation," "You have my appreciation for making something of yourself," "I give you moral credit for being true to yourself."

Chapter 4 defines human dignity as the value that the enlightenment-based world ascribes to the abstract concept of our universal humanity; to the idea of an all-human common denominator, humanness. This value is, by nature, too minimalist and static to generate a full set of rules that can structure every aspect of social interaction. Dignity merely marks a *floor* of conduct not to be descended: it prohibits torturing any human being, raping, silencing, or depriving them of nourishment and medical assistance. This narrow human dignity, with its derivative value system, code of conduct, and relevant range of emotions, cannot outline and instruct the full extent of any social order. It aims merely to prevent dehumanization, but not to guide and navigate us through the rich spheres of our individual and social lives.

Yet, as testified by my cosmetics bag, there is a distinct enlightenment-bound value, also emergent over the last few centuries, which can—and does—pick up where human dignity leaves off, attributing worth to those very parts of our diverse personalities that exceed and transcend the minimal human common denominator. This is the value of each and every one of our unique, incomparable, specific personal features, and accomplishments; it is the worth of the singular development and fulfillment of each human potential at any given time. This value, respect, commands that we allow each other to grow and blossom and that we recognize, accept, and cherish such personal realizations. It yields human rights that are not fundamental as dignity-based rights are, but rather secondary, *respect based*. The right to be the best version of me by becoming an astronaut and flying to the moon is respect based, and is clearly tentative and limited.

I am by no means the first to distinguish the notion that I call respect from the idea of human dignity. Several writers on human dignity differentiate, in various ways, the merit of humanness as our kernel common denominator, from the virtue of the unique singularity of every particular individual. For example, distinguishing between what he calls "human dignity" and "dignity of the person," in *Neither Beast nor God*, Gilbert Meilaender states that "perhaps slavery demeans human dignity embodied in the slave, yet is utterly incapable of actually depriving him of the personal dignity he shares equally with all of us."[2] He goes on to offer a respective distinction between "harms" (in reference to human dignity) and "wrongs" (in reference to dignity of the person), and states that "the dignity of each human person is to be respected, which is quite different from being valued."[3] He argues that dignity discourse confuses undifferentiated references to both types of dignity:

> For example, the language of dignity may be used to mark either a "floor," a kind of respect and care beneath which our treatment of any human being should never fall—or it might be used to mark a "height" of human excellence, those qualities that distinguish some of us from others. Similarly, [. . . in dignity discourse there is] a difference between an "ethic of equality" (valuing all human beings in light of their common humanity) and an "ethic of quality" (valuing life when it embodies certain humanly fitting characteristics or enables certain humanly satisfying experiences).[4]

I agree with Meilaender that these two values are widely conflated, despite their very different logic and psychology. This leads me to believe that they should be clearly distinguished through definition and name, hence my choice of "respect" over his term "dignity of the person" or other suggestions that have been made.

The English root "respect" is often used in connection with the meaning I propose to ascribe it. "I respect your choice" clearly means that I attribute positive value, merit, to your choice, and that I call that merit respect. Yet common usage does not distinguish the word respect from the specific meanings of the values that I propose to label *honor*, *dignity*, and *glory*. Indeed, the concept that I call "respect" is not necessarily associated with this word, and it is not under the banner "respect" that the concept developed in the last few centuries. In fact, this notion is frequently not labeled with any clear name. This is probably why it is so difficult to express and to refer to. It is referred to in the context of autonomous human development, growth, realization, and flourishing; it is closely associated with liberty, spontaneity, and authenticity. Yet none of these terms quite captures it.

Freedom and *authenticity*, of course, denote values, but are not typically applied to the *actual product* of the process of self-creation, the *me*. Evaluative labels such as "free spirit," or "authentic character," usually refer only to very specific aspects of a personality, highlighting its less conventional elements. Which is why I suggest that we use the noun "respect" to denote the value of all aspects of a specific, particular, realized self per se. "You deserve respect for becoming a kind, earnest, hardworking individual," or "for becoming such a wonderful piano player," or "for being such a compassionate, loyal friend," or "for being a patient and loving parent." Once we establish this, we can ask how much respect each of us has in view of our self-creative achievements. We can estimate and evaluate that Wendy has succeeded in building a mature, accepting, and responsible persona more than Peter. That she, therefore, earned and deserves more respect than he. Alternatively, we can accept each individual's self-respect, and award Tinker Bell the respect that she assigns herself for her ingenuity and resourcefulness.

In the second decade of the twenty-first century, there are countless voices presenting the value of the singular personality. My cosmetics bag's motto has become prevalent and self-explanatory thanks to innumerable thinkers and writers, who introduce and promote the concept—even if under diverse names. Of the myriad voices, I chose those of two founding fathers of this discourse: social psychologist Erich Fromm and philosopher Charles Taylor. The one focuses on "positive freedom" and spontaneity and the other on the ethics of authenticity and recognition.

Following the brief presentation of their insights, this chapter situates respect vis-à-vis human dignity and honor. It scrutinizes the claim that whereas "human dignity" marks the absolute, unchanging value of core, universal humanness, "respect" complements it and bestows tentative, changing value on the expansive zone of specific, diverse realizations of our multitude abilities and inclinations. The chapter concludes by introducing the category of "respect-based rights" (vis-à-vis "fundamental dignity-based human rights").

ERICH FROMM: POSITIVE FREEDOM TO SPONTANEOUSLY LOVE AND WORK

Born in Germany in 1900 to a Jewish family, Erich Fromm was a member of the Frankfort school of critical theory and a psychoanalyst. He left Germany in the early 1930s for the United States and later moved to Mexico. His interdisciplinary scholarship combines not merely philosophy, sociology, and psychology, but also deep humanism and political commitment. I understand much of his scholarship as an extensive exposé of what I term respect. In the second decade of the twenty-first century, many of Fromm's insights regarding human identity have become popular to the extent of cliché; their popular versions are elaborated in countless self-help books, stickers, and refrigerator magnets. Nevertheless, his many treaties are still powerful in their soulful humanism and precise reading and anticipation of the evolving human condition.

In his seminal work *Escape from Freedom*,[5] presented in detail in chapter 6, Fromm differentiates between "negative freedom," the freedom *from* external restriction and oppression, and "positive freedom," which he defines as the active, creative use of one's abilities for autonomous, authentic, integrated self-development. For Fromm, negative freedom is merely the indispensable precondition; positive freedom is the willful, committed process by which a human being realizes themselves as a unique, richly diverse yet intensely integrated entity, an entity both individuated from the world and deeply engaged with it. Positive freedom is the condition of spontaneous, excited engagement with oneself, others and the world, which, for Fromm, is the only way to achieve connected yet autonomous subjecthood. Love and work pursued with such spontaneous engagement are the main avenues to constitute positive freedom. Such love and work are never merely intellectual, rational endeavors; like any other significant human action, they must include and integrate intellect with emotion and body.

In terms of honor and respect Fromm's argument is as follows: individuals must achieve negative freedom from the external restrictions that are imposed on them by honor-bound social institutions and conventions. Positive freedom is the spontaneous realization of the self, which constitutes it as distinct from the world—yet united with it. This multifaceted yet integrated entity commands respect.[6]

Of Fromm's abundant references to positive freedom, I have chosen the following:

> We believe that . . . man can be free and yet not alone, critical and yet not filled with doubts, independent and yet an integral part of mankind. This freedom man can attain by the realization of his self, by being himself. What is realization of the self? . . . We believe that the realization of the self is accomplished not only by an act of thinking but also by the realization of man's total personality, by the active expression of his emotional and intellectual potentialities. These potentialities are present in everybody; they become real only to the extent to which they are expressed. In other words, positive freedom consists in the spontaneous activity of the total, integrated personality. . . .
>
> Spontaneous activity is the one way in which man can overcome the terror of aloneness without sacrificing the integrity of his self; for the spontaneous realization of the self, man unites himself anew with the world—with man, nature and himself. Love is the foremost component of such spontaneity; not love as the dissolution of the self in another person, not love as the possession of another person, but love as spontaneous affirmation of others, as the union of the individual with others on the basis of the preservation of the individual self. The dynamic quality of love lies in this very polarity: that it springs from the need of overcoming separateness, that it leads to oneness—and yet that individuality is not eliminated. Work is the other component . . . work as

creation in which man becomes one with nature in the act of creation. What holds true of love and work holds true of all spontaneous action. . . .

Positive freedom as the realization of the self implies the full affirmation of the uniqueness of the individual.[7]

If this sounds familiar, echoing contemporary spiritual teachings such as, perhaps, the immensely popular Eckhart Tolle's writings, please consider that Fromm's *Escape from Freedom* was written in 1941, when it was insightful, prophetic, and inspirational. The fact that his vision is so familiar testifies to its central role in contemporary modernity.

Fromm continued to develop his vision of positive freedom and its merit—respect—in many subsequent publications, perhaps the most popular of them being *The Art of Loving* (1956).[8]

CHARLES TAYLOR: RECOGNITION OF AUTHENTIC SELF-DEVELOPMENT AND CREATION

Like Fromm's social psychology, Canadian Charles Taylor's moral philosophy has reached and touched many around the world. Taylor's vast philosophy of the self, authenticity, and recognition resonates with Fromm's writings, and is similarly an elaboration of respect.[9] He repeatedly differentiates respect from honor, suggesting that each of them is the focal point of a "framework," that is, a systematic order of meaning:[10]

> Alongside ethics of fame [that is, honor,] there has grown up in the last two centuries a distinction based on vision and expressive power. There is a set of ideas and intuitions, still inadequately understood, which makes us admire the artist and the creator more than any other civilization ever has; which convinces us that a life spent in artistic creation or performance is eminently worthwhile. . . . There is . . . something quintessentially modern in this outlook. It depends on that modern sense . . . that what meaning there is for us depends in part on our powers of expression, that discovering a framework is interwoven with inventing.[11]

Taylor narrates that in "earlier societies," honor-based ones,

> what we would now call a person's identity was largely fixed by his or her social position. That is, the background that made sense of what the person recognized as important was to a great extent determined by his or her place in society and whatever role or activities attached to this. The coming of a democratic society doesn't by itself do away with this, because people can still define themselves by their social roles. But what does decisively undermine this socially derived identification is the ideal of authenticity. . . . By definition, this cannot be socially derived but must be inwardly generated.[12]

Taylor claims that the dawning of authenticity was historically launched by the Reformation.[13] It marked the decline of exclusive adherence to honor in the making of identities, and the beginning of inward-bound self-generation of authentic "selves." In this new era, identity is modeled on creative, original art:

> Self-discovery involves the imagination, like art. We think of people who have achieved originality in their lives as "creative." And that we describe the lives of non-artists in artistic terms matches our tendency to consider artists as somehow paradigm achievers of self-definition.[14]

This modern era encouraged the finding of authentic meaning in what Taylor calls "the affirmation of ordinary life"; "the key point is that the higher is to be found not outside of but as a *manner of living* ordinary life."[15]

Recognition, Taylor claims, and more specifically *equal* recognition of each individual's authentically created identity, is a fundamental element of modernity: "Equal recognition is not just the appropriate mode for a healthy democratic society. Its refusal can inflict damage on those who are denied it, according to a widespread modern view."[16]

In this context, one of Taylor's principal arguments is that authenticity does not, cannot and must not flourish in a vacuum, "monologically":

> My discovering my identity doesn't mean that I work it out in isolation but that I negotiate it through dialogue, partly overt, partly internalized, with others. That is why the development of an ideal of inwardly generated identity gives a new and crucial importance to recognition. My own identity crucially depends on my dialogical relations with others.[17]

Taylor summarizes this part of his thesis as follows:

> Briefly, we can say that authenticity (A) involves (i) creation and construction as well as discovery, (ii) originality, and frequently (iii) opposition to the rules of society and even potentially to what we recognize as morality. But it is also true . . . that it (B) requires (i) openness to horizons of significance (for otherwise the creation loses the background that can save it from insignificance) and (ii) a self-definition in dialogue. That these demands may be in tension has to be allowed. But what must be wrong is a simple privileging of one over the other, of (A), say, at the expense of (B), or vice versa.[18]

He states his belief that

> in articulating this ideal [of self-development] over the last two centuries, Western culture has identified one of the important potentialities of human life. Like other facets of modern individualism . . . authenticity points us towards a more self-responsible form of life. It allows us to live (potentially) a

fuller and more differentiated life, because more fully appropriated as our own.[19]

It has become so central to our modern self-definition, "it is hard to find anyone we could consider as being in the mainstream of our Western societies who, faced with their own life choices, about career or relationships, gives no weight at all to something they would identify as fulfillment, or self-development, or realizing their potential."[20]

According to Taylor, then, in traditional societies a person's worth, their honor, derives from exemplary adherence to social convention and devotion to their social roles and standing. In modernity, quite differently, personal worth derives, to a great extent, from "authenticity," which "involves originality" and therefore "demands a revolt against convention."[21] Such modern personal worth is inseparable from the new concept of self, and the conception of each person as manifesting (artistic-like) self-development and fulfillment. This modern worth is linked not with outstanding heroic acts that would award honor, but with ways of living ordinary life, anchored in family and work, and in emotions such as love.

In his pivotal 1994 essay "The Politics of Recognition," which inspired much response and debate, Taylor distinguishes between human dignity and the other human value, which he links with unique identity, authenticity, and recognition:

> *Everyone* should be recognized for his or her unique identity. . . . With the politics of equal dignity, what is established is meant to be universally the same, an identical basket of rights and immunities; with the politics of difference, what we are asked to recognize is the unique identity of this individual or group, their distinctness from everyone else. The idea is that it is precisely this distinctness that has been ignored, glossed over, assimilated to a dominant of majority identity. And this assimilation is the cardinal sin against the ideal of authenticity.[22]

In view of Taylor's philosophy, then, self-realization happens first and foremost in the ordinary life and through manifestation of thoughts, emotions, and conscience. Respect, which Taylor refers to as recognition, is the focal point of a coherent order of meaning that he calls a framework. This respect-based framework is additional to that of human dignity.

In line with Taylor, if we were to imagine a prominent man of honor, we would think of a samurai warrior, or a Viking. If we were to imagine a prominent man of respect, we would think of Michelangelo or Leonardo Da Vinci. The great respect that we ascribe these men is the immense value we attribute their realization of their creative genius.

DEFINING RESPECT VIS-À-VIS HUMAN
DIGNITY, EQUALITY, AND LIBERTY

The Opposite of Minimalistic, Static, Difference-Blind and Universally Identical

Whereas human dignity is a minimalistic, leveling value, that addresses only our common basic human form, respect is quite the contrary: it addresses each of us differently, based on our numerous distinctive qualities and their manifold concrete realizations. Whereas human dignity refers to the static component of human existence (humanness; existence as human), which remains unchanging in every one of us from birth to death, respect refers to the growing, developing, ever-changing aspects that typify each of us.

Whereas human dignity is blind to our distinguishing characteristics (including race, gender, age, ethnicity, culture, and all aspects of character), respect refers to those parts of us that are related to, influenced by, and manifested through our distinguishing attributes. Whereas human dignity is universally identical in all of us, respect can and must take into account differences, which come to play through and are intertwined with our unique selves.

Whereas the logic and discourse of human dignity constitute a firm *floor*, meant to safeguard the fundamental, common humanness that is similarly manifested in each of us, the distinct logic and discourse of respect is an expansive one, pointing us to reach for our stars in our unique ways. I think of the one as pessimistic, struggling to defend the core, and the other as optimistic, bursting to reach out.

These comparative features of the two values reveal that one, human dignity, is more closely associated with equality, whereas the other—respect—with liberty.

Equality and Liberty

Since human dignity marks the worth of our common denominator, we are all, by definition, *equal in human dignity*. Since basic *liberty* and autonomy are essential elements of humanness, they are deeply linked with human dignity. Yet dignity's link with equality is more crucial to its character as universal and inclusive. Dignity is meant, above all else, to equally protect everyone's common human denominator.

Since respect evaluates concrete realizations of autonomy, it is inherently linked with liberty. The association of respect and equality is less obvious. As our personalities are diverse in very many ways, is not the respect that they command different by definition? Surely, I cannot hope to receive or feel as much respect for my realized personhood as Michelangelo or Leonardo Da Vinci. How and in what sense can respect be equal? Is there a sense in which we *ought* to all have equal respect?

I believe that the answer is that we should all be acknowledged as having an *equal opportunity* to achieve respect. What should be equally respected is our *entitlement to pursue* our self-determined development and fulfillment, that is, our optimal selves and the according respect. In Taylor's terms, I believe that we should all enjoy equal recognition as potentially capable and deserving of achieving respect. In terms of Fromm's "negative freedom" (the freedom from restriction), this means that we should all enjoy equal freedom from restriction and oppression that may block our ability to realize our chosen selves and achieve our potential respect. In terms of "positive freedom" (the freedom to actively pursue self-realization), there are grounds for profound debate whether—or to what extent—equal positive freedom justifies affirmative action and collective funding to support those who cannot finance their own pursuit of optimal self-realization. A proper discussion of this point is beyond the scope of this chapter.

Although the association of respect with liberty seems natural and obvious, it is more problematic than first meets the eye. In a liberal world, the ideal is that we each develop ourselves freely. But what about the real world, in which many people develop and grow less freely than we would wish them to? What about a person who develops abilities and personhood in a nonliberal community, under conditions that seem coercive? Should we not acknowledge this person's respect? Should we, perhaps, presume that any achievements must be and hence are, by definition, products of choice and autonomy, even if no such freedom is acknowledged by the individual and the surrounding community? This too requires and deserves serious discussion. I believe that every person's development should be awarded respect, whether or not we presume that such development was pursued and achieved *freely*.

A Broad Respect that Complements the Narrow Human Dignity

Human dignity and respect both belong to the humanistic and liberal worldview that emerged in the Renaissance (or during the Reformation) and matured in the era that is commonly labeled "the Enlightenment." In this, they are siblings. Nevertheless, each of them accords value to a distinct aspect or perspective of human existence, each following and dictating different logic, psychology, and economy. Once we distinguish between them, we may choose one over the other. I suggest, instead, that we view and constitute them as mutually complementary.

Let me once again make use of the imagery of the circle. In a circle symbolizing the worth of a human individual, human dignity should be marked as the very center. It embodies the value of the hard-core, common denominator of what we perceive as humanness. Quite distinctly, respect refers to the great bulk of the circle. Marking the virtue of our realized attributes, colored by personality, race, gender, ethnicity, sexual orientation, culture, language, religion, and many other affiliations, it constitutes the value of the vast majority of each person's full-blown humanness. Respect, therefore, occupies most of the circle's radius.

If we were to draw the merit of each and all of us as circles, our circles would all share the same center point, signifying the dignity of our common humanness. Yet the size and makeup of the rest of our circles would vary greatly, based on our individual potential and its realization. This would visually express the *equality* of our common human dignity; it would also exhibit that respect covers greater ground regarding each person.

Since human dignity refers to the abstract human stamp that is identical in all of us, its scope is narrow. At the same time, since it values what we consider the very essence of humanness, it must be understood as absolute. Quite distinctly, respect must be very broad, to envelop the endless variety of personal human manifestations. It must be varying and tentative, to allow diverse valuing of distinct human manifestations. It must also allow for curtailment of such manifestations when they clash and obstruct each other or human dignity. So, whereas the value of free thinking, feeling, imagining, and believing must be acknowledged as absolute and safeguarded uncompromisingly, the value of a person's singing as manifesting their unique authenticity must be weighed against the value of their neighbor's silent meditation as manifesting their unique authenticity. The value of each of these authentic human manifestations must be considered tentative, and may have to allow for their restriction to enable their fair balancing. To value the full range of human existence, we must cherish both human dignity and respect, applying their discrete modes of operation to distinct elements of humanness.

This compilation of human dignity and respect raises the inevitable question where to draw the line between their two spheres and how to justify this decision. In terms of the circle metaphor: How much of the innermost part of the radius should we consider as human dignity zone and where should respect zone start? What is the criterion for drawing the line?

Following Mill's formative *On Liberty*, the common liberal perception is that any and every thinking, feeling, imagining, and believing must be recognized as covered by human dignity. I believe that the wide acceptance of this view derives from our feeling that preventing a person from mental activity of any kind would be inhuman: it would be offensive to the common-denominator basic form of humanness, imposing a condition that we consider "less than human" and denying the value of humanity as we understand it. Similarly, we reject slavery, feeling that the complete *ownership* of a human and the permanent denial of freedom of action would be inhuman. The criterion is, therefore, that anything effecting core humanness involves dignity, whereas anything else involves respect.

Slavery and pure mental activity are the most obvious cases that touch on core humanness; but what about more controversial issues such as self-prostitution, or public expression of racist hate speech? Should we consider such instances of self-determination within the range of human dignity, or should we define them as manifesting respect? Would restriction of self-prostitution or racist public expression constitute a condition that we view as less than human? Would such restriction deny the value of humanity?

To address this, I suggest that we add a second criterion: restriction of something that is in itself significantly offensive to human dignity does not constitute a condition that is less than human. Hence, something that is in itself significantly offensive to human dignity is not a part of core human existence as such and should not be referred to in terms of human dignity.

According to this criterion, the query we must determine is whether self-prostitution or public racist hate speech is significantly offensive to human dignity. We are likely to differ on this. My answer would be such: any selling of a human person as *merely*[23] a sexual object for the use of another, degrades human subjecthood by objectifying it, and is thus significantly offensive to human dignity; a public racist hate comment seriously implying that certain people are inherently inferior, or do not deserve to live, is significantly offensive to human dignity.

In line with this answer, self-prostitution and blunt public racist expression, both significantly offensive to human dignity, should not be considered essential parts of core human existence as such; they are not cherished as parts of human dignity and should not be referred to in dignity terms. They are self-expressions that threaten human dignity and as such, command very little respect, if any. It is, therefore, possible and perhaps desirable to restrict them or even prevent them altogether.

This brief discussion demonstrates that the exact distinction of human dignity and respect in every concrete situation must be a highly nuanced, ongoing process that reflects our ever-changing moral convictions, sensitivities, and fears. It requires perpetual astute public negotiation. No formula could possibly draw a clear unchangeable line in the *right* place for every occasion.

Nevertheless, I believe that the framework of conceiving human dignity and respect as distinct yet complementary *layers of value* is reasonable, applicable, and useful. I believe that the reference to abstract concepts such as "humanness" and "inhuman" is the only tool we have. It is clearly not mathematical, and requires constant exploration, negotiation, and convincing. It further requires great commitment, moral assuredness, and careful communication. But such is the nature of values and their application, and formulas may only pretend to disguise it, never truly dodging or circumventing it.

DEFINING RESPECT VIS-À-VIS HONOR

In its accommodation of diversity, versatility, and change, respect may remind us of the honor that underlies honor-based societies. It is, therefore, worth pointing out the profound differences between these two values. Honor is acquired and bestowed on a person based on their objective (that is, external to themselves) measuring up to uniform social standards of conduct. Respect is felt, requested, and attributed based on the particular individual's own, subjective set of standards. For example, in a militaristic, honor-based society, honor may be gained by heroic militaristic service. Respect, quite distinctly, may be felt by a person (as self-respect) and requested by that person from others ("Respect me") for qualities and achievements that are not widely accepted by social standards. In the said militaristic society—or any other—one may feel, request and/or gain respect by showing empathy and compassion to animals or love of and devotion to music, whether or not either one of these is encouraged and honored by the surrounding society.

In this sense, respect is dependent on the individual's own standards, valuing their own choice of norms rather than upholding and enforcing common social norms—as is the case with honor. Yet, as Taylor reminds us, no person is (or ought to be) an island; we each construct ourselves, our values, standards, and appreciation in the context of dialogue with our surroundings. Respecting any person according to their own standards is inherently also respecting that person's choices of social and cultural affiliations. By definition, it therefore implies liberalism, pluralism, and multiculturalism of some kind and to some extent.

Whereas honor measures people against each other, setting them in hierarchy and instilling a zero-sum game among them, respect measures each person in reference to themselves, creating no hierarchy and instilling no competition between them. Whereas honor may be *seized* from one person by another, no such *taking* is possible regarding respect. If a person builds their self-respect on their dancing and asks that their dancing be respected by others, no one can take that respect away from that person and claim it as their own. Another person may out-honor that person in a dancing competition: receive a higher score and more honor than the other in reference to a performance of that person's dancing. But this is entirely distinct from the respect that that person may feel, request, or acquire in reference to their dancing per se.

Whereas the honor regarding the dancing is bestowed based on accepted social norms, respect regarding the same dancing is dependent entirely on the dancer's own standards, and the community's willingness to acknowledge and recognize their standards and value their dancing accordingly. In this sense, a community's willingness to respect individuals is inherently liberal, diversity friendly, and pluralistic.

In honor-based societies, the desired honor necessarily instills competition, fear of humiliation, mutual suspicion, and a conformist race to best uphold accepted, prevailing standards. In contrast, a society inspired by respect encourages individual self-determination that is based on attentive self-exploration. It promotes each person's dialogue with what they define as their social and cultural contexts. It requires mutual recognition and acceptance of others' individualistic life projects, inviting empathy and mutual support.

The inevitable price that a respect-oriented society must be willing to pay is in the spheres of uniformity, clear hierarchy, simplicity, and stability. A respect-based society must educate its members to determine themselves in terms of positive liberty—while trusting their neighbors to do the same. It must instill in them self-reliance and self-assurance in their self-determination—as well as humility regarding their fellow men and women. It must bring them up to cherish and celebrate the possibility of unforeseeable change that is unavoidable if each individual is truly allowed to follow their best judgment. A respect-based society must be deeply optimistic and confident in the inherent value of unrestricted, pluralistic manifestations of humanity.

To use the circle metaphor, in an honor-based world, the entire circle symbolizing the individual is determined by honor. It is in reference to honor that a person derives the full range of evaluation, including their innermost center point. Can human dignity be introduced into an honor-based system and serve as a focal point, marking the common center of gravity? I believe that it can and often is. Nevertheless, such a compilation of honor and human dignity is very different from the integration of human dignity and respect. In the first instance, people may ban mutilation, torture, and starvation (all prohibited by human dignity), yet continue to judge themselves and each other in a competitive, zero-sum manner in reference to uniform honor norms. The humanism of human dignity will not necessarily impact the systematic honor-bound social interaction, or turn it into a liberal, pluralistic one. It will merely serve as a "floor," on which honor will continue to determine the logic of social interaction. Transformation of an honor-based system into a respect-bound one requires conscious committed education.

An Ordinary Life Anecdote Illustrating Honor and Respect

How does this distinction between honor and respect come into play in real life? Since this discussion is highly abstract, let me illustrate with a miniscule example. On one of my trips, I stood in a security line in a big international airport. As the luggage stall was clogged with empty trays, and since the security person in charge seemed not to be paying attention, I took down some trays, stacking them orderly in what seemed to be their place. Having done this several times, I heard the security person mutter, "Idiot." Meeting my eyes, he said, "This is not helping." I asked him whether calling a passenger an idiot was a part of his official training, to which he turned to a colleague, repeating my question. I asked for his name and approached the supervisor.

As I was later debating whether to also launch an official complaint, I tried to assess whether my emotional response to the insult directed at me was triggered by honor- or by respect-related sensitivity. In publicly calling me an idiot, refusing to apologize, and making light of my reproach, the security person clearly offended my honor, compromising my status and standing among the passengers and gaining esteem at my expense. Simultaneously, he was also disrespectful of the responsibility, resourcefulness, and diligence I had exhibited, thus offending my respect.

The stain on my honor required *getting even*, which could be achieved by belittling him publicly, or even dismissing him demonstratively as though he was someone situated beneath me and unworthy of my attention. I asked myself whether this would afford me the needed satisfaction. I further pondered what response could recover my hurt respect. Reassurance from a witness to the incident that my conduct was reasonable and even commendable would have probably sufficed. In absence of such a witness, I reassured myself that my conduct was indeed faultless. I felt that the supervisor's reproach would probably prevent future disrespect of other passengers. I decided that the offense to my honor did not require vindication, and that an official complaint would be unnecessarily vengeful.

Absent the distinction between offense to my honor and offense to my respect, I might have felt compelled to commence an honor-driven blood feud that could have cost both parties stress and aggravation.

Compiling Honor and Respect: Basing Honor on Respect

Nevertheless, there is an important way in which respect and honor may be and sometimes are fused. In an exclusively honor-based world, honor is the only game in town. If you manage to fake heroism, and no one finds out, you can enjoy the honor, status, standing, and prestige that you acquired. The same holds true for winning a competition by using illegal substances. Of course the fear of exposure, haunting your every breath, may make you paranoid, edgy, and aggressive.

In a world that combines honor with respect, the honor code may stipulate that honor must result from respect and accord it. In this world, you would not use illegal substances to win a competition since such victory, even if never exposed, would not afford you a sense of honor. The gap between your respect (the value of the actual realization of your genuine potential) and your honor (based on the illegal use of substances) would torment you, undermining your sense of honor. Such linkage of honor with respect is possible and indeed familiar. Some social groups and individuals within them genuinely embrace it. It provides a stronger foundation for a person's self confidence in their honor, curbing tension and aggression. It does not, however, undercut the conceptual distinction between honor and respect. [24]

RESPECT-BASED RIGHTS

We are in the habit of classifying rights in categories. *Civil rights* are the first-generation, eighteenth-century liberties that Anglo-American legal systems cherish; *economic, social, and cultural rights* are the second-generation, nineteenth-century concepts, promoted by Socialist and communitarian ideologies. This distinction is useful mostly for conservative liberals in opposing the *new* rights and for progressive liberals in their endorsement. Another pervasive distinction is between positive and negative rights. You have a negative right to perform an abortion if the state and fellow citizens are prohibited from restricting this practice. You have a positive right vis-à-vis your state if it must provide you with facilities, or even sponsor the procedure.

The final section of chapter 4 proposes a category of rights that are based on human dignity. Analogously, this section proposes the category of *respect-based rights*. These are the rights that derive from, acknowledge, and uphold respect: the value of our singular identities.

Chapter 4 defines human dignity–based human rights as fundamental, as rights that must be defended for every human being in any given situation if humanness and its value are to be secured. Since humanness denotes merely the very core of our ideal of human essence, human dignity–based rights are minimal, yet crucial to human existence. In comparison, respect-based rights cover everything else: they are not the rights necessary to prevent dehumanization, but those needed to encourage and promote every individual's optimal development and prosperity. Whereas human dignity–based rights are minimal and protective, respect-based rights promote optimal growth and diversity. They are, hence, manifold, yet necessarily tentative and qualified. Whereas human dignity–based rights are primary, respect-based rights are secondary: they must yield to human dignity–based rights, and accommodate other, sometimes conflicting, respect-based rights. [25]

What distinguishes respect-based rights from human dignity–based ones is not the subject matter that they cover, but their extent; their *radius* if you like. It is *not* the case that, for instance, family rights are human dignity based, whereas labor right are respect based. The minimal—yet most crucial part of each of these rights—is human dignity based, whereas the many penumbra rights that surround the hard-core ones are respect based.

The rights not to be forced into marriage or childbirth are human dignity based. They are fundamental, primary, unconditional, and as absolute as a right can be. If such a right is threatened, the state must actively intervene in ensuring it, be the price what it may be. The right to live in close proximity to one's family members, so that family traditions may be celebrated together effortlessly, is respect based. We do not consider the denial of this right as inhuman, rendering a person less than human and renouncing the tenet of human dignity. A person may demand a negative right to live in close proximity to family members, that is, that no one prevent the realization of such desired accommodation. But even such a right would be tentative, if, for example, residency in the area where family members live is determined by lottery, or age.

Analogously, the right not to be prevented from pursuing work is human dignity based. We normally believe that it is inhuman to prevent a person from working and being self-supporting. But the right to get a job that you believe you are suited for is respect based: it must be balanced against similar competing rights of all other interested parties. In some contexts, everyone's rights to the job they desire may be conditioned on proving to be the most suitable candidate according to specified criteria. In other contexts no such rights will be acknowledged.

Similarly, the right to clothing in cold climate might be recognized as human dignity based (although such a right is both economic and positive). But if some of us feel that their self-expression requires the right to nudity in public and others feel that they can only flourish and observe their religion if women in the public sphere are completely covered, a society cannot grant either party the full extent of the respect-based rights it demands without completely depriving respect-based rights from the other group. *Compromise* is the only reasonable solution; both groups' rights must be somewhat curtailed. Seeking an egalitarian solution, we develop means by which to equally curtail clashing respect-based rights.

In his State of the Union address of January 1941, United States president Franklin D. Roosevelt famously submitted that people everywhere in the world should enjoy four freedoms: the freedoms of speech and worship, and the freedoms from want and fear. Whereas the first two "freedoms of" are acknowledged by the First Amendment to the Constitution of the United States of America, the two "freedoms from" are considered "second-generation" economic, social, and cultural rights. [26]

In terms of the distinction suggested here, each one of these four rights has a hard core that must be acknowledged as fundamental, absolute, human dignity based. Every person should be allowed to express a political view (that is not a dangerous hate speech), even if this requires the state to actively prevent attempts of silencing them. Every person should be allowed to practice their chosen religion (in a way that is not offensive to human dignity), even if the state must actively protect such right from violent opposition. No person should starve, even if this means that the state must actively support them through entitlement programs. No person should live in fear of arbitrary violence, even if the state must actively maintain a police force and an army to ensure this right. The absence of such rights would compromise human existence as we commonly view it, hence human dignity.

At the same time, rights to have one's views published in the newspaper, to hold services in a lavish house of prayer, to eat one's favorite food, and not to fear losing one's job are *not* fundamental. They do not derive from our common denominator humanness and its value, human dignity; their lack is not commonly viewed as constituting inhuman conditions. These rights, like many others, are, therefore, respect based. If they are acknowledged, it must be tentatively.

The distinction between human dignity and respect-based rights, just as the distinction between human dignity and respect, must be constantly formulated in reference to our assessment of what constitutes human existence and inhuman conditions. For example, only a decade or two ago, many people did not consider same-sex marriage a fundamental, human dignity–based right. Many people did not consider it inhuman to prevent same-sex couples from marrying. As a result of intense international advocacy, public perception in some places has changed significantly and many people now feel differently on this point. If same-sex marriage does not enjoy recognition as human dignity based, it is very likely to do so in some places in the near future.

The determination, definition, weighing, and balancing of respect-based rights is the ongoing social negotiation that most political debate, legislation, and advocacy are made of. When a community debates whether to prohibit workplace bullying, for example, a part of the debate should touch on whether the worst kind of such bullying must be acknowledged and defined as offensive to human dignity. But most of the debate should revolve on respect-related concerns, balancing the employee's rights to optimal self-development in the workplace against the employer's rights to run their business autonomously. Interests, liberties, entitlements, power dynamics, and group rights all effect this deliberation.

RESPECT-BASED HUMAN RIGHTS IN THE UDHR

The second section of the preamble to the UDHR refers specifically and explicitly to American president Roosevelt's four freedoms:

> Whereas disregard and contempt for human rights have resulted in barbarous acts which have outraged the conscience of mankind, and the advent of a world in which human beings shall enjoy *freedom of speech and belief and freedom from fear and want* has been proclaimed as the highest aspiration of the common people.[27]

In her comprehensive analysis, *A World Made New*, Mary Ann Glendon asserts in no uncertain terms that economic, social, and cultural rights were explicitly and deliberately fully embraced by the UDHR. "The controversy over social and economic rights was not, as many later came to believe, over whether such rights should be included in the document. Eleanor Roosevelt's presence assured that FDR's 'four freedoms' which included freedom from want, would be a constant touchstone for all members of the Commission."[28] One of Eleanor Roosevelt's amazing achievements was in persuading a reluctant US Department of State to accept the inclusion of social and economic rights in the UDHR. The controversies were merely over the amount of emphasis social and economic rights should receive in comparison with first-generation political and civil rights, how they should be phrased, and most importantly how they should be implemented and by whom.

Yet, if the distinction between human dignity– and respect-based rights differs from that between civil rights and economic, social, and cultural, the question remains: Does the UDHR acknowledge and cover merely the human dignity component of the *new* (economic, social, and cultural)—as well as *old* (civil)—rights, or does it also refer to the respect-based sphere of all these rights? I believe that although not using this terminology, the UDHR does cover respect-based rights of both civil rights and economic, social, and cultural ones.

Article 4 of the UDHR establishes the following fundamental human right: "No one shall be held in slavery or servitude; slavery and the slave trade shall be prohibited in all their forms." There can be no doubt that the right to freedom from slavery is human dignity based, and the UDHR offers it absolute protection. Most rights stated in the UDHR's first articles similarly enjoy absolute protection and seem to be human dignity based. So, for example, Article 5 determines that "no one shall be subjected to torture or to cruel, inhuman or degrading treatment or punishment." Article 6 determines that "everyone has the right to recognition everywhere as a person before the law."

But consider Article 3, stating that "everyone has the right to life, liberty and security of person." Surely, some parts of the right to liberty are respect based, including the specific rights to freedom of singing or drum-playing at all hours. . . . Further, consider sections 2 and 3 of Article 16:

2. Marriage shall be entered into only with the free and full consent of the intending spouses.
3. The family is the natural and fundamental group unit of society and is entitled to protection by society and the State.

It would seem that section 2 establishes a human dignity–based right: an "intending spouse's" right to enter into marriage with "free and full consent." Yet section 3's determination that the family "is entitled to protection" might be interpreted more broadly, to include respect-based rights. A family's right not to have its children forcefully taken to boarding school might derive from family members' human dignity. But a family's right to change its name might be considered respect based; the denial of such right might not compromise the core value of humanity as such.

Similarly, consider the first section of Article 21:

1. Everyone has the right to take part in the government of his country, directly or through freely chosen representatives.

A right to be acknowledged as worthy of partaking in the government of one's country is a human dignity–based right. But does "everyone" have the specific right to meet in person with a parliamentary representative in order to convince them to take a certain stand on a given point? Surely, to the extent that such a right is covered by the section, it must be respect based, and hence conditional. Like Article 16(3)'s "social right," Article 21(1)'s "civil right" covers respect-based rights as well as human dignity–based ones.

Particularly interesting in this context is Article 22's general proclamation that situates "free development of personality" next to "dignity":

> Everyone, as a member of society, has the right to social security and is entitled to realization, through national effort and international co-operation and in accordance with the organization and resources of each State, of the economic, social and cultural rights indispensable for his *dignity and the free development of his personality.*

Everyone, the article determines, is entitled to "realization" of the "economic, social and cultural rights" to the extent that they are indispensable for two things: (a) "his dignity," and (b) "the free development of his personality." In other words, some extent of economic, social, and cultural rights is indispensable for human dignity and some extent is necessary for the free development of a person's personality; insofar as such rights are indispensable to either dignity or free development of personality, everyone is entitled to realize them.

In Article 22, therefore, the UDHR pronounces quite explicitly that some measure of its human rights is crucial for the protection of human dignity, and some measure is necessary to ensure the merit of free development of the personality, which I call respect.

If the UDHR proposes that its rights entail some portion that is human dignity based and some portion that is respect based, why specify this statement only to "economic, social and cultural" rights? Having closely reviewed the UDHR's composition, Johannes Morsink offers a simple reply: because it was already obvious regarding the "old," civil rights, but needed stating regarding the "new" ones: "The majority of the drafters . . . believed that the social, economic and cultural rights required more material involvements and needed attention because they were so new."[29]

Morsink also determines that

> there was no long debate, but from the earlier discussion of Article 3 we know what the meaning of this abstract right to full development meant to the drafters. Together with the other rights in Article 3 they counted it among the most fundamental of all the human rights in the Declaration. Most of the rights that follow Article 22—those listed in articles 23 through 27—aim at the realization of the right to the full development of one's person.[30]

"Development of the personality" appears again, in Article 26(2), this time fortified by the adjective "full";[31]

> 26(2) Education shall be directed to the *full development of the human personality* and to the strengthening of respect for human rights and fundamental freedoms. It shall promote understanding, tolerance and friendship among all nations, racial or religious groups, and shall further the activities of the United Nations for the maintenance of peace.

Section 1 of this article constitutes what seems to be a human dignity–based right: "26(1) Education shall be free, at least in the elementary and fundamental stages. Elementary education shall be compulsory." The right to "elementary and fundamental education" seems to be presented as absolute, one that the deprivation of would threaten human dignity. The UDHR does not hesitate to take this stand even though the right to education is both "new" and "positive" (requiring the state's active investment). Section 2 of Article 26 adds that all education must enable "*full* development of the human personality." Whereas elementary schooling offering fundamental education is constructed as a human dignity–based right, education at large is presented as a far more extensive, respect-based right.

The historical origin of Article 26(2) adds an interesting twist to its character:

> When the nuts-and-bolts paragraph of Article 26 arrived at the Working Group of the Second Session, A. L. Easterman, the representative of the World Jewish Congress, immediately noted that "the article on education provided a technical framework of education but contained nothing about the spirit governing education which was an essential element. Neglect of this principle in Germany had been the main cause of two catastrophic wars." He therefore proposed to add [Article 26(2)].[32]

Chapter 4 notes the effort of the declaration's drafters to establish the new post–World War II world on human dignity as a conscious rejection of the Nazi denunciation of that tenet. Morsink's narration reveals that the drafters' choice to acknowledge respect as an additional basis for human rights—and specifically for the right to education—was similarly motivated by their understanding that insufficient recognition of respect was instrumental in facilitating the expansion of Nazism. The UDHR's choice of both human dignity and respect as the basis of human rights was thus directly influenced by the drafters' deliberate determination to construct an alternative foundation for the new world order.

In the eighteenth and nineteenth centuries, the era of and following the American and French Revolutions, equality and liberty, fused together as *equal liberty*, marked the core of the ethos of enlightenment and the basis of rights. I suggest that since the UDHR, the ideal at the heart of the modern ethos and the foundation of human rights is "human dignity and respect."

Respect-based rights constitute the vast majority of human rights. Their logic is different from that of human dignity–based, fundamental rights. Their economy is far more nuanced and complicated. The mechanisms of curtailing them must be—and have indeed been—carefully developed by countless legislators, judges, and theoreticians. I believe that this historic effort stands to benefit from clear conceptual differentiation of these rights from fundamental, human dignity–based ones.

NOTES

1. John Stuart Mill, *On Liberty* (1852; repr., London: Longman, Roberts, & Green, 1869).
2. Gilbert Meilaender, *Neither Beast nor God: The Dignity of the Human Person* (New York: Encounter Books, 2009), 83.
3. Meilaender, *Neither Beast nor God*, 86.
4. Meilaender. *Neither Beast nor God*, 99.
5. Erich Fromm, *Escape from Freedom* (1941; repr., New York: Avon Books, 1965).
6. Fromm contextualizes positive freedom, hence respect, stressing that it is era specific: European and American history since the end of the Middle Ages is the history of the full emergence of the individual. It is a process that started in Italy, in the Renaissance, and which

only now seems to have come to a climax. Fromm, *Escape from Freedom*, 52, see also 62 and 66–67.

7. Fromm, *Escape from Freedom*, 283–84, 286, 290.

8. Erich Fromm, *The Art of Loving*, ed. Ruth Nanda Anshen (New York: Harper, 1956).

9. In earlier work Charles Taylor refers to this subject matter, which I call respect, as "dignity." In his later work he seems to distinguish between human dignity and what I call respect, which he refers to as difference.

10. "Frameworks provide the background, explicit or implicit, for our moral judgments, intuitions, or reactions." Charles Taylor, *Sources of the Self: The Making of the Modern Identity* (Cambridge: Cambridge University Press, 1989), 26.

11. Taylor, *Sources of the Self*, 22.

12. Charles Taylor, *The Ethics of Authenticity* (Cambridge, MA: Harvard University Press, 1992), 47.

13. Taylor, *Sources of the Self*, 23.

14. Taylor, *Ethics of Authenticity*, 62.

15. Taylor, *Sources of the Self*, 23; emphasis in the original.

16. Taylor, *Ethics of Authenticity*, 49.

17. Taylor, *Ethics of Authenticity*, 47–48.

18. Taylor, *Ethics of Authenticity*, 66.

19. Taylor, *Ethics of Authenticity*, 74.

20. Taylor, *Ethics of Authenticity*, 75.

21. Taylor, *Ethics of Authenticity*, 65.

22. Charles Taylor, "The Politics of Recognition," in *Multiculturalism: Examining the Politics of Recognition*, ed. Amy Gutmann (Princeton, NJ: Princeton University Press, 1994), 38; emphasis in the original.

23. "Merely," of course, echoes Kant's categorical imperative. It is meant to distinguish between a transaction that is pure sexual objectification of a person, and interactions in which there is some such objectification mixed with other motives that do acknowledge the person's subjecthood.

24. I am grateful to Rivka Elisha, with whom I have been thinking and developing these thoughts.

25. This distinction, albeit not under this name, is, of course, familiar. Taylor, for one, aptly stated in 1994 that "one has to distinguish the fundamental liberties, those that should never be infringed and therefore ought to be unassailably entrenched, on the one hand, from privileges and immunities that are important, but that can be revoked or restricted for reasons of public policy—although one would need a strong reason to do this—on the other hand." Taylor, "Politics of Recognition," 59.

26. Franklin D. Roosevelt, "State of the Union Address (Four Freedoms)," January 6, 1941, 77th Congress (Washington, DC: GOP, 1941); transcript availablehttps://millercenter.org/the-presidency/presidential-speeches/january-6-1941-state-union-four-freedoms.

27. United Nations General Assembly, Third Session, Universal Declaration of Human Rights (UDHR), Resolution 217A, Paris, December 10, 1948,http://www.un.org/en/universal-declaration-human-rights/, Preamble; emphasis mine. All further quotation to the UDHR are found on this website.

28. Mary Ann Glendon, *A World Made New: Eleanor Roosevelt and the Universal Declaration of Human Rights* (New York: Random House, 2001), 42–43.

29. Johannes Morsink, *The Universal Declaration of Human Rights: Origins, Drafting, and Intent* (Philadelphia: University of Pennsylvania Press, 1999), 228.

30. Morsink, *Universal Declaration of Human Rights*, 212.

31. United Nations, UDHR, Article 29(1) combines "full" and "free" stating, "Everyone has duties to the community in which alone the free and full development of his personality is possible."

32. Morsink, *Universal Declaration of Human Rights*, 215.

Chapter Six

Escape from Dignity and Respect

In 1941, as the world was engaged in a destructive world war, the German Jewish psychoanalyst and social theorist Erich Fromm composed a penetrating critique of Western society. He titled it *Escape from Freedom*.

ESCAPE FROM FREEDOM

According to Fromm, the disintegration of Europe's feudal ancient regime afforded Europeans unprecedented "negative freedom": the freedom *from* overwhelmingly oppressive social organization and institutionalized religion. This liberating social process released Europeans from the traditional structural constraints in which their identities had been previously formed to fit their roles as lord, peasant, guild member, wife, priest, or outcast. Liberated from powerful external forces that molded every aspect of their selves, people could now choose to exercise "positive freedom" and become actively sovereign, self-determined, autonomous individuals. They could now practice the dynamic freedom of spontaneous self-determination and construct their own personalities and identities.

But, as Fromm had it, liberation from the tightly knit social structures was experienced by most as an unbearable loss.[1] People felt thrown into a vacuum of meaninglessness and hopelessness. They felt lonely and scared. Positive freedom was too demanding: they did not know who they were, what they wanted, or how to go about seeking the answers to these existential questions.[2] Most of them did not have the means or the know-how to pursue the process of self-discovery that is inseparable from self-creation.

In the grip of intolerable, anxiety-instilling emptiness, most people chose to flee the newly gained freedom. Yet it was impossible to go back and assimilate oneself into the cozy traditional world of the past; once dismounted, the Garden of Eden could not be reconstituted. Europeans felt pressed to seek new directions that would relieve the excruciating fear, loneliness, anxiety, and agony. One such major direction was Protestantism, which offered many Europeans new meaning. Simultaneously, it molded a new psychological pattern that facilitated the rise of a modern, capitalistic economy and society. However, in turn, a market economy further augments its members' negative freedom, enhancing the sense of loss and the fear of isolation and powerlessness. [3]

In the twentieth century, Fromm continued, many members of Western societies found refuge from their sense of alienation in modern totalitarian regimes, such as Fascism and Nazism. These were not the traditional communities, offering warm recognition and personal support; rather, they were modern, mass alternatives, processing persons into indistinct parts of gigantic social machines.

Similarly opting for conformism, other members of the liberated West found peace of mind in herdlike behavior within liberal democracies. "The principle social avenues of escape in our times are the submission to a leader as has happened in Fascist countries, and the compulsive conforming as it is prevalent in our own democracy." [4] People who chose this route succumbed to the relentless pursuit of accumulating material goods and information. They chose to keep forever busy by chasing achievements dictated by commercial corporations and mass media. They adopted a lifestyle in which they were perpetually measuring themselves against their neighbors, who, motivated by the same drives, similarly pursued the same achievements and adopted the selfsame lifestyle. All ended up entrapped in eternal competition for its own sake.

To reassure themselves that they were fulfilling their unique human potential, they found insignificant little ways of making themselves feel special. Yet, fearing the solitary existence in freedom, they deprived themselves of genuine, authentic positive freedom, of lively, spontaneous self-determination and development. This fearful self-denial is the cause of their automatons-like lives and a sense of death-in-life with which they are plagued. Therefore, Fromm asserts that Western man

> is dead emotionally and mentally. While he goes through the motions of living, his life runs through his hands like sand . . . he is on the verge of desperation. . . . But since, being an automaton, he cannot experience life in the sense of spontaneous activity he takes as surrogate any kind of excitement and thrill; the thrill of drinking, of sports, of vicariously living the excitements of fictitious persons on the screen. [5]

In conclusion, negative freedom becomes devoid of meaningful realization of positive freedom, that is, emancipation from traditional communities that is not facilitated by active self-development leads to authoritarian, destructive regimes, or to the conformist, soulless, unbounded pursuit of consumerism and of social recognition per se.

Fromm summarizes and warns:

> [Modern man] has become free from external bonds that would prevent him from doing and thinking as he sees fit. He would be free to act according to his own will, if he knew what he wanted, thought and felt. But he does not know. He conforms to anonymous authorities and adopts a self which is not his. The more he does this, the more powerless he feels, the more he is forced to conform. . . .
>
> The despair of the human automaton is fertile soil for the political purposes of Fascism. . . .
>
> Both helplessness and doubt paralyze life, and in order to live man tries to escape from freedom, negate freedom. He is driven to new bondage. This bondage is different from the primary bonds, from which, though dominated by authorities or the social group, he was not entirely separated. The escape does not restore his lost security, but only helps him to forget his self as a separate entity. He finds new and fragile security at the expense of sacrificing the integrity of his individual self. He chooses to lose his self since he cannot bear to be alone. Thus freedom—as freedom from—leads into new bonds.[6]

In the rest of this chapter, I suggest an analysis that is analogous to Fromm's, but instead of negative freedom, positive freedom, and oppression, my line of thought refers to human dignity, respect, and honor.

ESCAPE FROM FREEDOM AND FROM DIGNITY AND RESPECT

The world war during which Fromm's chillingly prophetic insights were written came and went. As a consequence, the United Nations was established, and the Universal Declaration of Human Rights (UDHR) declared human dignity to be the foundation of the desired world order. The United Nations was composed of fifty member states, and the document they signed was meant to guarantee universal freedom and rights, with the goal of preventing the horrors against humanity such as those committed by the Fascist and Nazi regimes.[7] Human dignity was proclaimed to be the universal standard and benchmark of a just world order; it was to be the yardstick for measuring our societies, cultures, and regimes. If we accept the distinction suggested in this book between dignity and respect, then it was the combination of both dignity and respect that was adopted as the new universal standard.

Looking at our modern history through the lens of human dignity yields a story of *escape from dignity and respect* that is in many ways analogous to Fromm's narrative with regard to our escape from freedom. Let me introduce this analogous narrative. The gradual dissipation of Europe's traditional *hon-*

or-based, feudal social organization slowly emancipated individuals from the oppressive method that categorized and evaluated them almost exclusively according to their mostly predetermined, traditional social roles. This disintegration of the Old World slowly cleared the way to a new form of evaluating human beings. The new evaluative standards descended from the long-standing Judeo-Christian theological notion of *glory*, that is, from innate human merit that came from being made in the image of God.

The doctrine of *imago Dei* prescribed that people be evaluated and treated as the bearers of godly form that is imbued with a divine spark. Over the last few centuries, the new evaluative standard gradually evolved in two directions: the acknowledgment of the innate worth of the core, generic human form as such, *human dignity*, and the complementary recognition and appreciation of the singular, individualistic worth of each specific human specimen, *respect*. Within the modern ethical system that combines the two, we all share identical human dignity while also enjoying incomparable respect based on what we have chosen and toiled to make of ourselves.

Collective and personal processes of adjustment to the new logic of human worth have been gradual and rough. Individuals and groups have found it difficult to abandon the comparative, competitive, dramatic logic of honor, and to find contentment in the value of our common denominator, human dignity. Individuals and societies similarly found it difficult to evaluate each person based on the realization of their self-determined, authentic self-development, that is, in terms of respect. Regression to an honor mentality has recurred repeatedly, taking many various forms. For example, the development of fierce capitalism and consumerism in wealthy countries went hand in hand with a growing honor-based mentality, in which persons are evaluated almost exclusively based on their comparative possessions and wealth—their relative materialistic success.

This revived honor mentality did not reinstitute people's traditional, role-based, feudal sense of unproblematic identity and worth. In return for affording some sense of meaning and value, the new, capitalistic honor mentality imposed great alienation, frustration, and emptiness. In the first half of the twentieth century, feeding on such widespread alienation, Fascist and Nazi European societies renounced human dignity and respect altogether, instead embracing a particularly rigid, ruthless, racist form of honor. Populist nationalism and racism afforded people honor-based value based on their affiliation and patriotism.

This aggressive, authoritarian escape from human dignity and respect proved far more destructive and deadly than any traditional social order, exacting incomprehensible cost. Clearly, such state-organized escape from human dignity and respect is significantly more murderous than the parallel escape in liberal democracies via individual conformism to materialistic honor codes. Nevertheless, even in 1941 Fromm's analysis warned against the prevalence of such conformist escape from dignity and respect. Using different terminology, he, nevertheless, stressed that conformism was precluding what I refer to as meaningful adherence to human dignity and respect, and undercutting the declared ideology and goals of liberal democracies and modern Western civilization at large.

Writing in 1941, Fromm ended his narration and analysis at that historical point. Almost eighty years later we may narrate how the escape from dignity to honor has continued, even as the world declared its allegiance to human dignity and rights.

Fascist and Nazi brutish revival of honor brought on unprecedented mass destruction beyond Fromm's—or anyone's—imagination. The consequent widespread horror in reference to this outcome brought representatives of the world nations who defeated Fascism and Nazism to collectively pledge collective allegiance to a universal moral order based on the firm acknowledgment of human dignity, recognition of respect, and enforcement of human rights. New constitutions, treaties, and policies were adopted, promoting these basic values and derivative standards, norms, and rights. Yet authoritarian states and movements claiming to be motivated by economic ideologies, national needs, ethnic entitlements, or religious commitments continued to enforce honor-based social orders and wreak destructive havoc on their own members, as well as on targeted *Others* and *enemies*. Concurrently, many people in liberal democracies continued to pursue conformity and seek worth through accumulation of material wealth. In fact, the rat race has merely escalated.

The second half of the twentieth century offers ample examples of authoritarian, totalitarian regimes that disregard human dignity and respect, openly and bluntly. Suffice it to mention the Union of Soviet Socialist Republics (the Bolshevik Soviet Union), the People's Republic of China, the Democratic People's Republic of Korea (North Korea), the military dictatorship of Chile, Islamic Republic of Iran, and the Islamic Republic of Afghanistan, among others. Such authoritarian regimes meant oppression, aggression, and massive destruction of lives, communities, cultures, and goods. In the name of honor and precedence—assigned to socioeconomic ideology, religion, nation, or leader—these authoritarian regimes denied and offended human dignity and respect in ways that are not essentially different from those of earlier Fascist regimes.

Simultaneously, liberal democracies pledged formal constitutional allegiance to human dignity, but often did not go very far beyond that point. Their commitment to dignity remained partial; their acknowledgment of respect was often minimal. The normative order was declared, but not fully realized. Individuals were frequently left to ensure their human dignity and create and develop their respect on their own. Feeling lonely and helpless in the face of this enormous task, many members of liberal democracies continued to escape to familiar materialistic honor-bound codes by conforming to ever-new fashions, lifestyles, standards, technologies, gadgets, and media.

To better substantiate the point with regard to materialistic conformity, let me integrate the argument made popular by the 2004 international best seller *Status Anxiety*.

ESCAPE FROM DIGNITY AND *STATUS ANXIETY*

Public intellectual Alain de Botton claims that, at the turn of the twenty-first century, our liberal democratic world is plagued by what he calls "status anxiety." His book of this title might be the most widely read and presumably endorsed honor-related analysis of contemporary human reality.[8] De Botton refrains from using the words "honor" or "shame," as well as from addressing the literature on honor-and-shame sociocultural structures. He rather focuses on "status," explaining that we crave it because it holds the promise of "dignity," "respect," and "love." In his account, it is our unnerving concern that we might not achieve sufficient status that instills the deep anxiety defining our existential condition.

Yet the status and anxiety that de Botton describes are indistinguishable from the honor-bound socialization and the fear of shame depicted by many anthropologists and presented in this book's chapter 2. His "dignity," "respect," and "love" are honor by many other names. In the terms suggested in the book you are currently reading, de Botton's argument is that the craving for honor—as well as the fear of not achieving enough of it—haunt, motivate, and overwhelm us today more than in any past generation.

Translated into honor-and-shame terminology, de Botton claims that we perceive honor as the single form of evaluation available to us; we crave it desperately because it is the only recognition that can secure us that which we most desire: a sense of worth affirmed by our social surroundings. He claims that in earlier, traditional, class-based societies, status was mostly predetermined by hereditary factors. In that world, few had status and enjoyed honor, while most did not. The many have-nots accepted their lot fatalistically; they were spared the torment of craving and envying status and honor, as well as the bitter disappointment and sense of failure at not achieving them.

But contemporary societies, structured on the US model and dream of equal opportunity, are meritocratic, liberal, and democratic. Status and honor are believed to be potentially available to us all; their achievement is, hence, dependent on will, effort, and potential. We are all presumed to be free to pursue and achieve honor—and are expected to fulfill that potential. And since status and honor are intertwined with materialistic manifestations, we are all expected to earn money, status, and honor; to keep up with the Joneses, and preferably to surpass them. If we do not, we are classified as losers; we prove ourselves lacking in potential, spirit, and will. This is why no one is spared status craving and envy; no one is spared feelings of self-judgment, disappointment, failure, and hence—constant anxiety.

Further still, we are now all expected to compare ourselves not merely to the Joneses, but to everyone else, hence to a gigantic group of potential competitors. Any traditional, class-based society socialized its aristocrat to compare himself and compete against the relatively small group of his peers; modern democratic meritocracy, denying hereditary class and status, encourages each of us to compare ourselves and compete against the open-ended category of *everybody*. To be considered successful, we must strive to earn as much as—or more than—the richest people in the world. According to de Botton, this traps us in a hopelessly futile competition, inevitably fostering anxiety—if not depression—in most (perhaps all) of us.

De Botton offers no support for his claim that craving for status dominates our contemporary lives more than it did our ancestors'. His pastoral account of lower-class statusless bliss in traditional societies overlooks the fact that competition for honor among peasants, servants, or working classes, while lacking the stylized, romantic elegance of aristocratic dueling, might well have been just as fierce. Recall the brutal combating, in the PBS television series *Downton Abbey*, over downstairs honors such the title "*first* footman." Laughable as it might have seemed to Lady Mary, it meant the world to the young men competing for precedence among their peers, as well as to their entire downstairs community.

Nevertheless, de Botton's basic argument, that our yearning for recognition pushes us to conform to prevailing materialistic social codes, clearly strikes a chord with large audiences around the world. The global popularity of de Botton's book seems to testify to the relevance of its argument. Significant numbers of members of more than thirty liberal democracies found the argument appealing enough to purchase the book and thus cast their vote in its favor.

In line with the "escape from dignity" account presented in the previous section, de Botton claims that, despite the UDHR's commendable intentions, many members of liberal democracies around the world do not derive their sense of worth from human dignity or respect. Instead, we are seduced by corporations and the media to view honor, earned and manifested materialistically, as the exclusive means of obtaining a sense of worth.

According to this line of thought, we are taught to believe that conforming to global materialistic codes and excelling by their lights is the way to achieve honor, and that in order to accomplish these goals we must earn money and spend it in certain ways. We are thus constantly comparing our materialistic achievements to everyone else's according to the prevailing codes. We are trapped in a hopeless, eternal competition, the rat race, which we cannot win or exit, and suffer great anxiety. What Fromm diagnosed, in 1941, as unbearable fear of individual loneliness, in 2004, de Botton calls status anxiety.

In this context, de Botton's argument suggests that escape from human dignity and respect to honor via conformism to materialistically defined standards was as prevalent in liberal democracies at the turn of the twenty-first century as it was when Fromm described it, more than half a century earlier.

What de Botton could not have foreseen in 2004 is the rapid expansion of new forms of status seeking, enabled and encouraged by the internet and social media. These types of status and the games played to win them are not necessarily based on materialism and competitive accumulation of wealth; they exist in virtual realities and adhere to the rules of these new spheres. In the twenty-first century, significant portions of the escape from dignity to honor is not materialistic, and happens in the virtual universe. When such pursuit of status/honor reaches beyond the virtual world into the physical social reality, it interacts with the contemporary manifestations of older, twentieth-century types of honor seeking: those that offer honor through extreme, populist versions of nationalism and fundamentalism, and through conformity to materialist competitiveness.

The following sections of this chapter introduce the new, twenty-first-century virtual avenues of honor seeking, as well as their interactions with contemporary manifestations of populist nationalism and fundamentalism.

THE UNIQUE TWENTY-FIRST-CENTURY ESCAPE: FROM DIGNITY TO NONMATERIALISTIC, VIRTUAL HONOR

This book was written in the second decade of the twenty-first century: a time in which right-wing populist parties and leaders are on the rise all over the world, religious fundamentalism is spreading rapidly, and mass virtual communication has become so popular that it may have reached the dimensions of an epidemic. At this point in time, some totalitarian, authoritarian regimes continue to oppress masses, to violate human dignity and to disregard personal respect, while honoring dictatorial rulers in familiar ways. North Korea and Eritrea are the most obvious example. In other parts of the world, fundamentalist religious regimes enforce ancient codes of conduct that deny human dignity and personal respect, and crush populations in the name of honoring God and his commandments. Daesh and Iran are obvious cases in point. More surprisingly, populist right-wing parties and leaders are gaining great support and power in continental European countries, in England and in the United States. At the same time, some escape from human dignity and respect to honor has taken on the mark of the time: it has become virtual. As such, it seems to have become *viral*.

The denial of dignity and respect in the name of personal or ideological honor, enforced by ruthless totalitarian regimes such as those ruling North Korea, Eritrea, and Iran, is no different, in substance, from parallel twentieth-century phenomena enforced by Fascist and Bolshevik regimes and leaders of military dictatorships. Offenses committed by such regimes against human dignity and respect are dreadful and appalling. Nevertheless, they are recurrent and familiar, and at this point in history their mechanisms of operation can be regarded as self-evident. The same can be said of additional authoritarian, right-wing regimes, such as Vladimir Putin's in Russia, that differ from the regimes mentioned above in scale, not in the preference of personal and ideological honor over universal human dignity and respect. Similarly, the rise of populist, extreme right-wing parties in European countries threatens human dignity and respect in obvious ways, promoting national honor and humiliating "Others."

This is why the remaining sections of this chapter focus on the novel and less familiar mechanisms of escape from dignity to honor: those that evolve in the new realms of virtual reality and leap from there into the real world, triggering new real-world avenues of departure from the commitment to human dignity and respect.

The twentieth century was the age of great ideologies, from Marxism through Socialism and capitalism to Fascism. It was also the age of rapid changes in lifestyle, starting with the telephone, radio, film, and television, and leading to the computer equipped with internet. Technological developments created mass media and communication appliances that changed the patterns of social interaction. Escape from dignity to honor occurred in this context, reflecting and refracting both the ideologies and the influence of mass media on lifestyles.

In the first half of the twentieth century, technology and mass media served Fascist, Nazi, and Bolshevik totalitarian regimes well, enabling them to spread their ideologies and dictates while efficiently monitoring the masses. In liberal democracies, telephone, radio, film, and television, the tools of mass media, were the vehicles of a conformist race for materialistically manifested personal honor. The second half of the twentieth century offered a variation on the same themes.

The first decades of the twenty-first century seem to be the era of internet and social media. Wikipedia, the voice of the time, currently defines social media as "computer-mediated tools that facilitate the creation and sharing of information, ideas, career interests and other forms of expression via virtual communities and networks."[9] In the present, more and more people spend more and more of their lives interacting with virtual communities and networks, rather than in person. When not on Facebook, Twitter, or YouTube they are in their many chat rooms and WhatsApp groups. The younger they are, the more capable and likely they are to be in several such virtual locations at one time. In fact, many report that they check messages even while attempting to sleep, not to mention while eating, working, studying, or driving. Despite economic disparities, this seems to be as true of China, Iran, and the Arab world as it is of liberal democracies. Given the overwhelming centrality of virtual existence, it seems almost inevitable that contemporary forms of escape from dignity and respect to honor should take on features of the virtual world.

Indeed, the virtual mode of human existence has enabled at least four important avenues for the pursuit of honor. Interestingly, they seem to mark the postmaterialistic era in the modern pursuit of honor. They do, however, interact with real-world avenues for the pursuit of honor through populist nationalism and fundamentalism. Let me delineate four new courses of honor that flourish in the era of virtual reality.

First, countless people all over the world conform to emerging social codes that control virtual existence in social media communities. They derive their sense of worth, in the form of honor, from their status within these virtual environments. This status and sense of worth are based on other members' quantified, ritualized, virtual responses (such as "likes," "shares," "follows," and "retweets"), and on adherence to the "popularity principle" that serves the commercial interests of conglomerates, and enforces the logic of zero-sum competition for precedence. Millions around the world participate in, or fall prey and succumb to "virtual shaming," used to determine the pecking order within any given virtual milieu. They call their fear of individual loneliness, their virtual status anxiety, FOMO: fear of missing out on virtual, honor-determining social interactions.

Second, some contemporary young Muslims who were raised in the liberal West experience rejection and denial of full subjecthood and recognition. In the virtual world of internet and social media they encounter innovative interpretations of the traditional Muslim notions of holy war, jihad, of martyrdom, and of an ideal, universal Muslim nation, neo-*umma*. In these platforms, jihad and martyrdom are fused together to justify suicidal warfare against what is portrayed as the West's humiliation of Islam and of Muslims. Young Muslims who buy into this narrative feel that by committing suicidal terror attacks they honor the neo-*umma*, as well as their own individual selves. By supposedly redeeming their honor as Muslims, they attempt to gain honor instead of the sense of worth that the dignity-and-respect-based societies refused them.

Third, faced with a jihadist opponent boasting of his own honor, significant portions of the population in Europe and the United States feel that if they are dragged into a fearful, ruthless honor game, Western countries must recall their own honor and charge an honor war. To survive and triumph in a vicious life-or-death honor battle, they feel that they need a "strong leader" who will not flinch and go "all out," uninhibited by "bleeding heart" concerns of dignity and respect, and human rights.

This was one of the factors that contributed to the remarkable popularity of Republican candidate Donald Trump in the US 2016 presidential campaign. Since Trump's election as president of the United States, his many supporters want to continue believing that he is, indeed, the honorable warrior that will save the free world. To sustain this belief, they denounce any information or criticism that might undercut their belief as "fake news." They seclude themselves in social and conventional media that supports their views and shelters them from any other point of view. The abundance of social and conventional media facilitates such self-imposed seclusion, even in the midst of the free world.

Virtual versions of jihad, martyrdom, and neo-*umma*, therefore, turn into real-world fundamentalism, and promote real-world populist nationalism that uses social media to reject opposition and criticism. Virtual jihad and martyrdom, real-world fundamentalism, and real-world populist nationalism shielded by social media all manifest escape from dignity and respect to honor.

Fourth, at the same time, young adults attending elite US universities have established what Bradley Campbell and Jason Manning call in their 2018 book *victimhood culture*.[10] This culture, which is greatly reliant on social networks, breeds social groups that define themselves in terms of their collective victimization. In each group, members compete for honor by claiming that they were victimized due to their group identity, or by announcing the complaints they filed or the expansive social media campaigns they launched against their victimizers. On a larger level, groups similarly compete among themselves for superior victimhood or for launching complaints and campaigns against their victimizers.

The following sections present these familiar phenomena as contemporary ways of escaping dignity and respect to honor. Unlike some of the subjects presented in previous chapters, these topics are very well researched and familiar to contemporary readers. Yet they are not typically framed as means of escape from dignity and respect to honor. My purpose is to show that professional scholarship analyzing each of them, even if it does not directly use the terminology of honor and dignity, portrays these phenomena as avenues of escape from dignity and embrace of underlying honor-based patterns. To sustain this claim, I bring some of the scholars' own voices and argumentation, weaving them into my storytelling.

HONOR VIA PARTICIPATION IN VIRTUAL
SOCIAL MEDIA AND VIRTUAL SHAMING

The virtual world, in particular social media, has opened up a new sphere for the pursuit of social connections. It was enthusiastically embraced by many around the world who, like most humans, seek sociality and connectedness. Yet what *type* of connectedness does this sphere encourage and construct? Which underlying pattern of sociality does social media endorse, how does it do so, and why? In terms of the underlying patterns of sociality presented in this book: Does the world of social media favor virtual social structures and interactions based on honor, glory, dignity, or respect? How does it manifest its preference, and what motivates it?

I suggest that the world of virtual social media constructs an honor-bound universe. This is driven by powerful commercial interests and is executed by the technology of algorithms, which is both sophisticated and well hidden. By joining social media, submitting to it, and developing dependence, reliance, and even addiction to it, one endorses an honor-based social sphere that does not necessarily cherish or enhance human dignity and respect. For young people it is the primary social arena, one that socializes and indoctrinates them into honor.

José van Dijck's groundbreaking 2013 monograph *The Culture of Connectivity: A Critical History of Social Media* is a stimulating analysis of virtual media. Van Dijck exposes the techniques used by the conglomerates that control the "culture of connectivity" to manipulate and indoctrinate us to conform to structures that serve their profit interests. Her challenge is "to make the hidden layer visible and show how software is increasingly quantifying and measuring our social and everyday lives."[11]

Relying on Van Dijck's critical analysis, I suggest that the technologically designed, profit-oriented virtual culture of connectivity that rules our lives, structures the new sphere of human relations as an intense honor game. This new, virtual, algorithm-structured, gain-bound culture is more cynical and ruthless, and less friendly to human dignity and respect than many traditional honor games ever were. Submission to the seduction of this culture of connectivity is escape from human dignity and respect into an extreme version of honor mentality.

Although she does not much use the terminology of honor, Van Dijck's analysis exposes social media as a platform that indoctrinates its users into honor culture. In the following discussion, I bring you excerpts of her own voice to substantiate this claim.[12]

Van Dijck notes that it is people's overwhelming desire for connectedness and sociality that drove over a billion individuals worldwide, within the short period of a decade, to join virtual social media and make this sphere an indispensable part of their social lives. In the first phase of this development (years 2000–2005), it seemed that the virtual social world was a sphere espousing individual personal growth and respect. But fairly quickly this democratic, individualistic, respect-friendly haven was taken over by corporations imposing their interests, profit-seeking ideologies, and utilitarian, competitive frames of mind. [13]

Wikipedia, the noncommercial endeavor, once testifying to the spirit of the virtual world, has become the last significant exception that testifies to the rule. As for the rest of the virtual world of connective media, Van Dijck declares that it is no longer social media at all, but rather media structured by automated technologies to manipulate users' needs to increase commercial profit. [14]

The corporations that own the virtual platforms of connectivity profit, above all else, from data collected from their clients. The more users, the greater the data and hence the profit. Users are not valuable to these corporations due to their innate universal merit (their divine glory or human dignity), nor due to their unique individual characteristics (those that may constitute respect). Users' virtual contributions are not valuable for the merit of their contents. Users and their contributions are valuable as extras that constitute masses, as items in a collection that derives its value from size. [15]

Nevertheless, not all users are similarly valuable; some are more valuable than others. This distinction in value derives from a user's connectivity with masses of other users. A user's value depends on its "popularity": the more users it is connected with, the more valuable it becomes. Van Dijck claims that unlike sociality and connectedness, connectivity

> is a quantifiable value, also known as the *popularity principle: the more con-*
> *tacts you have and make, the more valuable you become, because more people*
> *think you are popular and hence want to connect with you.* . . . People who
> have many friends or followers are touted as influential, and their social au-
> thority or reputation increases as they receive more clicks. Ideas that are
> "liked" by many people have the potential of becoming trends. Friending,
> following, and trending are not the same functions, but they derive from the
> same popularity principle underpinning the online economy of social media. [16]

> In fact, it has become a common marketing strategy to search for people with a
> large network of connected followers and friends, "influencers," to spread
> "recommendation" and so promote products online. [17]

The logic of popularity seeking does not remain within the confines of the virtual world; it is mirrored and enhanced by real-world dynamics: "Techno-logical pressure from multiple platforms to select the most popular and most connected person or idea, is, in turn, reinforced by peer pressure in real life. Peer pressure has become a hybrid social and technological force; connections between people inform automated connections and vice versa."[18] This dynamic produces a world that manifests every element of an honor culture:

> Connectivity derives from a continuous pressure—both from peers and from technologies—to expand through *competition* and gain power through *strategic alliances*. Platform tactics such as the popularity principle and ranking mechanisms hardly involve contingent technological structures; instead, they are firmly rooted in an *ideology that values hierarchy, competition, and a winner-takes-all mind-set.*[19]

What is true of each of the corporate connectivity giants is true of them as a powerful hegemonic group:

> Most platforms are compatible because they are staked in the same values or principles: popularity, hierarchical ranking, neutrality, quick growth, large traffic volumes, and fast turnovers. Moreover, social activities are inextricably bound up with economic pursuits in a culture of automated "personal" recommendations.[20]

To sum up: Billions of people worldwide join social media seeking connectedness. The platforms facilitating this virtual sociability (Facebook, Twitter, Google, Amazon, and Apple) have a commercial interest in increasing their users' connectivity; intense connectivity, coded "popularity," is profitable for the corporations. So they employ technology to construct the types of "popularity" that serve their purposes, and induce users to pursue these profitable types of "popularity." Users partaking in this are often unaware of the manipulation; they are enticed to achieve commercially promoted "popularity," believing they are advancing their own status and prestige "spontaneously."[21]

Much like in the brave new worlds described by Aldous Huxley and George Orwell almost a century ago, the manipulation of language is a crucial part of this enterprise. Think of the new meanings that commercial platforms such as Facebook have assigned everyday words such as "sharing," "friends," and "like."

> In less than eight years, the meaning of "sharing," once understood as user-to-user information exchange, has subtly been replaced by a meaning that naturalizes the sharing of personal data with anyone on the planet. Among teenagers, the idea of "friending" as building the largest possible network of contacts—*a social badge of honor informed by the popularity principle*—has been steadily on the rise. The concept of "liking" pushes popular ideas or things with a high degree of emotional value, arguably at the expense of rational judgments for which there are no buttons in the online universe; "difficult but important" is not a judgment prompted by social media sites. Sharing, friending, and liking are powerful ideological concepts whose impact reaches be-

yond Facebook proper into all corners of culture, affecting the very fabric of sociality.[22]

Facebook is, of course, not alone: Twitter uses "following" and "trending" much like Facebook uses "liking" and "friending."[23] Striving to gain "popularity" through "sharing," "friending," "liking," "following," and "trending," billions of users around the world engage in connectivity that is profitable for Facebook and Twitter. Simultaneously, experiencing "popularity" as personal status, prestige, precedence, these users of social media engage in a virtual honor game that is very real for their emotional lives and self-perceptions. Their pursuit of this honor-type social value involves zero-sum competition, hierarchical thinking (the "popularity principle" ranks "influencers" above all others), the upholding of group norms (encoded by the commercial platforms), and the formation of strategic alliances, the exposure of competitors, shaming, and many other features of any honor game. All this often comes at the expense of privacy, authenticity, and other features of the universe of dignity and respect.

Social media shaming has caused great angst, especially to parents who witness their children being taunted, insulted, verbally abused in public, and driven to despair—and even to suicide. Many around the world believe that shaming is a new phenomenon that emerged in the wake of connective media. But as chapter 2 explains, shaming is an innate part of an honor-based system. In a hierarchical, zero-sum honor world, the social rise of one member requires the demise of others. To gain status, prestige, honor, a member can excel in upholding the group's code of honor. But instead of displaying courage, generosity, or loyalty, he may choose a shortcut, and gain honor by taking it away from a peer. Shaming a peer is a fast and easy means of accumulating honor. It allows the shaming party to invite other group members to join and ascend with them, thus making the shamer a leader.

In the world of connective media, which seduces members to gain popularity at all costs (to better serve the platform's economic agenda), shaming is not a deviation: it is an inherent aspect of social interaction. It is not a feature that can be corrected; it is built into the underlying pattern of honor. It manifests the logic of honor and trains members of social media to play the game of honor. Yet social media shaming is likely to be more ruthless and cruel than the shaming that is practiced in traditional honor societies. As described in chapter 2, in a traditional, tightly knit honor society, shaming must follow strict rules, such as "Pick on people your own size," or "Nothing below the belt." Group members who violate such rules risk losing face. In contrast, Facebook users are not a tightly knit group; they have not been raised on a real society's code of honor, and Facebook has no vested interest in training them to *play fair*. Their shaming is unconstrained.

Furthermore, in traditional honor societies, shaming serves social purposes. For example, a woman, a servant, or an old man may shame a young man into performing an honorable duty that he is reluctant to take on.[24] In *Bloodtaking and Peacemaking*, William Ian Miller claims that in allowing the weaker members of society to shame a young man into performing his honorable task, an honor society is inclusive in its distribution of power and roles, allowing the weaker members to feel meaningful and useful. This, he claims, enhances social cohesiveness and effectiveness.[25] In contrast, social media shaming serves no social role. It is ruthless, poisonous, damaging, and yet people accept it, realizing that it is inseparable from the game, and fearing the alternative even more. The alternative is leaving the game altogether. And members of honor societies are group players; solitary life outside the group is inconceivable for them.

For members of traditional honor societies, the only thing worse than losing some honor is losing the right to participate in the game. Exclusion is a fate worse than death. Like many other researchers, Van Dijck finds that in this respect as well, users of social media are no different:

> For many of the plugged-in, opting out is not an option: it would mean opting out of sociality altogether, since online activities are completely intertwined with offline social life. . . .
> Connective media have almost become synonymous with sociality: you can check out any time you "like," but you can never leave.[26]

Connective media does not, usually, send its users to commit suicide attacks. It does, however, induce a new type of status anxiety: FOMO—fear of missing out; fear of losing their standing in their numerous virtual connectivity networks. This anxiety, young people narrate, keeps them hooked up to multiple virtual groups at all times, including in their sleep. It interferes with focusing, with their capability to choose freely, with their ability to create intimacy, with their capacity to simply be; in short, with any human activity that might give rise to respect.

Manipulating us to abide by transparent algorithm-fabricated honor norms that serve commercial platforms' profit interests, connective media does not treat us as human subjects, as ends in their own rights. We are all merely means—objects in the service of corporations. "Liking," "friending," and "sharing," thus, undermine the sanctity of human dignity.

Escaping dignity and abandoning respect, some find satisfaction in virtual honor rewards as well as in the virtual rat race itself. Others, not content with connective media virtual gratification, experience alienation, loneliness, anxiety. Sometimes their flight from dignity leads them to seek more visceral, "old-fashioned" honor, in the form of "Trumpism" or even jihad.

SEEKING HONOR THROUGH VIRTUAL VERSIONS OF
MUSLIM JIHAD AND MARTYRDOM

The shelves of libraries devoted to books on contemporary Islam and Muslims—particularly outside the Muslim world—are stacked these days. It is probably impossible to coherently integrate the abundant distinct analyses and interpretations put forth by various experts. I have, therefore, chosen one such analysis, which explicitly addresses the topic of virtual honor gained through contemporary jihad and seems to do so quite plausibly. Iranian sociologist Farhad Khosrokhavar has studied contemporary Muslim cultures and communities for several decades, publishing, in France and the United States, on modern jihad and the phenomenon that he calls radicalization. In his 2002 book *Suicide Bombers: Allah's New Martyrs*, he offers a comprehensive overview. Although he focuses on "al-Qaeda-style transnational terrorists," I believe that the parts of his analysis that concern my discussion here are just as relevant to Daesh-style terror.[27]

In the conceptual framework proposed by the first sections of this chapter, Khosrokhavar's argument is that "al-Qaeda-style transnational terrorists" aspire to be full citizens of our post–World War II era of dignity and respect. Raised in the hope of having their dignity and respect acknowledged and cherished, they feel disillusioned, let down, and deprived when realizing that full individuation, development, and self-manifestation are not accessible to them. This personal, modern-day frustration metamorphoses into feelings of collective Muslim victimhood and humiliation. Rather than focusing on the feeling that they are being denied personal dignity and respect, these modern, dignity-and-respect-oriented individuals now feel that they were robbed of their honor as Muslims. Once the pain is perceived in these terms of collective humiliation, it seems to them only natural to avenge it in a manner that they believe to be "authentically Muslim" and honorable: martyrdom packaged by radical, contemporary Muslim theoreticians as heroic holy war.[28]

Sacrificing themselves in what they perceive as Muslim holy war, "al-Qaeda-style transnational terrorists" feel that they gain honor for Islam.[29] Achieving honor through jihadist martyrdom, they finally feel that they come in contact with their fundamental, autonomous humanity, realizing the potential of their unique individuality and manifesting it. Giving their lives in jihad for collective Muslim honor, they finally experience the dignity and respect they felt they had been denied: "Dying a holy death allows them to accede to dignity through sacrifice, whereas everyday life is dominated by insignificance and lack of dignity. It gives meaning and dignity to those who have been dispossessed of them."[30]

Khosrokhavar repeatedly stresses that "in most cases, religion is no more than a pretext."[31] Islam merely offers the context and language through which these people express their frustration with the modern world that has failed them, denying them the human dignity and respect they were promised:

> Martyrdom gives individuals who are modern but cannot assert themselves in the way they would like, a formidable ability to assert themselves in death. In the absence of any real individuality or political, economic and cultural autonomy, martyrdom has a remarkable ability to facilitate individualism in death. . . . [A]n irrepressible desire for modernity is combined with what is experienced as an absolute impossibility, and this inverts the vector of life into a vector of death. [32]

At the beginning of the chapter I presented some Europeans' frustration at what they experienced as failure to achieve a real sense of dignity and respect in a world that seemed to value and promise it. Following Fromm's analysis, I suggested that this led them to turn their backs on the culture of dignity and respect and instead to pursue a sense of collective honor through Fascism and Nazism. According to Khosrokhavar's analysis, a century later, some Muslims respond in an analogous manner to an analogous predicament. The outcomes, al-Qaeda-and-Daesh-style terror, differ in many ways from Nazi and Fascist brutality, yet the two are analogous in their complete denial of human dignity and respect, and consequently, in their ruthless, inhuman ferociousness. In both cases, the very personal crisis and frustration of individuals who felt betrayed by the unfulfilled promise of dignity and respect were channeled to strengthen authoritarian groups, highly destructive for *outsiders* as well as *insiders*.

One major difference between the "al-Qaeda-and-Daesh-style transnational terrorists" and their twentieth-century predecessors is the central role that virtual reality plays in the former's escape from dignity and respect to honor. It is in the virtual sphere that these young, modern Muslims encounter the newly designed ideal of a universal Muslim *umma* (nation), as well as the claim that the West despises and humiliates both the sacred *umma* and them. It is the virtual world, therefore, that gives them the ideal for which they can fight and sacrifice themselves, as well as the honor-based motivation to do so. [33]

An "al-Qaeda-style transnational terrorist" craves dignity and respect, and fails to feel their achievement. Living in Paris or Brussels, he does not feel the real-world oppression that a Palestinian in the West Bank does. But his life in the virtual world of media and social media invites and enables him to construct himself as a Muslim who is, in his own mind, oppressed and humiliated as such. Virtuality offers him experiences and sensations that are shaped for him and by him as "oppression and humiliation of Muslims." In his virtual life he feels much like the Palestinian does in his real-life existence. In this virtual reality, "the West" is presented as a prosperous, arrogant, global, anti-Muslim entity that is inaccessible to Muslims, inherently scorning, threatening, and crushing Muslim ideals, ways of life and honor. "The West" is virtually fashioned as the Muslim's archenemy. It is constructed in the virtual world much as, according to Khosrokhavar, Israel is described by oppressed Palestinians in the occupied territories: unattainably prosperous and strong, and inherently oppressive and humiliating.

The virtually instilled real-world feeling of humiliation-as-a-Muslim induces the "al-Qaeda-style transnational terrorist" to adopt a virtual vision: that of the global Muslim *umma*, that stands for everything that is Muslim, pure, and good, and will eventually conquer the world.[34] To promote this utopian, virtual ideal, nurtured by contemporary Islamists and portrayed as "authentic Islam," the "al-Qaeda-style transnational terrorist" chooses what he considers jihad martyrdom. This very real choice and its real-world realization afford a sense of collective and personal honor, and perhaps also a perverse feeling of dignity and respect. The "al-Qaeda-style transnational terrorist" feels that he gains collective Muslim honor by hurting the diabolical enemy, the West. He feels he gains personal honor by rising above other Muslims who cower before the West. If he is brought up to seek dignity and respect, he may feel that the choice of jihadist martyrdom and its realization expresses his human autonomy and personal qualifications, thus manifesting his dignity and respect. Here is one of Khosrokhavar's many articulations of this process:

> Those [such as al-Qaeda-style terrorists] who live in the despair of others "in virtual reality" experience a loss of self. They take on the role of the righter of wrongs . . . to extend the meaning of their struggle to the whole world. We are seeing a "globalization" of holy death, and its anthropological and sociological content is different to that of martyrs whose goal of self-realization within a nation that cannot come into being. In this precise case, death establishes a new articulation between self and community. Most of those who choose this type of martyrdom are suffering from an identity crisis. They are young men who are stigmatized in European countries (such as France and England), converts who are seeking a part to play, and immigrants whose life in the West has convinced them of its proud immorality.[35]

Virtuality does not generate the frustration that leads some young Muslims to escape from dignity and respect to collective honor; but virtuality does foster and shape the escape, framing the context of terror. It is through their virtual participation in media and particularly in social media that potential terrorists feel humiliated as Muslims and that they tap into the shared vision of a universal Muslim utopia. The constructed "humiliation of Islam by the West" thrives, according to Khosrokhavar, in the virtual world, as does the global neo-*umma*, that is humiliated by the West and calls for honorable redemption through jihadist martyrdom. It is, therefore, in virtual reality that potential terrorists find both Muslim humiliation and its therapeutic anti-dot in the shape of jihad martyrdom as a means to cleanse the neo-*umma*'s stained honor. These virtual interventions trigger potential terrorism and unleash real-world destruction.

As noted above, adopting the posture of honor and feud triggers a similar response in the would-be opponent. The awakening of Muslim honor presses some Europeans and US citizens to put on their own honor caps. Hence phenomena such as Trumpism, discussed in the next section.

HONOR SEEKING IN THE FORM OF "TRUMPISM": REVIVING THE "CHRISTIAN KNIGHT"

The tremendous popular appeal of Donald Trump, the colorful businessman aspiring to lead the United States and the world, has caused both national and international interest, as well as shock and scandal. This section reviews the phenomenon in the context framed here, of escape from dignity and revival of honor.

In 2006, conservative journalist James Bowman published the riveting monograph *Honor: A History*.[36] In this captivating, well-researched, and well-argued book, Bowman does not merely document the history of a value-laden concept; he takes a strong, unequivocal stand, calling on Western civilization at large, and the United States in particular, to revive its abandoned honor culture and employ it to challenge the Muslim honor culture.

Through careful cultural analysis of historical events and literary texts, Bowman traces the sources, makeup, and evolution of what he perceives as the glorious honor culture of Western civilization. He compares it with alternative, "primitive," Eastern honor cultures, defining and illustrating its superiority. He points to Christianity as a major source of the uniqueness and supremacy of Western honor culture:

> The Christian knight, like so many other features of the religion he professed, was something of a paradox, but he proved to be immensely influential right down to the Renaissance and beyond. Along with the Greek and rationalist tradition in Western civilization, he was an important part of the reason why Western ideas of honor developed along quite different lines from honor in other parts of the world and ultimately diverged so widely from the nearly primitive or wild honor such as still found in Muslim and other societies outside the Christian tradition as well as in the gang culture of the streets. Where honor was local, Christianity was universal; where honor was elitist, Christianity was catholic and inclusive; where honor was warlike, Christianity was pacifist; where honor treated women only as property, Christianity treated them as human beings, if not yet as the equal of men. Though the two traditions continued to exist side by side for centuries, rarely (we should say, perhaps, too rarely) interfering with each other, honor could hardly fail to be influenced by the existence of Christianity in such close proximity.[37]

In Bowman's historical narration, the acidic, uninhibited liberal criticism of the American Civil War, the two world wars, and finally the American humiliation in Vietnam all caused the downfall of cultural honor in Western civilization. Simultaneously, honor was systematically replaced by what he considers to be the despicable reverence for "authenticity" per se and the "self-esteem" that people were now entitled to feel for their unheroic, mundane authenticity.[38] Bowman notes that, unlike honor, self-esteem—which this book calls respect—is egalitarian. It is, therefore, the death of honor: "Self-esteem, parceled out equally to all, is a sort of anti-honor, not only because it leaves out the most essential of honor's components but also because it makes shame impossible."[39] Instead of aiming to be men of Western honor, contemporary Westerners merely aspire to be authentic; their role models are no longer heroes, but "celebrities," people revered for their pronounced, subjective authenticity, rather than honorable distinction.[40]

Of the many sociocultural factors that conspired to crush the culture of honor in the West, Bowman highlights the devastating impact of three: "modern warfare, psychotherapy and feminism, all of which were individually influential at the time, but which also reinforced each other in one particular way—by undermining the corporate (as opposed to individual) and elitist assumptions on which traditional honor was based."[41]

In Bowman's narration, feminism, eroding the prestige of true manhood; therapy, replacing self-restraint with talkative, unmanly self-exposure; pacifistic aversion to conflict and violence; and veneration of authenticity for its own sake are responsible for the contemporary sociocultural climate of "anti-honor." This is dangerous—perhaps suicidal—because America is fiercely threatened by two ruthless antagonists: the exterior opponent, in the shape of primitive Muslim honor culture, and the interior threat, in the shape of primitive "minority" honor culture (that is, gangster culture of African Americans and Hispanic Americans): "The new and anti-honor official culture is thus caught between two primitive honor cultures, one Islamic and military and the other native or immigrant and criminal, which challenge its hegemony in ways that may require it to do something more than denounce them as unenlightened."[42]

To confront these two honor threats, America, as he calls the United States, must reclaim its own, superior honor culture and allow it to prevail. To revive America's honor culture and make America great again, Americans must "defeat our hatred and fear of war," make inequalities "socially acceptable again," break free from their "celebrity culture," which encourages the sickly egalitarian self-esteem, and, of course, undo feminism: "revamp and revitalize our political, social and intellectual assumptions about the differences between the sexes, in particular making the traditional role of women as wives, mothers and nurturers not only respectable again but the most honorable of female aspirations."[43]

Bowman concludes in no uncertain terms:

> The honor-crazed Muslim fanatics who are blowing up women and children along with themselves are, if not exactly cavemen, equally stark in the alternative they pose to Western ways. And unless those ways include, and are understood by all to include, honorable ways of making war on that alternative, the alternative must triumph. The same may be said of the primitive honor of the urban gang culture, in which women are reduced to "bitches" and "ho's."[44]

According to Bowman, Muslim, African American, and Hispanic primitive honor must be fought and conquered by supreme, Western honor at large, and American honor specifically. In his mind, the revival of this forsaken, abandoned honor culture must be accompanied by curtailing what he views as the rampant, castrating feminism; the whining culture of psychoanalysis; and the prevalent unmanly recoil from violence and conflict. This revival of Western honor must go hand in hand with the defeat of the respect-based culture, with its tolerance and appreciation of the egalitarian cultural mood of plurality, diversity, and multiculturalism.

Less than a decade after Bowman voiced and elaborated this stand so clearly, many millions of US citizens intuitively manifested it by supporting Donald Trump as the strong man they would want to lead them and the entire world. Although they did not use this precise terminology, it would seem that Barack Obama's reign was experienced by many of them as committed, above all else, to minimalistic, hard-core human dignity. This minimalism brought some citizens of the United States, particularly young left-wing liberals, to yearn for more active commitment to personal respect. This sentiment was expressed through support of the socialist Democratic candidate Bernard Sanders. But for many other US citizens, particularly right-wing conservatives, the dignity-bound Obama era may have been experienced as alienating and anxiety inducing; this inspired them to escape the dignity culture represented by Obama's legacy and seek honor in the shape of a strong leader that would "Make America Great Again," Donald Trump.

For those baffled by the inconsistency of deeply Christian Trump supporters, let me repeat Bowman's unashamed statement, quoted earlier, that "the Christian knight . . . was something of a paradox," yet constituted the essence of the superior Western honor culture. This paradoxical mythological figure seems to fuse—for Bowman, as indeed for many—glory-bound Christianity with a manly, militant honor culture. The "Christian knight" is a real man of honor in the service of the Christian Church, thus refining honor to encompass Christian spiritualism while *toughening* Christianity with the spirit of honor. He is not a meek, pious Christian *sucker*, nor a bloodthirsty, brutish, member of a primitive (read: Muslim, African American, Hispanic) honor culture, but a complex combination of the spirit of Christianity and the best of honor. This paradoxical fusion is, for Bowman, the quintessence of Western honor culture and the source of its superiority. It is the bedrock of Western power and strength. It is precisely this paradoxical fusion, together with the superior Western honor culture, that some right-wing US citizens yearn for in Donald Trump.

VICTIMHOOD CULTURE

In the very prologue to their well-researched and very timely 2018 book *The Rise of Victimhood Culture: Microaggressions, Safe Spaces, and the New Culture Wars*, sociologists Bradley Campbell and Jason Manning list a long line of cases in which, in 2016, after the election of Donald Trump for presidency, university students were so eager to present themselves as victims, that they staged their own victimization: Muslim students at the University of Michigan, at Lafayette University, and in New York City reported hate attacks that never happened; so did a bisexual student at Chicago's North Park University, an Afro-American student at Bowling Green State University, and Hispanic students at Elon University. [45]

The analysis of these and other such incidents leads Campbell and Manning to claim that such students were trying to heighten awareness of what they understood to be a rising cultural victimization of their respective minority groups. Campbell and Manning show that in 2016, some social media circles created such an overwhelming sense of threat to Hispanics, African Americans, Muslims, women, Jews, gays, and transgender persons that many expressed deep anxiety and a sense of emergency. [46] Some went further, and tried to call attention to this threat by producing false proof of its dangers. This is why they staged their own attacks and complained of victimization.

Additionally, Campbell and Manning conclude that the students who staged their own victimization did so believing that they stood to gain something by it. They state that "victimhood is in fact a social resource—a form of status. Manufacturing a case of victimhood allows the aggrieved to elicit sympathy or even to mobilize third parties such as legal authorities against their enemies." [47] Campbell and Manning, therefore, suggest that victimization is, in these circles, a status symbol—a badge of honor.

This brings to mind Khosrokhavar's analysis, presented above. Khosrokhavar claims that some young Muslims in Western societies suffer from identity crises. These young people, raised in the West, seek personal dignity and respect, yet feel barred from achieving them. They feel dismissed, and experience disappointment. In the virtual realities of social media they come to view themselves as Islamic victims of humiliation, and avenge themselves on the West through ultimate, deadly self-victimization.

I suggest that this analysis of "al-Qaeda-style transnational terrorists" may elucidate the phenomenon of young Muslim students who stage their own victimization by would-be Trump supporters—as well as the parallel and complementary phenomenon of young Hispanic, African American, and LGBTQ students who do the same.

Like the "al-Qaeda-style transnational terrorists," some students of Muslim, Hispanic, and African American heritage, as well as LGBTQ students, experience identity crises. The tension between their cultures of origin and those of their universities may undermine their integral sense of self. Their perception that Trump and his supporters represent dangerous, condescending hostility toward their communities of origin likely aggravates their identity crises. This might induce disappointment, alienation, and anxiety; they might fear that their hopes for dignity and respect in the university world are doomed to be frustrated.

Experiencing these difficult, lonely feelings, they may well plunge into the comforting world of collective honor. Within this sphere they may construct their self-perception as members of groups that are humiliated by their fierce, hegemonic enemies. They may choose a course of self-sacrifice that serves as a means to regain collective honor, as well as to elevate their own honor within their communities. They may take on the role of alerting their groups to the humiliation, as well as that of fighting for collective honor by complaining to authorities and rallying group members to take action. Demonstrating loyalty, courage, and self-sacrifice, they may feel redeemed and honored.

Khosrokhavar's "al-Qaeda-style transnational terrorists" take action, violently attacking members of the enemy group, even at the cost of sacrificing their own lives. It is easy to see how this can be an esteemed choice within a world based on militant honor. Yet, different as it may seem, the self-victimizing students may also be playing the honor game. In an honor culture, not everyone is a young man who can challenge his opponents to a duel, start a blood feud, or execute a suicide attack on his enemies. In fact, most group members are not expected or allowed to inflict violence on their offenders. Women, members of low classes, children, and old men are barred from actively avenging their stained honor. They are expected to mobilize their victimization, calling on other group members to rally and do the avenging on their behalf. This is how they are encouraged to gain honor (see reference below to two such courses of action).

Perhaps it is no coincidence that many of the events of self-victimization that Campbell and Manning survey were staged by young women, whereas most "al-Qaeda-style transnational terrorists" are young men. But, of course, men too can play the "feminine" honor role, just as women can play the "manly" one. Students of any gender who stage their own victimization to call attention to group humiliation and to generate a group response take on the role that traditional militant honor societies label "feminine."

Yet they do not do so because they are "sissies," "soft," or "effeminate." What traditional militant honor cultures consider "feminine" timidity is what contemporary mainstream culture considers normative, sane conduct. Blowing oneself up to take the lives of members of Western societies is considered criminal and perhaps insane. Filing complaints and generating social media interest is what law-abiding citizens do, even if sometimes they have to fabricate a few facts in the process. Elite university students are likely to be relatively well adjusted, normatively socialized individuals. It stands to reason that they would choose an honor-bound course of action that is well within their normative mode of conduct. This does not impugn the honor-bound meaning of such actions.

I should stress that my suggestion that some students' mode of action is in line with honor culture by no means degrades them, certainly not on the basis of their ethnic, racial, or religious background; sexual identity; or conduct. It suggests that in times of identity crises and anxiety, some of us find comfort in social patterns that are honor based. In difficult times, the emotions inspired by an honor culture can be more comforting than those inspired by dignity and respect; likewise with regard to people's flocking to social media. Further, honor-based patterns of conduct are in no way unique to members of minority groups. Many members of elite academic cultures participate in fierce and sometimes ruthless honor games and competitions among researchers and professors that are as militant as the extreme manifestations of victimhood culture.

Staged self-victimization is, of course, anecdotal, and not the essence of victimhood culture. Campbell and Manning claim that the essence of this culture is the heightened sensitivity and intolerance to any slight or offense; this, as they acknowledge, is a familiar characteristic of any typical honor culture.[48] This feature is best exemplified in students' embrace of the new term "microaggression." Campbell and Manning point to counseling psychologist and diversity training specialist Derald Wing Sue as the person most responsible for the success of the microaggression program, and quote his definition of the term:

> The brief and commonplace daily verbal, behavioral, and environmental indignities, whether intentional or unintentional, that communicate hostile, derogatory or negative racial, gender, and sexual orientation, and religious slights and insults to the target person or group.[49]

Examples of microaggressions include saying to an African American, "You are a credit to your race" or "You are articulate"; clutching your purse when an African American enters an elevator with you; complimenting an Asian American that she speaks English well; staring at lesbians holding hands; saying, "All lives matter" instead of "Black lives matter"; approaching a mixed group of men and women with "you guys"; complimenting a woman on the shoes she is wearing; changing "Indigenous" into "indigenous" in a student's paper.[50]

Campbell and Manning offer a definition of the ways of handling conflict in the microaggression-bound campus atmosphere that they call victimhood culture:

> First of all, they involve the public airing of grievances—complaining to outsiders. In this way microaggression complaints belong to a larger class of conflict tactics in which people who have grievances appeal to third parties. Second, microaggression complaints are attempts to demonstrate a pattern of injustice, and in this way they belong to a class of tactics by which people persuade reluctant third parties that their cause is just and they badly need help. And third, microaggression complaints are complaints about the domination and oppression of cultural minorities.[51]

The first two elements in Campbell and Manning's definition, the ways of handling conflict within victimhood culture, are customary courses of action open to the weaker members of traditional honor societies.

Campbell and Manning define the first element as "complaining to outsiders," but in fact, their detailed account reveals that students do not take their complaints to outsiders, such as the police, but to the authorities of their own universities. In traditional honor societies, "complaining to authorities" about humiliating slights and offenses meant that women, children, old men, and people of lower class complained to the patriarch of their clan or household, or to one of his representatives, such as a son. This type of complaining was a way of demanding that the clan or household authorities take action that the woman, child, or other lower-class member was not allowed or able to take. In the world of honor, this was also a type of shaming, meant to urge the authorities to do the honorable thing and redeem the group's stained honor. Consider Miller's explication of this type of conflict management in the traditional honor culture of medieval Iceland:

> Not having had an especially active juridical existence of her own, [a woman in saga Iceland] depended on her men for her status, her property, and safety. She had to act through them and she wanted them tough-minded, honorable, and punctiliously mindful of their rights and reputations. Women were not the only people who played this role. Old men goaded their sons, servants both male and female goaded their masters, and thingmen goaded their chieftains. What was common to all inciters was not their sex but their dependence on the men they incited. The verbal style they adopted . . . is clearly a type of shaming ritual well evidenced in the ethnographic literature as a vehicle for exercising

upward social control. Icelanders in the subservient position . . . had to shame and importune to get a hearing, since relative difference in power prevented them from being included as equals in deliberative sessions.[52]

In filing complaints with regard to microaggression to universities, students acknowledge the relative difference in power between themselves and their academic institutions. They accept this social order, and demand that the authorities use their superiority to avenge the slights that minority students have suffered. Students' adherence to the universities' rule goes hand in hand with the students' performance of a role within an honor game.

In this context, by approaching a university, a student states that the university is the superior member of the social group that was shamed. In so doing, the student constructs a social group that is bigger than the slighted minority group, and includes the university itself as a member. In this light, students' acceptance of university administrations as the authorities that they need to stir into action serves them well, because it expands the offended group that they are members of and strengthens it significantly. Once such a complaint is launched, the offended group is no longer "Muslim students at a certain university," but "the entire university community." The university is also served well, because it is invited to resolve conflicts that might otherwise spiral out of control and metamorphose into violence. This is a win-win situation for both universities and students, hence likely to endure.

The second means of action Campbell and Manning cite is the persuasion of reluctant third parties that the victim's cause is just and that they badly need help. This too is an age-old course of conduct in honor societies. So, for example, during their annual summer meetings at the Althing, Icelandic men would pass from one tent to the next, convincing their kin, peers, and neighbors to join them in avenging slights and offenses to their honor. Pursuing such missions, these men of honor used all their social clout, manifesting their best social skills. "The success of feud and dispute at the practical level meant influencing others, both the members of one's own support group and the great class of the uninvolved."[53] So they used storytelling, emotional blackmail, family ties, promises, liquor, and anything they could come up with. Twenty-first-century students in elite universities use these same tactics and tools to ensure that their social media posts, meant to mobilize others to join their crusades, reach maximum audiences and convince them to support and join.

A woman in saga Iceland who managed to convince a man to take on a cause and redeem their group's stained honor demonstrated her social skill, courage, persistence, and effectiveness, and was accordingly rewarded with increased honor. The same holds true for an Icelandic man who convinced other Icelanders at the Althing to join his quest for honor. The same also holds true for a student at an elite university who files a successful complaint with the university or mobilizes many students and supporters to join a grievance. From an honor point of view, both these courses of action are advantageous both for the group and the individual.

The third element in Campbell and Manning's definition is that microaggression complaints refer to domination and oppression of cultural minorities; they are filed on behalf of cultural pluralism and equal treatment of minorities. This element does not describe a way of handling conflict. Additionally, it is not typically associated with traditional honor societies. Does this undermine the identification of victimhood culture as honor based? Not necessarily.

Recognition of cultural pluralism and demands for equal treatment of minorities are values that derive from dignity and respect. But they can be adopted as a social norm by an honor society and become a tenet in its honor code. What this means is that the content of the norm is dignity and respect bound, but the social treatment of the norm follows the dynamics of an honor culture: people who adhere to it gain honor within the group, and those who do not, gain shame; members of the group compete for honor by demonstrating their zealous loyalty to the norm; group members feel justified in publicly shaming individuals that they suspect of not properly adhering to the norm.

Campbell and Manning's research offers ample evidence that the victimhood culture which they describe treats the dignity-and-respect-based norms that demand cultural pluralism and equal treatment of minorities in an honor-based manner. Students compete to prove their adherence to the norm as a means of gaining status, and they shame and humiliate whoever they accuse of not adhering to it vehemently enough.

All this suggests that victimhood culture is a contemporary version of an honor culture, one that cherishes certain dignity-and-respect-based norms. In chapter 3, I argued that in Christian Europe, glory-based tenets were adopted into honor-based cultures. I mentioned that the crusaders adhered to the dynamics of honor societies while championing religious notions of God's glory. This testifies to the fusion—perhaps confusion—of honor and glory. Similarly, victimhood culture fuses dignity-and-respect-based notions with the structure and the dynamics of honor. It is this underlying honor structure that allows Trump supporters to adopt the dynamics of victimhood culture.[54] Since both groups engage in honor-based tactics, they can structure their rivalry and conflict in the form of an honorable blood feud, even as their specific honor norms are different.

Beyond the tripartite definition, Campbell and Manning claim that within victim culture any suggestion that anyone who claims to have been slighted might also be at fault is denounced as "victim blaming." They present Richard B. Felson's explanation, that this is because "blame is often treated as a fixed quantity." A "zero-sum treatment of blame" means that "if we say a crime victim has made a mistake it implies that we are assigning less blame to the offender." If you want to assign maximum blame to the offender, then "you will prefer to deny any sort of blame to the victim."[55]

As presented in chapter 2, this zero-sum logic is a classic feature of honor societies. Since honor is treated as a fixed quantity, competition for it is a zero-sum game. Blame, in victimhood culture, seems to fill the role that shame does in honor culture. What it means is this: a complainant of victimization can bear no shame, and is completely honorable, so that the accused may be constructed as completely shameful and dishonorable.

The importance and centrality of gossip as a social tool is another feature that victimhood culture shares with other honor-based societies. Campbell and Manning claim that *hashtag activism* campaigns within victimhood culture

> are effectively episodes of mass gossip in which hundreds, thousands, or perhaps millions of third parties discuss deviant behavior and express support for one side against another. Like gossip in the small town or village, such public complaining may be the sole way of handling the conflict, or it might eventually lead to further action against the deviant, such as dismissal by supervisors or investigation by legal authorities.[56]

Gossip, as chapter 2 states, is a major, highly effective social tool in any honor society. It is a means of socializing and supervising group members, spreading the word of their shame, and goading them to take honorable action such as revenge. In many honor societies women are expected to gossip profusely; in so doing, they perform an important role and take part in socializing, supervising, and goading men to do the honorable things that women are barred from doing. But gossip is by no means exclusively a women's role; men too, even the most honorable and militant, engage in it abundantly. Miller quotes one of the Icelandic sagas' description of such social activity:

> There was much merriment and people talked about comparing men, who was the best men in the district, or the greatest chieftain. And people were not in accord, as is so often the case whenever people engage in a comparison of men.[57]

Last but not least, Manning and Campbell stress that in victimhood culture, any slight can be—and very often is—viewed as harmful and damaging as any other. Reference to a mixed group as "guys" (and not "guys and women") can be considered as bad as spitting in a person's face because he or she belongs to a minority group. This is so partly because every slight is considered of utmost significance, and partly because this culture renounces the use of external, objective standards to evaluate the severity of offenses: only the complainant is allowed to estimate the seriousness of the grievance he or she suffered.[58]

Traditional honor cultures may view any conduct that stains one's honor to be as serious and damaging as any other. Miller claims that the sagas reveal that "medieval Icelanders, living in an honor-based culture, perceived little difference in the amount of wrong done by a blow or a verbal insult, even a homicide or an insult."[59] But even this society, deeply entrenched in its honor culture, did not depend on offended parties' subjective assessment of the harm, and required that "objective" standards be met, that is, honor standards that the community approved as such. An individual could not decide that a certain conduct constituted an insult and justified gossip about the offender unless that type of conduct was socially accepted as insulting and deserving of reprisal.

Victimhood culture manifests many important features of honor cultures. But if it adheres to an important tenet of dignity-and-respect culture, cultural pluralism, and equal treatment of minorities—what is the harm in its use of honor tactics?

First, shaming is an honor-based tactic that does not value human dignity or respect. Shaming involves vicious attacks on a person with no regard to presumption of innocence or due process. These *procedural* guarantees are crucial to the protection of human dignity. Additionally, shaming mocks every aspect of a person's identity, thus denying him respect.

Second, Campbell and Manning claim that victimhood culture "is particularly hostile to free speech."[60] Their description of this culture indicates that, only partially committed to human dignity and respect, it silences views that are not considered politically correct, as well as any utterance that may be considered triggering bad memories of an unpleasant experience.[61] Such broad silencing is harmful and damaging to human dignity and respect.

Third, gossip, as a disciplinary tool that often replaces due process, is a grave offense to the respect of every accused, and even to human dignity. It allows society to badmouth an individual who has no means of making his case and presenting his side of the dispute. It often leads to spiraling vilification, which may be detrimental to a person's respect, and deny her equal human worth.

Fourth, the zero-sum logic of blame can easily become offensive to human dignity. If an accused is completely at fault, the road to full demonizing is short. This may lead to treatment of the accused as less valuable than other people.

Fifth, like other honor-based cultures, victimhood culture is not universalistic nor egalitarian: it clearly prefers members of minority groups over members of the hegemony. As Campbell and Manning state:

precise definitions of both honor and dignity in order to yield a precise analysis.

HOPE SPRINGS ETERNAL

The two centuries following the great American and French Revolutions, and the celebration of equal liberty as a fundamental human value, brought tremendous growth in many ways—as well as continuous attempts to escape from freedom. The seventy years following the UDHR's establishment of dignity as the foundational value of human rights have seen great advancement in many parts of the world—as well as continuous attempts to escape from dignity.

Can those of us who feel committed to human dignity and respect find a reason for optimism? Having carefully distinguished a narrowly defined human dignity from honor, glory, and respect, I believe that massive flight from dignity results from four major factors. First, postmodernism taught us to distance ourselves from values of any sort and view them cynically. If they are all stories we tell ourselves, or worse—stories that serve hegemonies that indoctrinate us for their own benefits, we should be very weary of them all. Second, in many countries, professed commitment to dignity made by institutions and leaders rings hollow, "fake," feeding the cynical, disillusioned impression that dignity, like all values, is merely a vague, pompous, meaningless moral promise. Some scholars of dignity bolster this view. Third, unlike the theological glory, dignity is often discussed and defined by rationally inclined philosophers and lawyers; it therefore lacks the spiritual depth, enthusiasm, and inspiration that many people need and seek in a fundamental value. Fourth, emphasis of human dignity and dignity-based fundamental rights is inherently minimalistic, schematic, and unsatisfying.

If I am right, hope depends on our collective, universal ability to generate, express, and distribute genuine, emotional, enthusiastic commitment to and faith in the combined notion of human dignity and respect, together with the full set of rights they generate. If we delight in dignity and respect wholeheartedly, celebrating and revering with awe the inherent merit of humanity, as well as the wonder of every individual's uniqueness and specialty, then there may still be hope for the world built from the ashes of two world wars. This is no easy task. We must take it on while overcoming our cynicism, skepticism, suspicion, and reluctance to engage in morality. Yet our humanity and human existence may depend on it.

Personally, I devoutly believe that dignity and respect should not be ascribed merely to humans, but to all living things, as well as the universe. I believe that we will enjoy no human dignity or respect until we cherish those of all life at large. This calls for a whole additional discussion.

NOTES

1. Erich Fromm, *Escape from Freedom* (1941; repr. New York: Avon Books, 1965), 119–20.

2. Fromm, *Escape from Freedom*, 278.

3. Fromm, *Escape from Freedom*, 143–44.

4. Fromm, *Escape from Freedom*, 155.

5. Fromm, *Escape from Freedom*, 280.

6. Fromm, *Escape from Freedom*, 280–83.

7. See United Nations [UN Charter], The Charter of the United Nations. And the Statute of the International Court of Justice, San Francisco, June 26, 1945, http://www.un.org/en/charter-united-nations/; and United Nations General Assembly, Third Session, Universal Declaration of Human Rights (UDHR), Resolution 217A, Paris, December 10, 1948, http://www.un.org/en/universal-declaration-human-rights/.

8. Alain de Botton, *Status Anxiety* (New York: Vintage Books, 2004).

9. Wikipedia, "Social Media," accessed March 28, 2019, https://en.wikipedia.org/wiki/Social_media, citing Jan H. Keizmann and Kristopher Hermkens (2011).

10. Bradley Campbell and Jason Manning, *The Rise of Victimhood Culture: Microaggressions, Safe Spaces, and the New Culture Wars* (Cham, Switzerland: Palgrave Macmillan, 2018).

11. José van Dijck, *The Culture of Connectivity: A Critical History of Social Media* (New York: Oxford University Press, 2013).

12. Van Dijck, *Culture of Connectivity*, 29.

13. Van Dijck, *Culture of Connectivity*, 4, 15.

14. Van Dijck, *Culture of Connectivity*, 13–14.

15. Van Dijck, *Culture of Connectivity*, 152, 170.

16. Van Dijck, *Culture of Connectivity*, 13; emphasis mine.

17. Van Dijck, *Culture of Connectivity*, 41.

18. Van Dijck, *Culture of Connectivity*, 157.

19. Van Dijck, *Culture of Connectivity*, 21; emphasis mine.

20. Van Dijck, *Culture of Connectivity*, 158.

21. Van Dijck, *Culture of Connectivity*, 62.

22. Van Dijck, *Culture of Connectivity*, 65–66; emphasis mine.

23. Van Dijck, *Culture of Connectivity*, 69.

24. William Ian Miller, *Bloodtaking and Peacemaking: Feud, Law, and Society in Saga Iceland* (Chicago: Chicago University Press, 1990), 53, 199, 210–13, and *Humiliation and Other Essays on Honor, Social Discomfort, and Violence* (Ithaca, NY: Cornell University Press, 1993), 104–6.

25. Miller, *Bloodtaking and Peacemaking*, 213.

26. Van Dijck, *Culture of Connectivity*, 173–75.

27. Farhad Khosrokhavar, *Suicide Bombers: Allah's New Martyrs*, trans. David Mace (London: Pluto, 2005), and in French, Farhad Khosrokhavar, *Les nouveaux martyrs d'Allah* (Paris: Flammarion, 2002). On Daesh, see chap. 1, n1.

28. Khosrokhavar, *Suicide Bombers*, 44–46.

29. "In their testaments, martyrs constantly refer to honor to justify their commitment to death." Khosrokhavar, *Suicide Bombers*, 64.

30. Khosrokhavar, *Suicide Bombers*, 49.

31. Khosrokhavar, *Suicide Bombers*, 47.

32. Khosrokhavar, *Suicide Bombers*, 49. Khosrokhavar repeats this point incessantly (for example, p. 66).

33. Khosrokhavar, *Suicide Bombers*, 60.

34. Khosrokhavar, *Suicide Bombers*, 66–67.

35. Khosrokhavar, *Suicide Bombers*, 67.

36. James Bowman, *Honor: A History* (New York: Encounter Books, 2006).

37. Bowman, *Honor*, 51.

38. Bowman, *Honor*, 202.

39. Bowman, *Honor*, 260.

40. "As the reality-TV phenomenon has shown us, 'how you feel' has become the guarantor of a would-be celebrity's authenticity—that Whitney Houston–style catch in the voice of nearly all the vocalists on Fox's American Idol bespeaks strong emotion barely contained—and his or her potential ticket to stardom." Bowman, *Honor*, 279.

41. Bowman, *Honor*, 106.

42. Bowman, *Honor*, 287.

43. Bowman, *Honor*, 307.

44. Bowman, *Honor*, 323.

45. Campbell and Manning, *Rise of Victimhood Culture*, xvii.

46. Campbell and Manning, *Rise of Victimhood Culture*, 112, xiii–xvi.

47. Campbell and Manning, *Rise of Victimhood Culture*, 106.

48. "Honorable people are sensitive to insult, so they might understand how microaggressions could be severe offenses demanding a serious response." Campbell and Manning, *Rise of Victimhood Culture*, 16.

49. Campbell and Manning, *Rise of Victimhood Culture*, 3.

50. Campbell and Manning, *Rise of Victimhood Culture*, 4.

51. Campbell and Manning, *Rise of Victimhood Culture*, 40.

52. Miller, *Bloodtaking and Peacemaking*, 212.

53. Campbell and Manning, *Rise of Victimhood Culture*, 188.

54. Campbell and Manning, *Rise of Victimhood Culture*, xvii, 165.

55. Richard B. Felson, "Blame Analysis: Accounting for the Behavior of Protected Groups," *American Sociologist* 22, no. 1 (1997): 7, quoted in Campbell and Manning, *Rise of Victimhood Culture*, 177.

56. Campbell and Manning, *Rise of Victimhood Culture*, 63.

57. Miller, *Bloodtaking and Peacemaking*, 302.

58. Campbell and Manning, *Rise of Victimhood Culture*, 85, 90–92, 95, 216.

59. Miller, *Humiliation*, 83.

60. Campbell and Manning, *Rise of Victimhood Culture*, 216.

61. Campbell and Manning, *Rise of Victimhood Culture*, 74–78.

62. Campbell and Manning, *Rise of Victimhood Culture*, 115.

63. Campbell and Manning, *Rise of Victimhood Culture*, 160.

64. Campbell and Manning, *Rise of Victimhood Culture*, 12.

65. Campbell and Manning, *Rise of Victimhood Culture*, 229.

66. Campbell and Manning, *Rise of Victimhood Culture*, 14, 73.

67. Campbell and Manning, *Rise of Victimhood Culture*, 14.

68. Bowman, *Honor*, 75–80.

Bibliography

Abu-Lughod, Lila. *Veiled Sentiments: Honor and Poetry in a Bedouin Society*. Berkeley: University of California Press, 1986.

Afsaruddin, Asma, ed. *Hermeneutics and Honor: Negotiating Female "Public" Space in Islamic/ate Societies*, Cambridge, MA: Harvard University Press, 1999.

Alfredsson, Gudmundur, and Asbjørn Eide, eds. *The Universal Declaration of Human Rights: A Common Standard of Achievement*. The Hague: Martinus Nijhoff, 1999.

Anonymous/Pseudo Brunetto Latini. "Cronica" (alate 13th century). In *Medieval and Renaissance Florence*, by Ferdinand Schevill, 1:106–7. New York: Harper & Row, 1961. Available online athttp://courses.washington.edu/hsteu401/Buondelmonte.htm; andhttps://sourcebooks.fordham.edu/search.asp.

Appiah, Kwame Anthony. *The Honor Code: How Moral Revolutions Happen*. New York: Norton, 2010.

Barak, Aharon. *Human Dignity: The Constitutional Right and Its Daughter-Rights*. 2 vols. Jerusalem, Israel: Nevo, 2014.

Bauman, Zygmunt. *Liquid Modernity*. Cambridge, UK: Polity, 2000.

Benesch, Oleg. *Inventing the Way of the Samurai: Nationalism, Internationalism, and Bushidō in Modern Japan*. Oxford: Oxford University Press, 2014.

Berger, Peter L. "On the Obsolescence of the Concept of Honor." In *Revisions: Changing Perspectives in Moral Philosophy*, edited by Stanley Hauerwas and Alasdair MacIntyre, 172–81. Notre Dame, IN: University of Notre Dame Press, 1983.

Berlin, Isaiah. *Four Essays on Liberty*. Oxford: Oxford University Press, 1969.

Bourdieu, Pierre. "The Sentiment of Honor on Kabyle Society." In *Honor and Shame: The Values of Mediterranean Society*, edited by John G. Peristiany, 191–241. Chicago: Chicago University Press, 1966.

Bowman, James. *Honor: A History*. New York: Encounter Books, 2006.

Burrow, Rufus, Jr. *God and Human Dignity: The Personalism, Theology, and Ethics of Martin Luther King, Jr.* Notre Dame, IN: University of Notre Dame Press, 2006.

Campbell, Bradley, and Jason Manning. *The Rise of Victimhood Culture: Microaggressions, Safe Spaces, and the New Culture Wars*. Cham, Switzerland: Palgrave Macmillan, 2018.

Campbell, J. K. [John Kennedy]. *Honor, Family and Patronage: A Study of Institutions and Moral Values in a Greek Mountain Community*. Oxford: Clarendon, 1964.

Caulfield, Sueann, Sarah C. Chambers, and Lara Putnam, eds. *Honor, Status, and Law in Modern Latin America*. Durham, NC: Duke University Press, 2005.

De Botton, Alain. *Status Anxiety*. New York: Vintage Books, 2004.

Du Boulay, Juliet. *Portrait of a Greek Mountain Village*. Oxford: Clarendon, 1979.

Düwell, Marcus, Jens Braarvig, Roger Brownsword, and Dietmar Mieth, eds. *The Cambridge Handbook of Human Dignity: Interdisciplinary Perspectives.* Cambridge: Cambridge University Press, 2014.

Felson, Richard B. "Blame Analysis: Accounting for the Behavior of Protected Groups." *American Sociologist* 22, no. 1 (1997): 5–23.

Frevert, Ute. "The Taming of the Noble Ruffian: Male Violence and Dueling in Early Modern and Modern Germany." In *Men and Violence: Gender, Honor, and Ritual in Modern Europe and America,* edited by Pieter Spierenburg, 37–63. Columbus: Ohio State University Press, 1998.

Fromm, Erich. *The Art of Loving.* Edited by Ruth Nanda Anshen. New York: Harper, 1956.

———. *Escape from Freedom.* 1941. Reprint, New York: Avon Books, 1965.

Germany. Basic Law for the Federal Republic of Germany. Bonn. May 8, 1949.

Gewirth, Alan. "Human Dignity as the Basis of Rights." In *The Constitution of Rights: Human Dignity and American Values,* edited by Michael J. Meyer and W. A. Parent, 10–28. Ithaca, NY: Cornell University Press, 1991.

Gilmore, David D., ed. *Honor and Shame and the Unity of the Mediterranean.* Washington, DC: American Anthropological Association, 1987.

Glendon, Mary Ann. *A World Made New: Eleanor Roosevelt and the Universal Declaration of Human Rights.* New York: Random House, 2001.

Goodwin, Jan. *Price of Honor: Muslim Women Lift the Veil of Silence on the Islamic World.* Rev. ed. New York: Plume, 2003.

Goshen-Gottstein, Alon. "The Body as Image of God in Rabbinic Literature." *Harvard Theological Review* 87, no. 2 (1994): 171–95.

Greenberg, Kenneth S. *Honor and Slavery: Lies, Duels, Noses, Masks, Dressing as a Woman, Gifts, Strangers, Humanitarianism, Death, Slave Rebellions, the Pro-slavery Argument, Baseball, Hunting, and Gambling in the Old South.* Princeton, NJ: Princeton University Press, 1996.

Harari, Yuval Noah. *From Animals into Gods: A Brief History of Humankind.* Charleston, SC: CreateSpace, 2012.

———. *Homo Deus: A Brief History of Tomorrow.* [Toronto, ON]: Signal, 2015.

Hebrew Bible (HB). 2019.https://biblehub.com/.

Hicks, Donna. *Dignity: Its Essential Role in Resolving Conflict.* Foreword by Archbishop Emeritus Desmond Tutu. New Haven, CT: Yale University Press, 2011.

Highfield, Ron. *God, Freedom and Human Dignity: Embracing a God-Centered Identity in a Me-Centered Culture.* Downers Grove, IL: IVP Academic, 2013.

Hittinger, Russell. "Toward an Adequate Anthropology: Social Aspects of *Imago Dei* in Catholic Theology." In Howard, *Imago Dei,* 39–78.

Horden, Peregrine, and Nicholas Purcell. *The Corrupting Sea: A Study of Mediterranean History.* Oxford: Blackwell, 2000.

Howard, Thomas Albert, ed. *Imago Dei: Human Dignity in Ecumenical Perspective.* Washington, DC: Catholic University of America Press, 2013.

Israel. Basic Law: Human Dignity and Liberty, 12th Knesset, March 17, 1992.

Johnson, Lyman L., and Sonya Lipsett-Rivera, eds. *The Faces of Honor: Sex, Shame, and Violence in Colonial Latin America.* Albuquerque: University of New Mexico Press, 1998.

Kamir, Orit. "The Dignitarian Feminist Jurisprudence with Applications to Rape, Sexual Harassment, and Honor Codes." In *Research Handbook on Feminist Jurisprudence,* edited by Robin West and Cynthia Grant Brown, 303–20. Northampton, MA: Edward Elgar, 2019.

———. *Framed: Women in Law and Film.* Durham, NC: Duke University Press, 2006.

———. *Sheela Shel Kavod: Yisraeliyut U Kvod Haadam* [Israeli honor and dignity: Social norms, gender politics and the law]. Jerusalem, Israel: Carmel, 2004.

Kant, Immanuel. *Groundwork of the Metaphysics of Morals* (1784). Translated by Thomas Kingsmill Abbott. Peterborough, ON: Broadview, 2005.

———. *Groundwork of the Metaphysics of Morals (1785).* In *Immanuel Kant: Practical Philosophy.* Translated by Mary Gregor. Cambridge: Cambridge University, 1996: Refers to Preussische Akademie edition by volume and page.

————. *Grundlegung zur Metaphysik der Sitten.* Riga, Latvia: bey Johann Friedrich Hartknoch, 1785.

Kateb, George. *Human Dignity.* Cambridge, MA: Harvard University Press, 2011.

Khosrokhavar, Farhad. *Les nouveaux martyrs d'Allah.* Paris: Flammarion, 2002.

————. *Suicide Bombers: Allah's New Martyrs.* Translated by David Mace. London: Pluto, 2005.

King James Bible (KJV). 2019.https://biblehub.com/.

Kirchhoffer, David G. *Human Dignity in Contemporary Ethics.* Amherst, NY: Teneo, 2013.

Latin Vulgate Bible (VUL). 2019.https://www.biblestudytools.com/vul/.

Lewis, C. S. "The Weight of Glory." *Theology* 43, no. 257 (1941): 263–74. Repr. London: Society for Promoting Christian Knowledge, 1942. Preached originally as a sermon in the Church of St. Mary the Virgin, Oxford, on June 8, 1941; seehttp://www.verber.com/mark/xian/weight-of-glory.pdf.

Lewis, Orion A., and Sven Steinmo. "How Institutions Evolve: Evolutionary Theory and Institutional Change." *Polity* 44, no. 3 (July 2012): 314–39.

Lorberbaum, Yair. *In God's Image: Myth, Theology, and Law in Classical Judaism.* New York: Cambridge University Press, 2015.

Lutz-Bachmann, Matthias. *Human Rights, Human Dignity, and Cosmopolitan Ideas.* Burlington, VT: Ashgate, 2014.

MacIntyre, Alasdair. "Disquieting Suggestion." In *After Virtue: A Study in Moral Theory,* 1–6. 2nd ed. Notre Dame, IN: University of Notre Dame Press, 1984. First published in 1981.

Mandelbaum, David G. *Women's Seclusion and Men's Honor: Sex Roles in North India, Bangladesh, and Pakistan.* Tucson: University of Arizona Press, 1993.

Meilaender, Gilbert. *Neither Beast nor God: The Dignity of the Human Person.* New York: Encounter Books, 2009.

Mill, John Stuart. *On Liberty.* 1852. Reprint, London: Longman, Roberts, & Green, 1869.

Miller, William Ian. *Bloodtaking and Peacemaking: Feud, Law, and Society in Saga Iceland.* Chicago: Chicago University Press, 1990.

————. *Eye for an Eye: Justice Anatomized.* New York: Cambridge University Press, 2005.

————. *Faking It.* Cambridge: Cambridge University Press, 2003.

————. *Humiliation and Other Essays on Honor, Social Discomfort, and Violence.* Ithaca, NY: Cornell University Press, 1993.

Mitchell, C. Ben. "The Audacity of the *Imago Dei*: The Legacy and Uncertain Future of Human Dignity." In Howard, *Imago Dei,* 79–112.

Moltmann, Jürgen. *On Human Dignity: Political Theology and Ethics.* Translation, with introduction by M. Douglas Meeks. Minneapolis, MN: Fortress, 2007.

Morsink, Johannes. *The Universal Declaration of Human Rights: Origins, Drafting, and Intent.* Philadelphia: University of Pennsylvania Press, 1999.

Newman, Gerald L. "On Fascist Honor and Human Dignity: A Sceptical Response." In *Darker Legacies of Law in Europe: The Shadow of National Socialism and Fascism over Europe and Its Legal Traditions,* edited by Christian Joerges and Navraj Singh Ghaleigh, 267–74. Oxford: Hart, 2003.

Nisbett, Richard E., and Dov Cohen. *Culture of Honor: The Psychology of Violence in the South.* Boulder, CO: Westview, 1996.

Nye, Robert A. *Masculinity and Male Codes of Honor in Modern France.* New ed. Berkeley: University of California Press, 1998.

Ober, Josiah. "Meritocratic and Civic Dignity in Greco-Roman Antiquity." In *The Cambridge Handbook of Human Dignity: Interdisciplinary Perspectives,* edited by Marcus Düwell, Jens Braarvig, Roger Brownsword, and Dietmar Mieth, 52–63. Cambridge: Cambridge University Press, 2014.

Oprisko, Robert L. *Honor: A Phenomenology.* New York: Routledge, 2012.

Pardo, Osvaldo F. *Honor and Personhood in Early Modern Mexico.* Ann Arbor: University of Michigan Press, 2015.

Péristiany, John G., ed. *Honor and Shame: The Values of Mediterranean Society.* Chicago: Chicago University Press, 1966.

Pettit, Philip. *Republicanism: A Theory of Freedom and Government.* Oxford: Oxford University Press, 1997.

Pitt-Rivers, Julian. *The Fate of Shechem, or the Politics of Sex: Essays in the Anthropology of the Mediterranean.* Cambridge: Cambridge University Press, 1977.

Pope, Nicole. *Honor Killings in the Twenty-First Century.* New York: Palgrave Macmillan, 2012.

Roosevelt, Franklin D. "State of the Union Address (Four Freedoms)." January 6, 1941. 77th Congress. Washington, DC: GOP, 1941. Transcript available online at https://millercenter. org/the-presidency/presidential-speeches/january-6-1941-state-union-four-freedoms.

Rosen, Michael. *Dignity: Its History and Meaning.* Cambridge, MA: Harvard University Press, 2012.

Schevill, Ferdinand. *Medieval and Renaissance Florence.* 2 vols. in one. New York: Harper & Row, 1961.

Spaemann, Robert. "Human Dignity and Human Nature." In *Love and the Dignity of Human Life: On Nature and Natural Law,* 27–44. Grand Rapids, MI: Eerdmans, 2012.

Spierenburg, Pieter, ed. *Men and Violence: Gender, Honor, and Ritual in Modern Europe and America.* Columbus: Ohio State University Press, 1998.

Steinmo, Sven. "Evolutionary Narratives." In *The Evolution of Modern States: Sweden, Japan, and the United States,* 1–29. Cambridge: Cambridge University Press, 2010.

Stewart, Frank Henderson. *Honor.* Chicago: University of Chicago Press, 1994.

Taylor, Charles. *The Ethics of Authenticity.* Cambridge, MA: Harvard University Press, 1992.

———. "The Politics of Recognition." In *Multiculturalism: Examining the Politics of Recognition,* edited by Amy Gutmann, 25–74. Princeton, NJ: Princeton University Press, 1994.

———. *Sources of the Self: The Making of the Modern Identity.* Cambridge: Cambridge University Press, 1989.

Twinam, Ann. *Public Lives, Private Secrets: Gender, Honor, Sexuality, and Illegitimacy in Colonial Spanish America.* Stanford, CA: Stanford University Press, 1999.

United Nations [UN Charter]. *The Charter of the United Nations. And the Statute of the International Course of Justice.* San Francisco. June 26, 1945. http://www.un.org/en/charter-united-nations/.

United Nations General Assembly. Third Session. Address by Mr. Saint-Lot (Haiti). Rapporteur of the Third Committee, 853–54. Paris. December 9, 1948. https://undocs.org/A/PV. 180.

———. Third Session. Universal Declaration of Human Rights (UDHR). Resolution 217A, Paris. December 10, 1948. http://www.un.org/en/universal-declaration-human-rights/.

Van Dijck, José [Johanna Francisca Theodora Maria]. *The Culture of Connectivity: A Critical History of Social Media.* New York: Oxford University Press, 2013.

Villani, Giovanni. *Nuova Cronica* [New icleschronicles] (ca. 1300–1337). In *Florentine Chronicle,* translated by David Burr. Available online at Fordham University, Internet Medieval Sourcebook, http://www.fordham.edu/halsall/source/villani.html.

Waldron, Jeremy. *Dignity, Rank, and Rights.* Edited by Meir Dan-Cohen. Oxford: Oxford University Press, 2012.

Whitman, James Q. "On Nazi 'Honour' and New European 'Dignity.'" In *Darker Legacies of Law in Europe: The Shadow of National Socialism and Fascism over Europe and Its Legal Traditions,* edited by Christian Joerges and Navraj Singh Ghaleigh, 243–66. Oxford: Hart, 2003.

Wikipedia. "Social Media." Accessed March 28, 2019. https://en.wikipedia.org/wiki/Social_media.

Withnall, Adam, and John Lichfield. "Charlie Hebdo Shooting: At Least 12 Killed as Shots Fired at Satirical Magazine's Paris Office." *Independent,* January 7, 2015. https://www.independent.co.uk/news/world/europe/charlie-hebdo-shooting-10-killed-as-shots-fired-at-satirical-magazine-headquarters-according-to-9962337.html.

Wyatt-Brown, Bertram. *Honor and Violence in the Old South.* New York: Oxford University Press, 1986.

———. *Southern Honor: Ethics and Behavior in the Old South.* New York: Oxford University Press, 1982.

Zahavi, Amotz, and Avishag Zahavi. *The Handicap Principle: A Missing Piece of Darwin's Puzzle*. Translated by Naama Zahavi-Ely and Melvin Patrick Ely. New York: Oxford University Press, 1997.

Index

About the Author

Orit Kamir is a researcher and professor of law, culture, and gender. She received her LLM and SJD from the University of Michigan Law School in 1995. Her main areas of research are human dignity and honor, feminist jurisprudence, and law and film. Kamir is a social activist and a contributor to public discourse in Israel, where she lives. She drafted Israel's Sexual Harassment law, which was enacted in 1998, and has had an immense impact on gender norms in Israel. Her most recent activism is in the promotion of a bill she drafted to prevent workplace bullying.

In 2004, Kamir founded, together with Rivka Elisha, the Israeli Center for Human Dignity. The nonprofit organization applies Kamir's theory of dignity and honor through workshops and interventions in public and private organizations (such as schools, prisons, hospitals, municipalities, and workplaces).

www.ingramcontent.com/pod-product-compliance
Lightning Source LLC
Chambersburg PA
CBHW021817270326
41932CB00007B/218